a-z of transitions

Professional Keywords series

Every field of practice has its own methods, terminology, conceptual debates and landmark publications. The *Professional Keywords* series expertly structures this material into easy-reference A to Z format. Focusing on the ideas and themes that shape the field, these books are designed both to guide the student reader and to refresh practitioners' thinking and understanding.

Available now

Mark Doel and Timothy B. Kelly: *A–Z of Groups & Groupwork*
David Garnett: *A–Z of Housing*
Jon Glasby and Helen Dickinson: *A–Z of Interagency Working*
Richard Hugman: *A–Z of Professional Ethics*
Divya Jindal-Snape: A–Z *of Transitions*
Glenn Laverack: *A–Z of Health Promotion*
Glenn Laverack: *A–Z of Public Health*
Jeffrey Longhofer: *A–Z of Psychodynamic Practice*
Neil McKeganey: *A–Z of Addiction and Substance Misuse*
Steve Nolan and Margaret Holloway: *A–Z of Spirituality*
Marian Roberts: *A–Z of Mediation*
Fiona Timmins: *A–Z of Reflective Practice*
David Wilkins, David Shemmings and Yvonne Shemmings:
   A–Z of Attachment

Coming soon

Angela Olsen, Andrea Pepe and Dan Redfearn: *A–Z of Learning Disability*

a–z of
transitions

Divya Jindal-Snape

BLOOMSBURY ACADEMIC
LONDON • NEW YORK • OXFORD • NEW DELHI • SYDNEY

BLOOMSBURY ACADEMIC
Bloomsbury Publishing Plc
50 Bedford Square, London, WC1B 3DP, UK
1385 Broadway, New York, NY 10018, USA
29 Earlsfort Terrace, Dublin 2, Ireland

BLOOMSBURY, BLOOMSBURY ACADEMIC and the Diana logo
are trademarks of Bloomsbury Publishing Plc

First published 2016 by PALGRAVE

Reprinted by Bloomsbury Academic

A catalogue record for this book is available from the British Library.

A catalog record for this book is available from the Library of Congress.

ISBN: PB: 978-1-1375-2826-1
ePDF: 978-1-1375-2827-8
ePub: 978-1-3503-1377-4

To find out more about our authors and books visit
www.bloomsbury.com and sign up for our newsletters.

contents

acknowledgements

I am indebted to numerous people, families, professionals, and academics, from whom I have learned a lot about transitions and continue to do so. I would also like to thank the following for their valuable constructive feedback on the book: Katrina Cuthbertson, Deepak Gopinath, Tim Kelly, Dianne Mitchell, Jonathan Snape, and Lorna Strachan.

I am grateful to Peter Hooper and his colleagues from Palgrave for bringing this book to fruition.

Finally, I would like to express my love and thanks to my family for their unwavering support and patience.

using this book

In keeping with the focus of the Professional Keywords series, this book has been written with an interprofessional and international audience in mind. This book aims to be a one-stop source book for students and professionals working in the caring professions across a range of transitions. It will also be of use to policy makers and academic researchers. The book uses a navigation structure that should make it easier for you to see the links between various entries. As you will probably dip in and out of this book, each entry has been written in a way that it is free standing. Each entry makes connections with the implications for you as practitioners or future practitioners. This book embeds theory and latest research into each entry, with clear signposting to indicate additional reading that might be beneficial for you.

For those of you who want to read the book differently, there is cohesiveness built in to the narrative so that you can focus on particular aspects within the book through signposting. This will meet the demand of different readers, those who want to dip in and read only one to two entries, as well as those who want to follow a strand such as 'Transition Planning' and reasons behind it, such as 'Resilience', 'Familiarisation', etc.

The content of the book is based on several important aspects related to transitions, such as definition and conceptualisation of transition (e.g. Ongoing process, Educational and Life Transitions, Rite of passage), types of transitions (e.g. educational, bereavement, ageing, health), issues related to transitions (e.g. academic dip, well-being), positive aspects of transitions (e.g. increased choices), strategies to facilitate successful transition (e.g. induction, familiarisation), theories used to understand transitions (e.g. resilience theory, self-esteem theory), and research methods most appropriate to transitions (e.g. longitudinal studies, cohort studies). Therefore, the book covers a broad spectrum of information that you might require as a student or professional to work with individuals going through their transitions; indeed, also to understand your own transition to becoming a college or university student, from student to practitioner, moving into different roles as a professional, and the impact of your transitions on those you work with.

introduction

Transition is defined as an ongoing process which involves moving from one context to another as well as from one set of interpersonal relationships to another (Jindal-Snape, 2010), resulting in creation or renegotiation of relationships with others such as professionals, family members, and peers. All of us go through transitions, whether they are to do with starting school, moving house, or starting a new job. Most people find transitions to be fulfilling and are able to deal with them without any problems. However, some transitions such as bereavement or hospitalisation can be difficult to deal with. Further, research shows that even transitions that are usually positive and imply moving up and progression, such as educational transitions, can be stressful and traumatic for some people with significant negative impact on their well-being (Jindal-Snape & Miller, 2008). Professionals usually put planning and preparation in place for normative transitions, and in some cases it is a legal requirement (for example, The Education (Additional Support for Learning) (Scotland) Act 2004 (ASL), amended 2009; Individuals with Disabilities Education Act (IDEA) 1990, 2004). However, some non-normative transitions such as sudden death of a significant family member cannot be planned for. If any of these transitions become problematic, they can have an impact on all aspects of that individual's life as well as that of significant others around them.

Therefore, irrespective of the nature of transitions, professionals working in caring professions have an important role to play in supporting these individuals, either to prepare them or to support them through the transition process. Research suggests that to navigate transitions successfully, we need to be resilient. Resilience literature highlights that an individual's resilience is influenced by their internal attributes (e.g. self-esteem) and support networks (e.g. family). Professionals form an important part of the individual's support network; this is especially true for professionals working in a caring profession as they might be the only positive, stable, and secure support network that the individual has. However, if these professionals do not conceptualise or understand transitions appropriately, they cannot support the individual adequately. For instance, teachers who consider transition to be a one-off event would put something in place for children a couple of months before they leave school and for a couple of months after starting a new school. However, research shows that children who settled well in the first few months of moving to a new school experienced difficulties related to the move six months later, highlighting that transition is an ongoing process. Similarly, if the teacher does not put it in the context of other life transitions that the child is experiencing, such as parents separating, they might not be able to support them well with the educational transition. Therefore, it is imperative that professionals in the caring professions understand the life transitions of that individual even though they might be primarily supporting them through a specific transition.

referencing and further
reading

All references are included in the bibliography with some additional entries that are relevant for the reader. This bibliography includes international literature spanning a range of disciplines and types of transitions. After every entry in the book, readers have been guided to further reading for more in-depth information about that topic. Readers are encouraged to delve into reading from different disciplines and across stages as there is a lot to be learned from transitions across the life course.

a

Abcs (affect, behaviour, and cognition) of acculturation

SEE ALSO international students' transitions to higher education, readiness

Acculturation has been defined as a process of change as a result of the interaction of two or more cultures (Berry, 2005). ABC stands for the affective, behaviour, and cognitive response to a different culture in the new (host) country. Three theories that are more comprehensive and regard the individual as pro-actively responding to the environmental changes provide a framework for the ABC framework of acculturation (Ward, Bochner, & Furnham, 2001). These are 'stress and coping', 'culture learning', and 'social identification'. As mentioned earlier, they consider different components of response, namely affect, behaviour, and cognition. The stress and coping theories (affect) are based on the premise that life changes are inherently stressful and that an international sojourner needs to develop coping strategies to deal with this stress, and adjustment is dependent on personal (e.g. personality, attitude) and situational (e.g. social support) factors. Culture learning theories (behaviour) suggest that social interaction is important and the international sojourners need to learn culturally relevant social skills not only to survive but also to thrive. Social identification theories (cognition) assume that cross-cultural transition might involve changes in one's cultural identity and inter-group relations. This 'cultural synergy' ABC framework offers a multi-dimensional understanding of the processes involved in the acculturation of international sojourners, such as international students (Zhou, Jindal-Snape, Topping, & Todman, 2008).

Initial acculturation studies were based on the transition experiences of migrants and saw them as people experiencing culture shock. Culture shock implies that when a person experiences a new culture, due to the difference between their own culture and that of the host country, they will experience a shock and find the experience stressful. Research suggests that the larger the cultural distance between them and the host nation's culture, the bigger the shock (Beech, 2016; Tempelaar & Verhoeven, 2016). Over time, there has been a change in thinking, and theorists have moved from **culture shock** of migrants and sojourners towards **cultural adaptation**. It is important to note that shock is very different from adaptation. Shock implies that the person is passive and over-whelmed by the situation or incident, whereas the term 'adaptation' highlights a person taking control of the situation, modifying their behaviour according to the new environment they find themselves in and adjusting over time.

When applied to international students, for example, this suggests that they would experience cultural and *pedagogical shock*. Pedagogical shock would similarly be seen to be a result of the exposure to edu-cational experiences vastly different from their previous educational experiences in a new educational system, and, in the main, at a higher level, as they will embark on the next level of the degree.

The ABC model moves the thinking from '*cultural shock*' to '*cultural adaptation*', and with its application to international stu-dents, from '*pedagogical shock*' to '*pedagogical adaptation*' (Zhou, Todman, Topping, & Jindal-Snape, 2010). It emphasises that the individuals are not passive in this process and experiencing shock (see also entry on **international students' transitions to higher education**). They are, instead, actively adapting to the difference in culture and pedagogical approach of the host nation.

Another change in thinking is related to who is experiencing change or needs to acculturate. Initially, acculturation was seen as unidimensional, focusing on the immigrant who was considered to discard their culture to adopt the host culture (Schwartz, Unger, Zamboanga, & Szapocznik, 2010). However, over the last 40 years there has been a shift in thinking, with acculturation being concep-tualised as bi-dimensional (Berry, 2005, 2006; Smith & Khwaja, 2011). Berry's (2005) definition of acculturation highlights that acculturation is happening for both cultures; he proposed a taxon-omy to explain attitudes towards acculturation, namely integration, assimilation, separation, and marginalisation. Integration is seen to be the most desirable, in which the individual maintains their own original cultural identity as well as accepting the new culture. Assimilation implies a rejection of the original culture and identification with the host culture. Separation indicates a strategy where the migrant only identifies with their original culture, whereas marginalisation is the rejection of both cultural identities.

The interactionist approach suggests acculturation should be about mutual adaptation, which considers not only sojourners' readiness to adapt but also how the organisations and the host communities can be ready to adapt and work with them (see entry on *readiness*). For example, in an educational context, Zhou et al. (2010) found that staff participants in their research reported that they had adapted their teaching style and assessment practices to meet the needs of their international students.

Implications for practice
1. Professionals should consider familiarising the sojourner with the new environment and culture by providing information related to life in the host country *prior* to the move.
2. It is important to consider each individual's circumstances, including whether they have family moving with them and what their needs might be.
3. Professionals will also need training to enhance their cultural awareness and understanding to be able to work with people from a range of cultures. They might become the bridge builders between individuals from different nationalities as well as between the sojourners and the local community.
4. It is worth considering how the ABC framework can be applied to adaptation to different *organisational* cultures (i.e. beliefs, values, and norms held by an organisation, see Xenikou & Furnham, 2012), which can also be very different even within the same city but are usually very hidden and go unacknowledged. A child moving between the organisational cultures of the primary and secondary school needs to acculturate (Jindal-Snape & Foggie, 2008) and the ABCs of acculturation might be equally relevant to their context.

FURTHER READING
Berry, J. W. (2005). Acculturation: Living successfully in two cultures. *International Journal of Intercultural Relations, 29*(6), 697–712.

Jindal-Snape, D., & Rienties, B. (Eds.) (2016). *Multi-dimensional transitions of international students to Higher Education*. New York: Routledge.

Xenikou, A., & Furnham, A. (2012). *Group dynamics and organizational culture: Effective work groups and organizations*. Basingstoke: Palgrave Macmillan.

Ward, C., Bochner, S., & Furnham, A. (2001). *The psychology of culture shock* (2nd edn.). New York: Routledge.

additional support needs (ASN)

SEE ALSO **collaboration, creative approaches, multiple and multi-dimensional transitions (MMT) theory, nursery-primary school transition, parental participation, post-school transitions, readiness, self-determination, transition meetings, voice**

Additional Support Needs are long- or short-term needs that pose a substantial barrier to participation in school life and learning, indicating support that is required to get through a difficult period in the life of a child. The Education (Additional Support for Learning) (Scotland) Act 2004 (ASL), amended 2009, introduced the term 'Additional Support Need' (ASN). According to this legislation, the terminology 'special educational need' (SEN) was to be replaced.

There was also a philosophical shift in the conceptualisation of support needs. It moved away from a medical model of within-child needs to the social model of needs emerging due to environmental factors. ASN can include factors related to disability or health (e.g. ADHD, terminal illness), the learning environment (e.g. English as an additional language), family circumstances (e.g. looked-after-child), and social and emotional factors (e.g. experiencing bullying). Any child might have a support need emerging during their learning journey.

Research suggests that ASN can have an impact on the transition trajectory; for example, Jindal-Snape, Douglas, Topping, Smith, and Kerr (2006) reported different secondary school destinations for children with autism in their study and found that there were significant delays in placement, leading to anxiety and stress for families (see also Hannah & Topping, 2012). Similarly, research suggests that nursery to primary transitions and post-school transitions can be difficult for children and young people with additional support needs (see entry on *post-school transitions*). Gorton (2012) reported that parents chose to defer transition to primary school in the hope of their children moving to mainstream primary instead of special school, with professionals and parents alike waiting for the child to be 'mature' enough to move to school (see entries on *nursery-primary school transition, readiness*). As highlighted under *MMT theory*, environmental factors can have an impact on a person's ability to deal with transitions (see entry on *multiple and multi-dimensional transitions (MMT) theory*). On the other hand, it is important to acknowledge that for some people, transitions can make them vulnerable to anxiety and stress, thereby in turn potentially creating ASN for them.

The ASL legislation places specific duties on local authorities in Scotland, with clear time scales for transition planning and practice for children and young people who are identified to have ASN (no later than 12 months prior to the move local authorities/schools have to request and take account of information and advice from relevant agencies, and no later than 6 months prior to the move they have to give information to relevant agencies). The ASL Act also emphasises the importance of collaborative, multi-agency working and timely transition meetings to review aspirations and create transition plans (see entry on *transition meetings*). This is perhaps a more positive move towards timely planning for transitions; however, it could be argued that despite these being highlighted as the minimum time periods, organisations might start using them as the default time scale irrespective of needs which might warrant an earlier start.

Further, the legislation places emphasis on better interprofessional collaboration and listening to the voice of children and young people and their families (see entries on *collaboration, voice*). However, research suggests that some professionals ignore the views of children and young people with ASN, as they consider it difficult or even impossible to get their views (Dickins, 2008). In practice, others have found ways of listening to their views in ways that are meaningful to them (see *creative approaches, voice*), as they consider this to be essential for self-determination (see entry on *self-determination*). Similarly, some find interprofessional collaboration and parental involvement to be tricky, whereas others have found ways of making these happen (see *collaboration, parental participation*).

Although this terminology and legislation is specific to one nation, it resonates with conceptualisation of support needs elsewhere (e.g. Finland), and it is important to be mindful of this in the context of transition, potentially creating support needs for anyone at any time across the world and educational systems. Also, it is important to consider the significance of removing the focus from situating the support needs within the individual to the environment, thus moving to a social model of inclusive transition practice.

Implications for practice

1. There are legislative requirements for professionals in terms of transition planning and preparation. However, limiting this responsibility towards those already identified to have ASN does not support the ethos behind the Act and conceptualisation of ASN. To be fully inclusive, it is important to be mindful of support needs of every child and young person (or any individual in the context of other transitions) and to understand that significant transitions might create a need for additional support.

FURTHER READING

The Scottish Government. (2009). Education (Additional Support for Learning) Act (Amendment). Edinburgh: The Scottish Government.

ageing

SEE ALSO **additional support needs, bereavement, creative approaches, employment, health transitions, nursery-primary school transition, parental participation, resilience, self-determination, voice**

Ageing is a normative transition that everyone experiences. The changes associated with it can be psychological, physical, and/or social. These involve, for example, changes in relationships as one grows from being a child to a young person, or cognitive changes over time. Some of these changes and transitions are discussed elsewhere (for example, see entries on *nursery-primary school transition, parental participation, employment*).

With improvements in medical care, people are living longer, and most are active and content with their life (Berman-Rossi & Kelly, 2014). However, ageing in the late 50s and 60s brings about several changes that one has to adapt to, such as moving from full-time employment to retirement, having more leisure time, and potential isolation if the individual experiences ill-health or immobility. The challenges related to ageing across the life course can lead to mental health issues for some people. Ageing, as a life transition, is related to other transitions such as educational transitions over the life course, employment and retirement, emergence of additional support needs, bereavement, and loss (see entries on *additional support needs, bereavement, employment, health transitions*).

In this entry, we will focus on ageing for older people and other entries elsewhere will focus on ageing for other age groups. One transition that can be particularly traumatic for older people is the move to residential or community care, with the involvement of health and social care; this is known to have a profound impact on the older person and even the anticipation of moving to care can become a big source of concern and fear. This change also can signal other changes, such as loss of their own space or home when moving into residential care, loss of privacy and autonomy, change in identity from that of house owner to resident and potentially provider to receiver, change in relationships (losing old relationships due to death or moving away and having to form new relationships with professionals and other residents) due to the new environment, change in health and independence, and feelings of loss of dignity when accompanied with support for daily tasks such as personal and intimate physical care.

As with any other transitions it is important to consider the *resilience* of the individual to life changes, with identification of risks and protective factors. In the context of older people, Berman-Rossi and Kelly (2014) outline an 'older person: environment fit assessment tool' as a person-centred tool that can assist practitioners in maintaining the balance between the older person and their environment, taking into consideration formal and informal support networks and focusing on the strength and needs of older people with an emphasis on their voice (see entry on *voice*). They suggest using it at different time points to take cognizance of the changing person–environment fit (see also entry on *stage–environment fit*). This tool includes areas such as definition of the problem, client's expectations (including choice and control), knowledge of the client's life, client's strengths and limitations, environmental supports and obstacles, degree of congruity between personal and environmental resources, and practice direction (see Berman-Rossi & Kelly, 2014, pp. 428–429 for details; see entry on *self-determination*).

Research suggests that participation in art activities can support this transition as well as enhancing well-being (Creech, Hallam, Varvarigou, McQueen, & Gaunt, 2013; Liddle, Parkinson, & Sibbritt, 2012) by creating environmental conditions that facilitate the satisfaction of competence, autonomy, and relatedness (see entries on *creative approaches, self-determination*). Further, they were found to be important in counterbalancing mental well-being difficulties, decreasing the risk of low mood, anxiety, and social isolation.

Communication is essential for healthy ageing, perceived quality of life, maintaining social networks, and having a say in decisions related to one's life. However, although a majority of older people develop age-related hearing impairment, most do not have hearing aids or do not use them due to insufficient attention to supporting them with making the transition to life with hearing aids (Kelly, Tolson, Smith, & McColgan, 2010). The older people in Kelly and colleagues' study highlighted the need for information prior to the use of the aids and ongoing support, similar to other transitions' support needs, and the researchers suggested a group-based support system.

Implications for practice
1. As suggested above, ageing is part of a normative process and brings its own risks. Therefore, it is important to understand the existing protective factors, including support networks, in the person's environment and providing additional support networks accordingly.
2. As noted elsewhere, for successful transition the person's *agency, voice,* and sense of control are important. It is again important to be mindful of these given that these might be the areas in which they might be experiencing the most change and disempowerment.

FURTHER READING

Berman-Rossi, T., & Kelly, T. B. (2014). Older persons in need of long-term care. In A. Gitterman (Ed.), *Handbook of social work practice with vulnerable and resilient populations.* (3rd edn., pp. 415–440). New York: Columbia University Press.

Sole, C., Mercadal-Brotons, M., Gallego, S., & Riera, M. (2010).
Contributions of music to ageing adults' quality of life. *Journal of Music Therapy, 47*(3), 264–281.

agency

<small>SEE ALSO</small> **games-based approaches, self-determination theory**

Agency has been defined as the ability to make choices and act on these in a way that transforms independently one's life activities (Davydov, Slobodchikov, & Tsukerman, 2003). Engeström (2006) has defined it as potential for '…intentional collective and individual actions aimed at transforming the activity' (p. 4). These definitions focus on the potential to take initiative to make judgements for intentional transformative actions. There is a belief that one has control over, and can shape, one's life. Biesta and Tedder (2006, 2007) have highlighted that agency should not be taken as something that an individual possesses, but it is something that can be achieved in and through interaction with a particular environment or situation, thereby highlighting its ecological nature. Therefore, one can be agentic in one context but not another, and this can change over time.

According to Bandura (2000), a person's belief of efficacy determines whether they believe that they can change anything; whether that is producing desired effects or stalling undesired ones. Social Cognitive Theory acknowledges three types of agency: personal, proxy, and collective. Personal agency is when a person believes in their personal efficacy and is motivated to act in particular ways accordingly. However, when they feel that they do not have this efficacy, or do not want to take responsibility for the action, they exercise agency by proxy, i.e., through another person they think has power and would be able to have an agency and bring about desired action. Collective agency is a collective belief in the efficacy and power of the group to exercise agency. Bandura also highlights the importance of agency for well-being.

Therefore, agentic action can bring about transformation and transition that is intentional. For instance, in the context of offending behaviour, it was found that the person's agency played a major role in their transition to a life of desistance (King, 2013; Healy, 2014; Lloyd & Serin, 2012). On the other hand, during times of transition, if rapid changes take place and the person starts feeling overwhelmed, they might feel that they have no agency, or their belief about their personal efficacy or competence to take agentic action might be low (Jindal-Snape & Miller, 2008). In the context of school transitions, Pietarinen, Soini, & Pyhältö have focused on the learner agency. They defined it as 'a capacity for intentional and responsible management of new learning within and between school transitions' (p. 144) and see it as crucial for children's well-being (see entry on *self-determination theory*).

However, this agency needs to be achieved and opportunities created for the individual to feel in control during transitions by enhancing their sense of control, autonomy, and self-esteem. Jindal-Snape and Miller (2008) suggest that active involvement in transition planning supports and enhances self-esteem through an increased sense of self-competence and self-worth. For example, an off-the-shelf computer game Guitar Hero was used as a contextual hub to facilitate transition from primary to secondary school (Jindal-Snape, Baird, & Miller, 2011; see entry on *games-based approaches* for details). In one particular primary and secondary school cluster, children were given complete choice to put themselves forward as not only musicians but also as manager and publicity personnel. They could choose any role according to their interest and perceived ability. They could also choose the songs from a playlist. Within a couple of hours, children had to learn to work together with others, many of whom they did not know, and take responsibility for every aspect of setting up a band. This process had started in primary school, where they had chosen the song list that was then used at secondary school induction day. They were also involved in setting up their own targets and aims for this part of the induction day. Professionals highlighted that the project was effective as children had autonomy and also knew more than the teachers. They were put in situations where they were teaching the teachers how to set up the console or use the game. It provided an opportunity for active learning, active agency (Pietarinen, Soini et al., 2010; Pietarinen, Pyhältö, & Soini, 2010), and perceived sense of personal and collective efficacy (Bandura, 2000). On the other hand, the same project when implemented in a school environment that was more teacher-centred, rather than passing on the control to children, did not seem to have the same impact.

Implications for practice
1. It seems that giving an individual control of their transitions and planning/preparation for those transitions can have an impact on their self-esteem, as it might be an indication to them that the professional considers them worthy of trust as well as competent.
2. Agency should not be seen as a given and static. It changes over time and in different contexts. Opportunities should be created for individuals to exercise their agency to bring about the changes they desire.

FURTHER READING

Bandura, A. (2000). Exercise of human agency through collective efficacy. *Current Directions in Psychological Science, 9,* 75–78.

Biesta, G. J. J. & Tedder, M. (2007). Agency and learning in the lifecourse: Towards an ecological perspective. *Studies in the Education of Adults, 39,* 132–149.

Pietarinen, J., Soini, T., & Pyhältö, K. (2010). Learning and well-being in transitions – how to promote pupils' active learning agency? In D. Jindal-Snape (Ed.), *Educational transitions: Moving stories from around the world* (pp. 143–158). New York: Routledge.

attachment

SEE ALSO **collaboration, emotional intelligence, parental participation, resilience, self-esteem**

Attachment is considered to be an innate biological instinct to seek proximity to an attachment figure when an infant perceives threat and is looking for security. This attachment figure for an infant is usually the primary care giver, but it shifts to other care givers or significant others such as partners in later life. John Bowlby was the first attachment theorist; he believed that the earliest infant bonds and quality of relationships with the care giver influenced their behaviour for life.

The central tenet of the attachment theory is that mothers (or primary care givers) who are available and respond to their child's need in a consistently positive manner establish a sense of security in their child, creating a secure base from which the child can explore the world (Bowlby, 1988). Bowlby suggested different styles that were then evidenced through Ainsworth's 'Strange situation' studies and proposed three clear styles of attachment along with one that was later called 'disorganised attachment' by Main and colleagues (Ainsworth, Blehar, Waters, & Wall, 1978; Main & Solomon, 1990). The four styles are secure attachment, insecure avoidant attachment, insecure resistance attachment, and disorganised attachment. Children with secure attachment are found to be confident that the attachment figure will meet their needs, and they use this figure as a safe base for exploring the world around them. It is suggested that this is developed when care givers are sensitive to their signals and respond appropriately to their needs in a consistent manner. Avoidant attachment children do not turn to the attachment figure when distressed or exploring their environment, and it is suggested this is the case for those who have attachment figures who are not sensitive to their needs or leave them at times of difficulty. Resistant or ambivalent attachment behaviour involves being clingy towards the attachment figure but also rejecting them during interaction and being difficult to calm down by the presence of the attachment figure. It is believed that this is due to inconsistent support from the attachment figure. Disorganised attachment is seen in children who have been mistreated or abused (or whose primary care givers have experienced abuse and show signs of fear when their child turns to them for support), with patterns of behaviour suggesting fear when the primary care giver or assumed attachment figure enters the room/situation: termed as 'fear without solution' (Main & Solomon, 1990).

The time scale for forming attachment patterns suggested by Bowlby has been contested by others, who see it as more dynamic. Further, although the influence of the quality of early parent–child attachments is seen to be evident over time, research suggests that changes are possible based on later positive and negative life experiences, with individuals breaking cycles of negative parenting histories.

In the context of life course transitions, the Dynamic-Maturational Model of Attachment and Adaptation (DMM) is useful, as it emphasises the dynamic interaction of the maturation of the individual with the contexts in which maturational possibilities are used to protect the self and significant others (Crittenden, 2005). Also, this helps consider the possibility of professionals breaking negative attachment patterns for individuals by creating opportunities for secure attachment.

Attachment is seen to have an impact on learning and socio-emotional well-being. The patterns of attachment change as young children move from home to nursery, leave behind their nursery 'helpers', learn to interact with different adults, and begin to internalise the new messages received. Gilligan (2000) suggests that providing a child with a secure base (e.g. secure attachments with parents and siblings, enabling examination, and exploration of the greater environment) will support the development of self-esteem as well as acting as a protective factor in its own right (Jindal-Snape & Miller, 2008; see entries on *resilience* and *self-esteem*). Professionals need to understand the role attachment plays, as they become important attachment figures for some children. This is particularly true for those where the primary care givers are not providing a secure base.

Secure attachment is seen to be associated with greater emotional regulation, social competence, and willingness to take on challenges (Bergin & Bergin, 2009) and can therefore be important during times of transition (see entry on *emotional intelligence*). Attachment is most often referred to in literature in the context of early years' transitions, such as starting formal child care and/or nursery and moving from nursery to primary school. However, as can be seen from the discussion earlier about different types of attachment behaviours, it is relevant to all types of transitions. Individuals will be able to explore the new environment differently based on their attachment patterns across the life course.

A longitudinal study conducted 20 years after the first set of data collected through Ainsworth's Strange Situation at 12 months of age (Waters, 1978, followed by Waters, Merrick, Treboux, Crowell, & Albersheim, 2002) found support for Bowlby's expectation that individual differences can be stable across significant portions of the lifespan along with them being open to change based on real experience. They also argue that their study provides strong evidence for the value of the secure base concept and that strong social support networks might reduce the impact of negative life experiences.

During transitions relationships can be in a state of flux, and therefore professionals need to develop nurturing relationships so that individuals can develop a secure sense of belonging by developing enduring positive relationships (Baumeister & Leary, 1995) not only with them but also their peers. This can be difficult, for example, when individuals move from a smaller teacher–child/learner ratio of nursery to primary school to secondary school and then in further and higher education. Further, other changes associated with transitions can be difficult for an individual to navigate if they do not have a secure base to explore them from or have not learned how to regulate their emotions. This again highlights the importance of developing secure attachments; close partnership between home and school, and different professionals (see entries on *parental participation* and *collaboration*); a key transition person or *key worker* who is consistent throughout; early planning and preparation; familiarisation and meeting with significant others from the new context whilst the individual is in their old/familiar context; opportunity for the individual to maintain links with those known to them (including moving to the new context with known peers or significant others); and opportunities to discuss concerns and have a voice throughout the transition process.

Implications for practice
1. A person-centred approach is required to understand the attachment styles and needs of different individuals. Secure attachment and base is crucial during transitions for an individual to explore the unknown without becoming anxious.
2. Trusting and consistent relationships have to be built in the new context for the well-being of the individual.
3. Organisations should consider implications for their systems of guidance, counselling and pastoral support; for example, through mentors for probationers in the workplace. In the context of educational transitions, there could be a system of providing non-stigmatising secure attachments in nursery, schools, and tertiary education; for example, through buddy systems and peer tutoring.

FURTHER READING

Ainsworth, M. D. S., Blehar, M., Waters, E., & Wall, S. (1978). *Patterns of attachment: A psychological study of the strange situation.* New York: Lawrence, Erlbaum Associates.

Bowlby, J. (1988). *A secure base: Parent-child attachment and healthy human development.* London: Routledge.

Crittenden, P. M. (2005). Teoria dell'attaccamento, psicopatologia e psicoterapia: L'approccio dinamico maturativo (The theory of attachment, psychopathology and psychotherapy: The dynamic-maturational approach). *Psicoterapia, 30*, 171–182.

adaptation

SEE Abcs of acculturation in the context of pedagogical and cultural adaptation

autonomy

SEE self-determination theory

b

belonging

SEE group identification

bereavement

SEE ALSO **additional support needs, multiple and multi-dimensional transitions, resilience, self-esteem**

Bereavement refers to the feeling of loss experienced by someone, for example due to the death of a significant other, separation or divorce, natural calamity, substance abuse and recovery, illness, trauma, and/or career change (Horn, Crews, & Harrawood, 2013). Therefore, it is important to remember that this loss might not only be of a significant person, but can be of a pet or significant object or status and identity. However, in the main the term 'bereavement' is used in the context of death of someone significant to the individual and that is how it will be used here. Bereavement is a transition in itself, leads to other transitions, as well as interacting with other transitions of those affected by it and of those supporting them.

Each individual might be affected differently by loss and the process of adaptation might be substantially different, e.g. depending on the relationship with the individual they have lost, their resilience and support networks, age and stage, expected and unexpected nature of the bereavement. This can also be dependent on the cause of bereavement, i.e., whether it was due to natural causes, accident, homicide, or suicide. In a study undertaken by Jindal-Snape and Foggie (2006), it was found that the stigma attached to the death of a father due to alcohol overuse had a substantial impact on the child's ability to deal with that bereavement and led to problems in forming positive relationships with peers and teachers in the new secondary school. Similarly, in a study of parents bereaved because of the violent death of their child, Murphy, Johnson, Wu, Fan, and

Lohan (2003) found that nearly 70% of their participants reported that it took them 3 to 4 years to deal with their child's death and to move on with their own lives, thereby suggesting a substantial impact of bereavement on other life transitions. Another study found that carers of those people who died due to health conditions also experienced burden and reported that they had received inadequate support and had unmet palliative care needs (Hasson, Spence, Waldron, Kernohan, McLaughlin, Watson et al., 2009). Murphy, Chung and Johnson (2002) found that decrease in a family's distress over a period of time was due to higher levels of affective coping, lower repressive coping, and higher self-esteem (see entries on *resilience, self-esteem*).

Healthy grieving follows a natural course. According to Dowdney (2011), in the context of children affected by the death of a parent or sibling, grief symptoms attenuate within 4 months of the death, although a minority of bereaved children evidence emotional and behavioural disturbance up to 12 months. However, unresolved grief due to bereavement can lead to trauma and post-traumatic stress. For optimum resolution, children need accurate information about the death and relevant events along with reassurance that they are not responsible for them or could not have changed them (Dowdney, 2011; Sweeney & Boge, 2014). Research suggests that professionals and other adults such as parents can be misguided, and in an attempt to protect a child or young person might withhold information about the cause of death, which then leads to a spiral of lies and lack of trust (Sweeney & Boge, 2014). The discussion of death, for example, can also be influenced by adults' beliefs, values, religion and culture. This can then have an impact on how they or children/young people deal with bereavement.

This is complicated by professionals not being ready to support people affected by bereavement. Horn et al. (2013) reported that grief and loss coursework is not included in the curriculum for counsellors in America despite the high probability of counsellors coming in to contact with, and supporting, people experiencing it. Similarly, in a survey of professionals from various backgrounds from a Scottish region, Jindal-Snape and Sweeney (2011) found that when asked where staff would refer a child if they discovered that s/he was bereaved, staff named 23 different services, including child adolescent mental health team, school counsellors, educational/school psychologist, general practitioner/family doctor, school guidance staff, school health nurse, and social worker. There was a circular referral, with professionals referring on to *other* professionals assuming that other professionals have more expertise in providing bereavement support; highlighting a haphazard system that lacked understanding and coordination amongst professionals with ultimately no actual source of bereavement support. This was due to their perception of their own lack of confidence, knowledge and skills on the subject of death, and there were clear indications of lack of adequate professional training in this area. Interestingly, these professionals rated their own confidence to support children to be lower than their confidence in their organisation's ability to support children and young people, suggesting a misguided dependence on each other's ability to support the children and young people. This suggests clear training needs in the context of supporting children and young people affected by bereavement. It is worth noting that bereavement is legislatively seen as an additional support need (see entry on **additional support needs**).

This is concerning, as other studies indicate that high numbers of children and young people experience bereavement; for example, Ribbens McCarthy, and Jessop (2005) highlighted that as many as 92% of young people will have experienced a significant bereavement before the age of 16, and Fauth, Thomson, and Penny (2009) reported that around 1 in 29 children and young people of school age at that time had experienced the death of a parent or sibling, with many more affected by the death of someone else close to them. Research also highlights the potential increased risk of negative outcomes in areas such as education, mental health, and risk-taking behaviour for children and young people who are bereaved. Compared to their peers, bereaved children and young people can be more likely to display conduct problems, use substances, truant school and engage in offending behaviour (Akerman & Statham, 2011). Similar to any other transition, Sweeney and Borg (2014) suggest that it is a good idea to plan and prepare for the inevitability of death and how it affects individuals of all ages.

Planning and preparing for death can be difficult in some cases, again where adults including professionals might be misinformed. For example, some believe that young children or people with learning disability lack the capacity to understand complex concepts such as death and/or might not experience bereavement in a similar manner to others (Doka, 2002). However, research with people with profound and multiple learning disabilities suggests that they experience bereavement and grief similar to others (Blackman, 2003) and that bereavement can be a key factor related to their poor mental and physical health (Phillip, Lambe, & Hogg, 2005). Also, it is important to be mindful that they will be affected not only by the death of family members but also that of long-term professional carers, which will not only lead to the loss of the person but also have an impact in other ways, such as influencing their level of daily activity and independence.

It is important to remember that adults are equally affected by bereavement, as could be seen earlier. Similarly, those who have children with profound complex needs or those who are caring for partners or parents with substantial needs might find that they are so focused on that role that they might find that on the death of the person they were caring for they do not have any support networks external to the ones they had developed due to the caring role, which are then no longer available to them due to the death of that person. This can leave them with multiple loss and support needs. In cases where the bereavement was related to health needs that were genetic, there is additional burden of guilt as well (Jindal-Snape, Johnston et al., 2015).

People's multiple and multi-dimensional transitions (see entry on *MMT*) should be kept in mind as well. For example, parents and other adults such as professionals might not be able to support individuals experiencing any transitions if they are dealing with their own bereavement. For example, after the sudden death of her father two weeks prior to the child going to school, a mother felt unable to support her child at the time of starting school, which then led to her son experiencing problems as she was not able to support him fully whilst dealing with her own transition related to the bereavement (Jindal-Snape, 2009). Therefore, the child and mother were both experiencing multiple transitions that had an impact on their ability to deal with their own grief as well as supporting each other through those transitions. Similarly, caring for those with life-limiting conditions, in palliative care, or supporting families affected by bereavement can be stressful for professionals with presence of secondary traumatic stress-like symptoms (Jindal-Snape, Johnston et al., 2015). This would then have an impact on the professionals' own life transitions and how they can support others in their personal and professional life.

Implications for practice
1. Bereavement can have a substantial impact on the mental and physical well-being of an individual. However, there is a lack of discussion of death and dying within homes and schools, the primary sources for getting information about them. There are myths around how people, especially children and young people or those seen to be 'vulnerable', should be protected from the information about significant others' death, including keeping them away from funerals. This could instead leave them with a sense of confusion about the disappearance of an individual from their life and lack of closure. A healthy and supportive discussion of death that is shared with families is required earlier on in life. Several such opportunities are present naturally for professionals, such as when discussing the life cycle of a plant in early years or change of season.
2. Research suggests that professionals might not have been provided bereavement training unless they are specifically working in that field. As every professional who comes in to contact with a person affected by bereavement should be able to provide some support, it is important that a training needs analysis is undertaken and training is provided.
3. As with any other transition support, professionals should also consider their own support needs either when providing support to those affected by bereavement or when affected by bereavements themselves.

FURTHER READING

Dowdney, L. (2011). Children bereaved by parent or sibling death. In
D. Skuse, H. Bruce, L. Dowdney, and D. Mrazek (Eds.), *Child psychology and psychiatry: Frameworks for practice* (2nd edn.). Chichester, UK: John Wiley & Sons Ltd.
Gerrard, B., Young, H., & Lambe, L. (2014). *Bereavement and loss: Supporting bereaved parents and carers who have cared for someone with profound and multiple learning disabilities*. Dundee: PAMIS.

Murphy, S. A., Johnson, C., Cain, K. C., Gupta, A. D., Dimond, M., Lohan, J., et al. (1998). Broad-spectrum group treatment for parents bereaved by the violent deaths of their 12- to 28- year-old children: A randomized controlled trial. *Death Studies, 22*, 209–235.

Young, H., Gerrard, B., & Lambe, L. (2014). *Bereavement and loss: Supporting bereaved people with profound and multiple learning disabilities.* Dundee: PAMIS.

big fish little pond effect (BFLPE)

SEE ALSO familiarisation, international students' transitions to higher education, self-esteem

As the name suggests, Big-Fish-Little-Pond implies someone who is important within their own small world but might not be as influential in a bigger arena; with the converse being Small Fish in a Big Pond. Herbert Marsh and colleagues (Marsh, Trautwein, Lüdtke, Baumert, & Köller, 2007; Seaton, Marsh, & Craven, 2009) used the terminology Big-Fish-Little-Pond Effect (BFLPE) in the context of highly selective schools with students of high ability level, with those students moving from schools where they were in the top ability grouping to actually becoming small fish in the new big pond of several children with the same or higher ability level. They saw a negative impact of this on those students' academic self-concept after leaving school. Cross-nation studies have found similar effect (Seaton et al., 2009). Research indicated that despite having the same ability levels, those in high ability classes rated their ability as low compared to those in low ability classes (Zell & Alicke, 2011). In a study that examined BFLPE in the context of academic self-concept, test anxiety, and school grades of gifted children participating in special homogeneous classes for the gifted and regular mixed-ability classes, the data supported the BFLPE for all three variables (Zeidner & Schleyer, 1999). The children in the classes for the gifted perceived their academic ability and chances for academic success less favourably compared to students in regular mixed-ability classes, and their low academic self-concept resulted in higher levels of test anxiety, and had an impact on school grades.

Several authors have subsequently used this phrase in similar contexts and provided further data to support this effect. However, some have used this to explain what is happening to children as they move from small primary schools to a bigger secondary school, and the impact of this transition on their self-esteem (Jindal-Snape & Miller, 2008). Children who might have led in several domains in the old context come together with others equally able from other primary schools. Also, it is possible that children who were seen to be performing at a high level, both academically and non-academically, might find it difficult to perform at that same level when coming together with other children from other schools who might be more academically able or socially adept. This might also be the case for children who were less able in the primary school but their teacher, who knew them well, had matched work with their ability in a small classroom, keeping their sense of self-competence intact. In a bigger secondary school, with fewer opportunities for teachers to get to know each child, they might feel more exposed and less competent than they did before. This can create difficulties and a lowering of the sense of *self-esteem* (see entry on *self-esteem*) for all children, especially when several changes are taking place for them developmentally and socially. Further, when children leave primary school they move from being the oldest and perceived to be the ablest to being the youngest in the secondary school. Their self-concept of their ability level might change with concerns about not being able to meet the 'high academic level' of the secondary school. Therefore, these children might feel like a small fish in a big pond.

This can of course apply to university students (Jackson, 2003) and international students as they move from their 'small world' to a different and 'bigger world'. For example, an international student who might have received a prestigious scholarship to study abroad might have been chosen out of several hundred in their university and country, and will come together with several other students including other international students who will be functioning at the same ability level as them in the new university (see entry on *international students' transitions to higher education*). Further, for example, they might find that the academic style that was highly regarded in their country and university might not be highly regarded or might actually be unacceptable in the new context. This can cause a level of discomfort and disorientation for the individual as they might be out of their comfort zone, and, more importantly, it can have a negative impact on their academic self-concept and self-esteem.

At times, transition authors have used the terminology to show the change in the size of the organisation that the person moves to rather than any direct links with academic level, self-concept, or self-esteem. In this context, it is used to imply a big jump and to indicate that a person might experience difficulties due to the change in size from the old to the new environment.

Implications for practice

1. The terminology of BFLP, or rather the converse LFBP, can have negative connotations associated with the image it generates of a small person in a big, uncertain world. It is important to discuss any concerns with individuals in this context and to provide them with as much information about the new physical, social, and academic environment as possible. However, it is also important that professionals use their own judgement to understand the needs of different individuals, as some might feel overwhelmed with too much information, whereas others with high Need for Cognitive Closure (see entry on *familiarisation*) might need it to reduce their anxiety.

FURTHER READING

Jackson, C. (2003). Transitions into higher education: Gendered implications for academic self-concept. *Oxford Review of Education*, 29(3), 331–346.

Marsh, H. W., Trautwein, U., Lüdtke, O., Baumert, J., & Köller, O. (2007). The big-fish-little-pond effect: Persistent negative effects of selective high schools on self-concept after graduation. *American Educational Research Journal*, 44(3), 631–669.

border crossing

SEE ALSO agency, collaboration, parental participation, multiple and multi-dimensional transitions, self-determination

The term 'border crossing' refers to moving between two spaces, such as home and school (Fabian & Dunlop, 2007), or home and work (Campbell Clark, 2000). This is seen to be a *horizontal transition* that an individual experiences daily or within moments (Vogler, Crivello, & Woodhead, 2008). It is based on the assumption that there are domains of life (e.g. home, workplace, school) that are separated by borders that an individual must successfully cross every day in order to perform their roles in that domain (Campbell Clark, 2000). It is suggested that there needs to be a good balance between the two domains, and that the individual's role, identity, behaviour, and even appearance (such as in terms of clothes) change as they cross domains. To cross the borders successfully, the individual needs to be able to identify with their roles in both domains.

However, in practice it is more likely that an individual inhabits multiple domains with complexities attached to each one, and several borders are crossed in one day. These borders will not only be tangible and physical ones but also cultural and social borders that might be invisible or subtler. For example, even within the domain of school, some researchers have indicated multiplicity of interactions and identities that someone might adopt when interacting with teachers or peers (Pietarinen, Soini, & Pyhältö, 2010). It is also important to consider that they might identify more with one domain than another. Also, one domain might stay constant, such as home, whereas others might change, such as moving to a new job, which would then lead to a vertical transition along with new horizontal moves.

The term 'border' is also seen to imply that the domains are different, with borders being controlled and managed by others, with individuals integrating and separating these domains (Vogler et al., 2008). This then highlights the issues of continuity and ongoing communication between the domains that the individual inhabits, e.g. clear communication and partnership is required between primary and secondary schools and families during primary–secondary transition (see entry on *parental participation*) along with that with other agencies who might be involved due to health and social care needs. Issues of *continuity* between different domains have been highlighted in literature with regard to curriculum and pedagogical approaches. Of course, these are also relevant in the context of continuity of expected behaviours, culture, and rules between different domains, such as home and school or paediatric and adult palliative care.

The concept of borders that are controlled and managed by others challenges the notion of autonomy and agency (see entry on *agency*). Some researchers have welcomed the notion of 'borderlands', spaces that exist around borders, where individuals do not have to give up one domain or identity for another. They have also been described as spaces where individuals might bump into each other when crossing borders, with the possibility of a shared space for co-existence, dialogue, and effective transition work (Britt & Sumsion, 2003; Peters, 2010). These are the spaces where there can be effective collaboration between professionals and parents, and with those who are experiencing that transition (see entries on *collaboration, parental participation* and *multiple and multi-dimensional transitions*) with more opportunities for agency and self-determination (see entry on *self-determination*).

Implications for practice

1. Border crossing provides a good way of visualising the transition between different domains an individual has to make on a daily basis and helps us understand the complexity of transitions. However, these seem to refer to tangible and physical spaces. It is important to remember that an individual will cross multiple borders within the same domain every day; not all borders will be tangible, and they might need support for all of them.
2. This conceptualisation also helps with understanding ways in which significant others from different domains need to communicate with each other for successful horizontal transitions.

FURTHER READING

Campbell Clark, S. (2000). Work/family border theory: A new theory of work/family balance. *Human Relations, 53*(6), 747–770.

Vogler, P., Crivello, G., & Woodhead, M. (2008). *Early childhood transitions research: A review of concepts, theory, and practice.* Working Paper No. 48. The Hague, The Netherlands: Bernard van Leer Foundation.

c

case studies

SEE ALSO ecological systems theory, longitudinal studies, multiple and multi-dimensional transitions theory

A case study is used to explore the characteristics of a single, *unique* individual unit, namely, a student or an organisation (Jindal-Snape & Topping, 2010). A case study examines a phenomenon in-depth and in its natural context (Yin, 2009). Normally, the purpose of a case study is to get in-depth information which goes beyond what is happening to why it might be happening and what the effect of that is on that case (e.g. Rienties, Johan, & Jindal-Snape, 2015). Case studies are usually used in qualitative research, although there are instances when they are used in experimental research designs involving interventions (e.g. Jindal-Snape, 2005).

The case is a single unit and can be one person or a larger unit such as an organisation/country, and can be at different eco-systemic levels (Swanborn, 2010; see entry on *ecological systems theory*). A single case study of a larger unit can also have embedded single or multiple case studies within it (Yin, 2009). So, for example, a hospital can be one case study and within that there can be multiple case studies of different medical wards. Or as can be seen from Figure 1, within the case study of a country, there might be multiple case studies of different regions that have particular characteristics. Within each region there might be further case studies embedded, for example, of rural and urban areas; with further case studies of public and private schools, and within them case studies of children from a variety of family backgrounds.

Usually in a case study data are collected from various sources; e.g. the child's case study might involve data collected from the child, family, teacher/s, assessment scores, assignment, youth worker at an after school club. The purpose of this is to look at a case in a holistic manner to fully understand the reasons behind what is happening

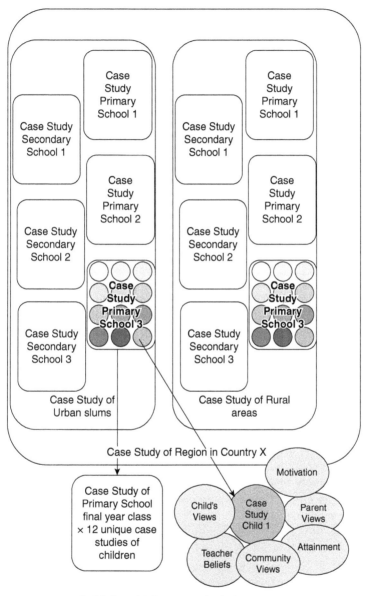

FIGURE I   *Embedded multiple case study design*

for that person, why it is happening, and its effect on different parts of their life.

In transition research, case studies are used to understand an individual's journey, changes that they are experiencing, and how they are dealing with that change. As data are collected from different sources, they can also start giving information about what might be happening from the family, friends, or staff perspective. There is a recognition that despite going through the same change, such as starting university, individuals will perceive and experience that change differently based on what else is happening in their environment, including other changes they are experiencing (e.g. bereavement) along with the transitions of significant others (see entry on *multiple and multi-dimensional transitions theory*). A case study can capture this information in a meaningful and effective manner.

Case studies are usually used with a **longitudinal study** (see entry on **longitudinal studies**) design so that an individual can be followed over time to understand their transition experience, impact of transition planning and preparation on their transition experiences, and/or to identify and respond to their ongoing support needs. For example, a case study of a child starting primary school could involve data collection from them through sketches and photos, and their parent/carer through interviews whilst in nursery and then a few weeks after starting primary school and a few weeks before finishing the first year in primary school. Similarly, the nursery and primary school teachers could be interviewed at least once or twice. Their class work or information passed between nursery and primary school could also form part of the data. Observations in nursery, primary school (classroom, playground), and home could also take place. All of these would provide a holistic picture of what is happening and why.

Case studies not only capture various perspectives; they can also be used to observe how an individual might behave or function in different contexts, with different people. So, for example, an individual might be followed as a case study with data collected in a new and an old setting to gauge their self-esteem levels during transitions. It can help understand how one transition might be impacting on them in other settings. Also, it can help understand how one setting might work as a support system or buffer for other contexts. The in-depth information provided by a case study is very useful in understanding any phenomena in detail.

In transitions research, several researchers use mixed methods with initial data collection through a survey, followed by case studies (e.g. Rienties, Johan, & Jindal-Snape, 2015). For example, to be able to collect information about the transition experiences of a large group, it is possible to collect the information of 'what' from all and then follow up by case studies of a few to understand 'why' that might be the case.

Although case studies provide research data and unique stories, they are resource intensive and difficult to generalise across the population. However, as the transition process and experiences are unique to individuals, they provide the real picture of how things might be different for different people. If undertaken over time, they can be very helpful in tracking an individual's transition journey and seeing the tipping points as well as understanding how the individual adapted to change. They are also good for unpacking the interactions between people, policies, environment, and practice. They can feed into the case notes that professionals might pass on to each other about the individual experiencing transition, and might help plan and prepare for future transitions.

Due to the unique nature of each case, it is difficult to protect the identity of the individuals. For example, Jindal-Snape, Johnston, and colleagues' (2015) study of the transitions of young adults with life-limiting conditions was conducted as a longitudinal case study. Data were collected over time from 12 young adults and significant others nominated by them such as family members and professionals as well as from their case review notes. However, the unique combinations of health condition, gender, age, family members' background, and professionals' background meant that if the findings were reported as case studies, some young adults would have been identifiable. Therefore, based on the initial research ethical approval of the assurance of confidentiality to the participants, a decision had to be taken to present the findings thematically rather than as case studies. This still ensured the benefits of in-depth data collection, understanding the context of data clearly, and appropriate interpretation. However, it was difficult to clearly show the unique journeys over time. It is important therefore to consider the extent of anonymity and confidentiality that can be provided for case studies prior to starting the study, especially if the sample is small. Ethical approval and participant consent should be obtained with that in mind.

Implications for practice
1. It is important to understand and see every individual as unique and recognise that their life experiences and environment will make their transition experiences different from those of others. Therefore, when undertaking transitions research or evaluation of the effectiveness of transition practice it is useful to consider undertaking case studies.
2. It is important to be mindful that case studies, if done in a meaningful manner, are resource intensive due to the importance of collecting rich and in-depth data from multiple sources (and ideally over time). Case studies, due to their focus on uniqueness, need to be presented carefully and the reality of whether it would be possible to make the participants unidentifiable should be considered and discussed appropriately with the case study participants. Again, due to the uniqueness of each case, it is difficult to generalise the findings to others. However, conducting a range of case studies could help provide a good picture for a group.

FURTHER READING

Swanborn, P. G. (2010). *Case study research: What, why and how.* London: SAGE.

Yin, R. K. (2009). *Case study research: Design and methods* (5th edn.). California: SAGE.

collaboration

SEE ALSO **additional support needs, parental participation, special education needs, voice**

Collaboration involves working with others to achieve a common goal. In the context of transitions, collaboration can be between professionals from two contexts or agencies working with each other or, more importantly, the professionals working with others most affected by the transitions, e.g. child starting secondary school and their parents/carers (see entries on *parental participation* and *voice*), or the adult returning to work after long-term illness and their employer. In the case of the former, for example, when a child moves from primary school to secondary school, teachers and head teachers from both schools need to collaborate to ensure accurate and meaningful academic, emotional and social information about each child is passed on, there is curricular and pedagogical continuity across the two schools, and that the feedback loop is closed. They also need to have effective collaboration between the staff within the same organisation, e.g. guidance staff and class teacher. In this example, all professionals are in the main educationists. Research suggests that not only collaboration but also simple communication between professionals from the same profession or organisation does not always work. For example, parents in several transition studies were unaware of the communication and collaboration between nursery and primary school, primary and secondary school, and the professionals themselves raised concerns about lack of effective communication (Hannah et al., 2010; Jindal-Snape & Mitchell, 2015).

Consider the situation when the child has additional support needs or special educational needs (see entries on *additional support needs* and *special education needs*) with a history of abuse in the family, and social work, educational psychology (school psychology), and health are involved. This then requires interprofessional collaboration and multi-agency working. Interprofessional collaboration can be challenging for professionals, and several barriers have been identified in the literature (Jindal-Snape & Hannah, 2014a, b). This can become worse as a young person with additional support needs leaves educational or children's services at post-school and moves to adult services (Pilnick, Clegg, Murphy, & Almack, 2010). This is despite a strong view and agreement that for strong integrated practice and seamless transitions from one context to another, it is very important for professionals to collaborate and provide a seamless service. Inter-agency and interprofessional collaboration are strongly encouraged during transitions even within legislation, e.g. The Education (Additional Support for Learning) (Scotland) Act 2004, amended 2009, and IDEA 2004, also highlighting it as an imperative especially in the context of those with special educational or additional support needs (Mittler, 2007; Bangser, 2008), and some improvements have subsequently been observed (Richardson, 2015).

In another context, young adults with life-limiting conditions and their families (parents, siblings, grandparents) were working with several professionals such as family doctors, paediatricians, health visitors, community nurses, hospice services, social workers, paid carers, and volunteers (Jindal-Snape, Johnston et al., 2015). The strong collaboration between these professionals and families was crucial for good transition support.

Interprofessional collaborative working can provide new learning opportunities for professionals working together, but professionals themselves are not always convinced about the effectiveness of interprofessional collaboration (Jindal-Snape & Hannah, 2014a, b; Warmington, Daniels, Edwards, Brown, Leadbetter, Martin, et al., 2004). Some factors that have been reported to leading to the failure of interprofessional collaboration include poor communication systems and difficult power dynamics (Zwarenstein, Goldman, & Reeves, 2009), and cultural differences between different professionals, the organisational culture and ethos (Brown & White, 2006). In the context of transitions, Kaehne and Beyer (2008, 2009) reported professionals' perspective of the desired outcomes of collaborative transition planning for young people leaving school, and found that most believed that they were raising awareness of post-school options, college-placements, and employment. However, some reported that the purpose of collaborative meetings was improving collaboration between children and adult services. In the US, Finn and Kohler (2010) found that professionals used a checklist linked to legislation, the Individuals with Disabilities Act (IDEA revised 1990), to ensure transition guidelines were followed to meet the outcomes for young people.

For collaboration to happen, it has been suggested that several factors are crucial and organisations can play an important role in making this happen (Hanna, 2014), including sharing of mental models, closing the communication loop, and developing trust amongst the professionals (Salas, Rosen, Burke, & Goodwin, 2009); sharing knowledge and respectful relationships (Bamber, Gittell, Kochan, & von Nordenflycht, 2009); identifying and working towards shared goals (Hackman, 2002); and provision of adequate resources, rewards, incentives (Baggs, Norton, & Schmitt, 2004), time and scheduling (Smith, Lavoei-Tremblay, Richer, & Lanctot, 2010) for collaboration to take place.

Several ways have been suggested to make interprofessional collaboration effective; this of course applies to collaboration within the same profession as well (Hanna, 2014; Jindal-Snape & Hannah, 2014). These include:

- Open dialogue and debate between professionals about their value base, principles, and professional code to ensure everyone is aware of where the other professional is coming from.
- Critical reflection and reflexivity that can be undertaken individually or in a group.
- Prequalifying training and continuous professional development, where students and staff from different professions get a chance to study together, and debate and discuss about their practice.
- Managers or organisational leaders taking a key role in supporting collaboration as organisations do not tend to specify how collaboration should take place.
- Change in the wider organisational culture so that all staff can examine and modify the way they work collaboratively and interprofessionally.

As mentioned earlier, collaboration is not limited to professionals. There should be effective collaboration between professionals and the individuals who are experiencing transitions. There are further gaps in this area, as for collaboration to be effective both parties have to work on an equal footing. However, at times professionals are the ones who hold key information and become givers of information or gatekeepers in the process. Also, individuals need to be proactive and take responsibility for collaboration with the professionals as well. There can be several barriers to this, for example due to the roles and expectations, power dynamics, and lack of awareness of roles and responsibilities.

Implications for practice
1. Collaboration, although it might seem difficult or time consuming, is important for effective practice and seamless transition.

Similarly, interprofessional collaboration and collaboration between professionals and individuals experiencing transitions are crucial. It might be important to seek further learning opportunities in this area.

2. The organisational culture can sometimes hinder effective collaboration. It is important that those barriers and boundaries are lowered through mutual dialogue and organisational critical reflection.

FURTHER READING

Jindal-Snape, D., & Hannah, E. F. S. (Eds.) (2014). *Exploring the dynamics of personal, professional and interprofessional ethics*. Bristol: Policy Press.

communication

SEE **collaboration, parental participation, transition partnerships, voice**

conceptualisation

SEE **transition, educational transition, life transition, border crossing, rite of passage, multiple and multi-dimensional transitions, educational and life transitions**

continuity

SEE ALSO **Games-based approaches**

Continuity during transitions can take many forms. In an educational transitions context, in the main it is used within the context of curricular continuity, especially during primary–secondary transitions. This includes children understanding and being prepared for the expectations and level of work at secondary school and ready to build on their learning in primary school (Evangelou, Taggart, Sylva, Melhuish, Sammons, & Siraj-Blatchford).

The issue of continuity in curriculum is not new and has been highlighted by researchers, practitioners, and policy makers for decades (Galton, 2010). Several countries have aligned their school curriculum to ensure that there is a seamless transition. Despite this, there is always a narrative of a 'big gap', for example, between the primary and secondary school curriculum. Interestingly, research suggests that some children find that when they start secondary school, there is a repetition of the curriculum which they find very boring as well as other research pointing to teachers underestimating children's abilities (Galton, Gray, & Rudduck, 2003). They are ready to move on but this overlap in the curriculum can be frustrating and tedious for them. There are also reports of reduction in homework in the secondary school compared to what they were used to in the final year of primary school, with their teachers trying to prepare them for the 'big school' by giving them extra work. It seems that in trying to reduce the gaps, schools might have gone too far in terms of curricular continuity.

On the other hand, where gaps and lack of continuity are really evident to children are in the context of pedagogical approach and pupil–teacher interaction. These gaps seem to be related to the unspoken rules, values, and cultural norms of primary and secondary schools. For example, Jindal-Snape and Foggie (2008) found that children, parents, and professionals reported differences in discipline in primary and secondary schools. A professional highlighted that if in the primary school a child was late for school they would be commended on coming to school and asked to come on time in future (especially in the case of children coming from difficult homes); however, in secondary school that would result in punishment. Similarly, differences are found in terms of pedagogical approaches with move from small groupwork to individual or bigger groupwork, or a move from a single-teacher classroom with a strong pupil–teacher relationship to several subject specialist teachers with children moving around the school to attend classes. To address issues of continuity, professionals in some schools in the UK, for example, work in each other's class for a few days, undertake peer teacher observations, and use bridging units, to ensure curricular and pedagogical continuity. Further, there is provision of some through-schools where children stay in the same physical location for their entire school journey.

Therefore, some curricular discontinuity might be important for some children, whereas for others curricular continuity might be more important. However, without doubt, continuity in pedagogical approaches and expectations with subtle changes over time are required. To this effect, some schools organise reciprocal staff and pupil visits, teachers from primary and secondary schools work together and bridging activities are undertaken. A good example of this was seen in Scotland, where an off-the-shelf computer game was used to bridge the gap and to ensure continuity but with progression (see entry on *games-based approaches*).

In health and social care transitions, continuity is referred to in the context of service provision, either during the move from child to adult services or hospital to community care. This is considered to be the cornerstone of effective medical care. Gulliford, Naithani, and Morgan (2006) propose two conceptualisations of continuity of care; that based on the patient receiving care from the same health care professional or from different providers that is seamless due to optimum coordination and sharing of information between different health care providers. However, another review of literature found that there were different conceptualisations of continuity of care in the literature, with different indices used to ascertain it, classified as duration of provider relationship (this took account of duration of relationship without frequency of care sought during that time), density of visits (frequency with which care is sought from the same provider), dispersion of providers (continuity seen as the degree to which care is sought from alternate providers), sequence of providers (order in which providers are seen to see if follow up is from the same provider), or subjective estimates (used primarily in paediatric literature, it uses more qualitative measures to ascertain continuity of care) (Jee & Cabana, 2006).

Therefore, there are different conceptualisations of 'continuity', depending on the types of transitions and professions/populations. As continuity has been seen to be important, it is crucial that it is conceptualised accurately within a range of contexts.

Implications for practice

1. In the context of educational transitions, it is important to realise that along with curricular continuity it is essential that students feel there is some progression as they move up. Curricular continuity in itself is not enough. There needs to be continuity of pedagogical approach and expectations with

gradual change over time rather than at the time of the move when children are experiencing various other life transitions, such as developmental transitions, travelling independently, and change in identity. It is worth noting that this becomes even more important for children with additional support needs. In health and social care, continuity of service provision is seen to be crucial.

2. Collaboration (also interprofessional collaboration) and communication are key to ensure continuity in a range of contexts.

FURTHER READING

Galton, M., Gray, J., & Rudduck, J. (2003). *Transfer and transition in the middle years of schooling (7-14): Continuities and discontinuities in learning*, Research Report 443, Annesley, Department of Education and Science.

Gulliford, M., Naithani, S., & Morgan, M. (2006). What is 'continuity of care'? *Journal of Health Services Research & Policy, 11*(4), 248–250.

Jee, S. H., & Cabana, M. D. (2006). Indices for continuity of care: A systematic review of the literature. *Medical Care Research and Review, 63*(2), 158–188.

coping skills

SEE resilience

creative approaches

SEE ALSO agency, emotional intelligence, self-esteem, resilience, voice

Creative approaches in this context imply ways of engaging with individuals that can lead to imaginative, innovative, and active learning, where the individual has a voice and agency (see entries on *voice* and *agency*), i.e. they feel in control. These can include drama, sketches, photography, play, music, stories, Photovoice, Photo-novel, and visual arts. Research suggests that creative approaches can lead to increased levels of motivation and engagement (Bancroft, Fawcett, & Hay, 2008; Craft, Chappell, & Twining, 2008; Wood & Ashfield, 2008), improvement in academic achievement (Schacter, Thum, & Zifkin, 2006), increased levels of confidence and imagination associated with creative environments (Galton, 2010), enhanced ability to face challenges (Galton, 2010), increases in resilience (Bancroft et al., 2008), enhancement of emotional development and social skills (Bancroft et al., 2008; Galton, 2010; Matthews, 2007; Whitebread, Coltman, Jameson, & Lander, 2009); and positive effects on health and well-being irrespective of age (Toma, Morris, Kelly, & Jindal-Snape, 2014). Creative approaches can also facilitate transition by building in strategies to enhance an individual's self-esteem, resilience, emotional intelligence, and agency (Jindal-Snape, 2012).

Marsh (2012) looked at the role of music in refugee and newly arrived immigrant children's and adolescents' lives within a range of extracurricular school, home, and community contexts in Australia. The research suggests that the music project contributed to fostering social and group cohesion and helped overcome perceived separation and marginalisation, thus facilitating their transition to a new country. Similar positive outcomes were reported by Barrett and Baker (2012) for young offenders who participated in the Australian Children's Music Foundation's (ACMF) 'Youth at Risk' music initiative, with transferable skills being developed, and by Wood, Ivery, Donovan, and Lambin (2013) for at-risk young people who participated in a drumming project. Professionals were positive of the impact; for example, in the Wood et al. study they highlighted positive changes in behaviour, outlook on future opportunities, willingness to learn and follow instructions, confidence, interactions with others, sense of pride and belonging, group cohesion, improved communication skills, all seen as important for their life transitions.

Jindal-Snape argues that creative approaches can on one hand have the above-mentioned impact and on the other they also provide the child/young person/adult with an opportunity to express themselves in ways meaningful to them and have a real voice (see entry on *Voice*) in matters related to their transitions. She provides some examples of creative approaches and activities that are grounded in the theories of self-esteem (see entry on *self-esteem*), resilience (see entry on *resilience*), emotional intelligence (see *emotional intelligence*), and agency (see entry on *agency*). These are, for example, using photographs taken by children and adults to familiarise with the new environment, both physical and human. It also includes the use of Photovoice technique to enable even very young children to give their views about what is important to them in their current environment, for instance, or what might become important in the new environment.

Jindal-Snape (2012) cites two studies in which the use of sketches by children and young people to express themselves was found to be more effective than at times words can be, as well as using them for further discussion with disaffected young people who had initially found it difficult to engage in sustained conversation with the researcher. Similarly, board games, particularly for younger children, can be used to hear their voices in a playful way that might be more meaningful to them (see entry on *games-based approaches*).

Other approaches such as story books and creative drama have also been used to give children and adults a chance to practice activities and rules that are new to them in a simulated setting or to help deal with any confrontation or concerns. Story books and creative drama (based on Boal's Forum Theatre approach, see entries on *resilience* and *relationships*) with age-appropriate characters in a relevant context can give individuals opportunities to personalise (I would...) or depersonalise (She should...) and practise within a safe environment what they would do in a similar scenario. Some of these creative approaches can also be effective for individuals with communication difficulties.

Transition practice using creative approaches is not limited to children or young people. Others have used creative approaches for the transition of students to and within higher education (see entry on *games-based approaches*, QR Whodunnit). Similarly, within the context of life transitions and ageing, an innovative Photo-novel project involved 12 older people with disability in Canada to capture their voice regarding participation in society and how they brought about change, as well as including them in participatory action research (Raymond & Grenier, 2015). The authors argue that this provided an opportunity for changing and blurring of identities, voicing and raising awareness of the experiences of people with disabilities about their ageing, and disseminating through the format of engaging graphic stories that could easily capture the attention of policy makers and the community.

Despite the positive impact of creative approaches, research has also suggested that professionals can be worried about the use of creative approaches, as they might not see themselves to be creative or worry about 'wasting time' within a pressured week with focus on measureable outcomes (Davies, Jindal-Snape, Digby, Howe, Collier, & Hay, 2014), and some are worried about 'letting go of control' as their students might be more skilled than them (Jindal-Snape et al., 2011). Professionals can only promote creative approaches if they are confident and model creative behaviour, can build positive and trusting relationships, and understand others' needs and learning styles. Therefore, their professional development, whether pre- or post-qualifying, should focus not only on enhancing their creativity but also self-efficacy, risk-propensity, and leadership skills. This should be supported by an organisational culture and ethos that provides them with autonomy and space to explore creative approaches for transitions. It also requires an open and honest dialogue about what creativity and creative environments mean to different people, for further exploration of any myths and realities of these concepts as well as the impact of creativity on the individuals.

Implications for practice
1. Creative approaches have been found to be effective and can be used in an age-appropriate manner to listen to the voice of individuals experiencing transitions irrespective of their age group.
2. They can not only be effective in listening to their voice but also help with maintaining their self-esteem and resilience, which are very important when an individual is facing or dealing with change.
3. Professionals might need training and ongoing support to use creative approaches effectively.

FURTHER READING

Raymond, E., & Grenier, A. (2015). Social participation at the intersection of old age and lifelong disability: Illustrations from a Photo-Novel Project. *Journal of Aging Studies, 35*, 190–200.

Wang, C., & Burris, M. A. (1997). Photovoice: Concept, methodology, and use for participatory needs assessment. *Health Education and Behavior, 24*(3), 369–387.

Wang, C. C., Yi, W. K., Tao, Z. W., & Carovano, K. (1998). Photovoice as a participatory health promotion strategy. *Health Promotion International, 13*(1), 75–86.

cultural adaptation

SEE ABCs (affective, behaviour, and cognitive) of acculturation

culture shock

SEE ABCs (affective, behaviour, and cognitive) of acculturation

d

diagnosis

SEE health transitions

dip in attainment

SEE ALSO big-fish-small-pond effect, emotional intelligence, longitudinal studies, self-esteem, stage-environment fit, resilience

Several studies have defined 'dip' in attainment as lack of expected progress and sometimes regression, especially in literacy and numeracy at the time of transitions. There has been a lot of discussion about academic attainment and learning dip (sometimes used interchangeably) during educational transitions, in particular when students move to secondary school (e.g. Anderson, Jacobs, Schramm, & Splittgerber, 2000; Eccles et al. 1993; Galton, Gray, & Ruddock, 1999, 2003; Galton & Willcocks, 1983; Galton, Morrison, & Pell 2000; Galton & Morrison 2000; Reyes et al. 2000). Various reasons have been given for this dip in attainment (academic attainment to be precise) such as lack of curricular continuity between primary–secondary, differences in pedagogical approaches, difference in expectations of teachers in the two contexts, alongside lowering of *self-esteem*, especially self-competence and self-worth associated with the *big-fish-small-pond* effect, and mismatch between *stage-environment fit* (see entries on *self-esteem*, *big-fish-small-pond effect* and *stage-environment fit*).

International datasets have been used to emphasise this connection between the dip and primary–secondary transitions; for example, Alexander (2010) reported dip in attainment evidenced in research from various countries, namely Germany, Ireland, Italy, Scotland, Spain, Tasmania, and England. As school starting age and primary–secondary ages are different around the world, and no other connections such as with development stage can account for it, professionals and researchers have taken this to be evidence for the impact of moving to secondary school. However, others have argued that this evidence can be contested as *co-existing* but *not* necessarily providing a *causal relationship* (West, Sweeting, & Young, 2010). Further, some of the studies mentioned above also noted dip in motivation to learn and dip in self-esteem alongside dip in attainment.

Similar discussion has come from other educational transitions, with dip in attainment during early years or higher education. However, this dip in attainment (or other aspects) seems to fade off after some time; although studies collecting appropriate longitudinal data are somewhat limited (see entry on **longitudinal studies**). A worthwhile question to consider is whether this dip in attainment (or motivation) is surprising, as the researchers reporting this are all focusing on 'academic' aspects? Research suggests that at transition times, learners, and indeed their families and professionals, are more focused on social aspects such as dealing with losing old and making new friends and forming positive relationships with teachers; or survival, such as finding their way around the 'big' secondary school, or avoiding being bullied or being isolated (Jindal-Snape & Foggie, 2008; Jindal-Snape, 2013). Similarly, those moving to higher education reported that they were most excited and worried about making new friends (Muszynski & Jindal-Snape, 2015). If one was to 'measure' their attainment and motivation in these social or personal relationship contexts, it might be that there is a 'rise' in those aspects, which might balance out the 'dip' in academic attainment or academic motivation. So are we looking at only a partial picture when we know transitions and their impact are so complex? It is of course important to generate a strong evidence base to make this assertion, but it is probably something that professionals should be mindful of given the belief that learners experience these issues due to lack of curricular continuity, and there is good pastoral support in place. If we fail to identify what is of utmost importance to learners during transitions, we will be measuring the wrong aspects, and if so, will we be able to provide the support they require for issues that are of the most urgency to them at that time? A more rounded perspective is required, and, most importantly, we need to ask the learners and families what is most important to them at different times of their transition journeys. Therefore, a longitudinal approach with continual need and support analysis is crucial to understand any 'dip' along with a more holistic focus on not only academic but also socio-emotional aspects.

Implications for practice

1. It is important to be mindful of the dip in (academic) attainment but to take cognizance of the learners' all round development and attainment during transitions. Support should be provided accordingly, with careful consideration of what type of support is required in the short term and then in the long term.

2. Again, the importance of longitudinal studies that track the learner over a period of time cannot be overstated, as that is when we will be able to understand where the dips might be, what type of dips, and the reasons behind them. The focus from academic attainment and motivation has to be widened out to take cognizance of social attainment and motivational factors that might be heightened during transitions.

FURTHER READING

Eccles, J. S., Midgley, C., Wigfield, A., Buchanan, C. M., Reuman, D., Flanagan, C., & MacIver, D. (1993). Development during adolescence: The impact of stage-environment fit in young adolescents' experiences in schools and families. *American Psychologist*, 48, 90–101.

Galton, M. (2010). Moving to secondary school: What do pupils in England say about the experience?'. In D. Jindal-Snape (Ed.), *Educational Transitions: Moving Stories from around the world*, pp. 107–124. New York: Routledge.

Jindal-Snape, D. (2013). Primary-secondary transition. In S. Capel, M. Leask, & T. Turner, Learning to teach in the secondary school: A companion to school experience (6th edn.). New York: Routledge, 186–198.

West, P., Sweeting, H., & Young, R. (2010). Transition matters: Pupils' experiences of the primary–secondary school transition in the West of Scotland and consequences for well-being and attainment. *Research Papers in Education*, 25(1), 21–50.

e

ecological systems theory

SEE ALSO ageing, educational and life transitions (ELT), multiple and multi-dimensional transitions (MMT), parental participation, social network analysis

Bronfenbrenner (1979, 1992) conceptualised ecological systems theory in terms of hierarchical systems ranging from those closest to the individual to those most remote, namely the microsystem, mesosystem, exosystem, and macrosystem, to which chronosystem was added at a later date. This theory posits that an individual's development is influenced by the environment around them and their interaction with it, and that these interactions do not happen in a vacuum but are embedded in the larger social structures of society, economy, and politics. He viewed human development as part of a life course and presented these as concentric circles each nested within the next, or as highlighted by him as a set of Russian dolls. These systems are based on settings. At the lowest level of this hierarchy is the microsystem, where the individual in the centre plays a direct role, has first-hand experiences, and has social interactions with others, such as the family or school. The next is the mesosystem, where two or more of the individual's settings interact, such as interaction between family and school, i.e. child's mother and class teacher. The next is exosystems, which include settings that have an influence on the individual in the centre but this individual has no direct interaction with them. This can be, for example, an educational policy that will have an impact on the individual's educational experience, or a change in the parent's employment status. Beyond this is the macrosystem, which includes values, culture, and ideologies that have long-term consequences. He later introduced the chronosystem to reflect change or continuity across time that has an influence on the other ecosystems

(Bronfenbrenner, 1986a, 1986b). This could be, for example, environmental changes such as earthquake or life course transitions such as ageing.

This theory has been criticised as being too simplistic, not taking account of individual differences and how each individual interacts with their ecosystems, that an individual would inhabit several different ecosystems at the same time and that these systems interact with each other (Darling, 2007; Neal & Neal, 2013). Neal and Neal (2013) suggest that Bronfrenbenner himself was aware of the complexity of the systems and therefore the simple concentric circles representation of his theory does not do justification to his thinking, but neither would moving these from nested or concentric circles to 'overlapping configuration of interconnected ecological systems' (Neal & Neal, 2013, p. 735). They present a networked model after redefining each of the systems based on patterns of social interaction, which they call a Social Network Model of Ecosystems. They argue that this draws attention to *social interactions* as the building blocks of ecosystems and that ecosystems overlap in complex ways (see Neal & Neal, 2013 for examples and figures). This reconceptualisation has much to offer to the understanding of what is happening for individuals during transitions and how each individual would interact differently with different systems, and that the control or interaction they have might be quite different. For example, two children might have the same microsystem of the same school. However, whether they interact with it will have an impact on their transition experience rather than just the assumption of the existence of that system or particular group. Neal and Neal suggest that this link with Social Network Analysis is another benefit of their proposed model (see entry on *social network analysis*).

Some educational transition researchers have used this theory to understand transitions by putting the learner in the middle of the ecosystems, with home and educational institutions in close proximity to the learner, and looking at the impact of the learner's interaction with them as well as the impact of the interaction of those in the mesosystem such as parents with nursery staff, and nursery staff with primary school staff on the transition experience of the learner (see Broström, 2000; Dockett & Perry, 2001; Fabian

& Dunlop, 2002; Hannah, Gorton, & Jindal-Snape, 2010; Ledger, Smith, & Rich, 2000; Margetts, 2007). When transition is viewed from this perspective taking cognizance of the individual differences and interaction of ecosystems, and keeping in mind the *educational and life transitions (ELT)* and *multiple and multi-dimensional transitions (MMT)*, theories discussed elsewhere, it emphasises that transition preparation and planning needs to take account of significant others in the learner's environment. It also highlights the importance of parental participation in the learner's learning and transitions (or spouse and children in the adult learner's case, see Jindal-Snape & Ingram, 2013; Jindal-Snape & Rienties, 2016) (see entry on *parental participation*). This theory has not only been applied to educational but also to other life course transitions, such as ageing (see entry on *ageing*) (e.g. Jindal-Snape, Johnston, Pringle, Gold, Grant, Scott et al., 2015; Santariano, 2006).

However, in practice, the picture is more complex than presented by the concentric and nested circles or by overlapping networked circles. It is important to be mindful that all individuals within each system will have their own corresponding potentially unique systems. So, for example, if we look at the microsystem of a young person, it might include family, college staff, and peers from another context. Each family member will have a common aspect of the microsystem but then they will have their own microsystems. In this instance, a sibling who might be attending school would then have a microsystem that involves the family but also school teachers and peers from school or other out of school activities/clubs. Similarly, the college staff and peers will have other microsystems. These microsystems of the young person will interact with their mesosystem as well as with other mesosystems. Each member of the mesosystem will have their own exosystems and so on. Even at a microsystems level, then, these overlapping networked systems will have an impact on the transition experience of the young person who is interacting with these different individuals (see Figure 2 and entry on *multiple and multi-dimensional transitions (MMT)* for another way of conceptualising the dynamic interaction between different systems). This also reminds us of the complexity of transition experiences of individuals who might 'seem to' be making the same transition.

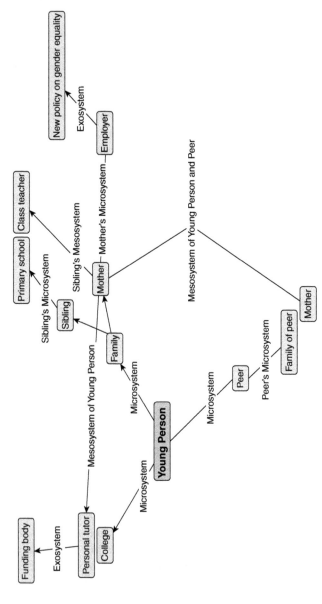

FIGURE 2 *Complexity of the interaction between ecosystems*

Implications for practice

1. It is important to consider each individual and their interaction with those in their immediate (and distant) environment. Depending on their age and stage, these might be different. These significant people in the environment have a vital role to play in supporting their transitions and are sometimes untapped resources available to the practitioners.

2. These significant others from different systems will also interact with each other and this interaction might have an impact on the individual's transition experiences. Further, the transitions that significant others in the ecosystems are experiencing will also have an impact on an individual's transition experience.

FURTHER READING

Bronfenbrenner, U. (1979). *The ecology of human development: experiments by nature and design.* Cambridge, Massachusetts: Harvard University Press.

Bronfenbrenner, U. (1992). Ecological systems theory. In R. Vasta (Ed.) *Six theories of child development.* London and Philadelphia: Jessica Kingsley Publishers, pp. 187–249.

Fabian, H., & Dunlop, A. W. A. (Eds.) (2002). *Transitions in the early years. Debating continuity and progression for children in early education.*London: Routledge Falmer.

Hannah, E. F. S., Gorton, H., & Jindal-Snape, D. (2010). Small steps: Perspectives on understanding and supporting children starting school in Scotland. In D. Jindal-Snape (Ed.), *Educational transitions: Moving stories from around the world.* New York: Routledge, pp. 51–67.

Neal, J. W. & Neal, Z. P. (2013). Nested or networked? Future directions for ecological systems theory. *Social Development, 22,* 722–737.

educational transitions

SEE ALSO **ABCs of acculturation, creative approaches, dip in attainment, induction, familiarisation, home-nursery transitions, primary school-secondary school transitions, post-school transitions, international students' transitions, parental participation, resilience, voice, educational and life transitions, multiple and multi-dimensional transitions**

Educational transition is an ongoing process which involves moving from one educational context and set of interpersonal relationships to another (Jindal-Snape, 2010). The educational context can involve change in educational systems or moving across different stages of education. Some examples include moving from one class to another, moving from one school to another, moving from school to university and moving from one country and educational system to another. The change in interpersonal relationships involves leaving old peers and staff, and forming relationships with the ones in the new environment. It also involves a change in identity, for example from being a nursery child to a primary pupil, with subtle and hidden changes in expectations and rules in the new educational context.

Individuals go through various educational transitions, starting from early years to adult returners to education as part of their continuous professional development (CPD) or for leisure. Some of these educational transitions are better researched than others. The one that has received the most attention is primary–secondary transitions. Please see entries on *home-nursery transitions, primary school-secondary school transitions, post-school, university* and *international students' transitions* for more details on different types of educational transitions.

Research indicates that most of the learners (whether children, young people or adults) make this transition successfully, and for some it involves adaptation and adjustment over a longer period of time. It is important to note that most educational transitions are satisfying and fulfilling, and individuals yearn for this change and the opportunity to 'move on' and 'move up' with increased choices (Jindal-Snape & Foggie, 2008; Lucey & Reay, 2000). In some cases, where there is competition involved to move to a particular educational stage or context, such as a university programme or getting a scholarship to study at a prestigious school, university or overseas, this might also be a marker of academic esteem and fulfilment of the learner's aspirations. However, some learners find educational transitions challenging and stressful (Jindal-Snape & Ingram, 2013). The stress can be due to moving to a fairly unknown environment with new staff; loss of friendship groups, familiar staff, and peers; the need to form new relationships; navigating the new physical, academic, and social environment; and fear of the unknown, especially due to the *horror stories* they might have heard from others and due to the high Need for Cognitive Closure (NCC). Previous research provides evidence of dip in attainment and motivation to learn in the short term (see entry on *dip in attainment*). For some, like international students, it might involve learning to study in a new language, live in a new country, and in some cases such as university students, leaving their family and friends behind, and learning to adapt to a new culture (see entry on *ABCs of acculturation*).

Research suggests that the same aspects of educational transitions can worry or excite different learners, as well as indeed at times the same learner. Please see entries on *nursery-primary, primary-secondary, post-school* and *ABCs of acculturation* for more information. These transitions can be even more complex for those with *additional support needs* or *special education needs*.

Most research on educational transitions focuses on particular stages, such as primary–secondary school transition. There is a dearth of research that tries to understand transition within the same educational setting but different contexts, e.g. moving from one class to another, transitions related to change in staff members. It is assumed that when the organisation stays the same, transition would be smooth. However, consider the case of a primary school that splits year groups into composite classes to keep numbers small in each class (the latter being done in the best interests of all children). Children can end up separating from peers when their class is split into different groups every year, and this can be stressful for some children. Also, contrary to the belief that communication must be good within the same school, at times information about the child is not passed from one class teacher to another. This has pros and cons, as the child could get a fresh start in a new class with different peers and a new teacher; however, it might repeat a pattern of problems for the child that they had experienced in the previous class.

This period is not challenging for learners alone. It can cause anxiety for parents/carers and family members, with some finding it equally difficult to adapt to changing systems, 'unspoken rules' of institutions, expectations of them as parents/carers/spouses, as well as the additional responsibility of working through this with their child/partner at home (Jindal-Snape & Foggie, 2008; Jindal-Snape & Hannah, 2014c; Jindal-Snape & Ingram, 2013).

Similarly, learners' educational transitions have an impact on professionals. They are expected to support the learners and families but with very little training or support for this. Further, their own emerging transition support needs go unnoticed.

To understand educational transitions, it is important to consider them within the context of other life transitions (see entry on *educational and life transitions*) as well as in the context of their impact on other transitions as well as that of others and vice versa (see entry on *multiple and multi-dimensional transitions*).

Implications for practice

1. Professionals working with the learners and their families have to learn to implement new strategies according to their varying needs and ways of dealing with educational transition (see entries on *creative approaches, induction, familiarisation, Multiple and Multidimensional transitions (MMT), parental participation, resilience* and *voice*).
2. To be able to do this effectively, it is important to understand what the individual experiencing the educational transition is excited and/or worried about and listen to their voice (see entry on *creative approaches*).
3. Adaptation happens over time. Also, the concerns and excitements change over time. Therefore, it is important that support is provided over time rather than just before or after the move to a new educational context.
4. Learners' transitions will have an impact on significant others in their ecosystems and trigger transitions for some. The significant others will also have transition support needs and should be supported over time.

FURTHER READING

Dockett, S., & Perry B. (2003). Children's views and children's voices in starting school. *Australian Journal of Early Childhood, 28*(1), 12–17.

Fabian, H., & Dunlop, A.-W. (Eds.) (2002). *Transitions in the early years. Debating continuity and progression for children in early education.* London: Routledge Falmer.

Jindal-Snape, D. (Ed.) (2010). *Educational transitions: Moving stories from around the world.* New York: Routledge.

Jindal-Snape, D., & Rienties, B. (Eds.) (2016). *Multi-dimensional transitions of international students to higher education.* New York: Routledge.

Yaeda, J., & Jindal-Snape, D. (2011). Post-school transitions of students with disabilities: The Japanese experience. *International Journal of Humanities and Social Science, 1*(17), 112–117.

educational and life transitions (ELT) model

SEE ALSO ABCs of acculturation, border crossing, resilience

Educational and Life Transitions (ELT) model was proposed by Jindal-Snape (see Jindal-Snape & Ingram, 2013) to unpack the academic and other aspects of transitions that an individual goes through at the same time. ELT model highlights that not only do learners experience educational transitions, they also experience other life transitions at the same time. These can happen in the same domain as the academic aspects or that of home or community (see entry on *border crossing* for the movement between domains). For example, when a young person moves to secondary school, they might experience changes in the curriculum and academic level along with other daily life aspects such as managing finances related to buying school lunch and taking the bus to the new school or forming relationships with new peers. Further, they can have different experiences in different aspects of their academic and everyday life, with one aspect being positive and the other negative at the same time. For example, a student whose academic work might not be going really well might find managing finances to be easy or might have formed really good friendships. These variations in different aspects of their transitions are bound to interact with each other and if the positive experience is stronger, it could act as a buffer for the negative aspects. Professionals could then build on the positives to provide a buffer for any (sometimes unavoidable) negative experiences. However, the model also highlights that if the negative experiences are too difficult to cope with, the positive experiences will not act as a buffer; in fact the student might not even feel the positives (see Figure 3). For example, a student experiencing extreme financial problems due to moving to a new educational environment with no possibility of support from others would focus on resolving that by seeking part-time employment, for instance, rather than focusing on academic matters.

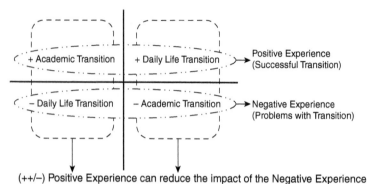

(++/–) Positive Experience can reduce the impact of the Negative Experience

(––/+) Negative Experience can reduce the impact of the Positive Experience

FIGURE 3   *Educational and Life Transitions (ELT) Model depicting relationship between academic and daily life transitions of international doctoral students (from Jindal-Snape and Ingram, 2013)*
The author has permission to reproduce Figure 3 under Creative Commons License.

Note: This is not a static model and individuals' experiences will fluctuate over the period of their study and stay. The overall experience can shift depending on the strength of the positive or negative transition experience.

This model is based on empirical research undertaken with international students and theories of the ABCs of acculturation and Resilience due to its link with the protective factors that can act as a buffer against any risks and the risk factors that can make the transition experience negative (see entries on **ABC** and ***resilience***). It is important to remember that these transitions and the ELT model are dynamic and individuals' experiences, as well as what they see as important during transitions, will fluctuate over the period of their study. For example, previous research suggests that initially the focus of the learner and families might be on relationship building and life issues rather than academic issues (Galton, 2010; Jindal-Snape, 2013; Jindal-Snape & Ingram, 2013). However, once these have been taken care of, the focus might shift to academic issues. In case of any further changes, such as emergence of financial issues, the focus might again move from academic to daily life aspects. Their ELT experience will be influenced by the transitions of significant others.

Jindal-Snape and Ingram (2013) developed the Supervision Remit Compatibility (SuReCom) model to show how support can be provided to learners by different support systems. They highlight the need for an honest discussion between the learner and professional as soon as possible about what the learner's support needs are (academic or daily life), who is best placed and able to provide the support, and how it can be accessed.

Implications for practice
1. It is important that professionals are aware of the positive and negative experiences of the learner so that they can minimise the negatives and build on the positives. As research suggests that learners focus on relationships more than academic aspects when they move to a new class, school or university, it is important that professionals focus on building good relationships with them and providing good opportunities to build strong networks with peers.
2. If the negative experiences are too strong, they can overshadow the positive experiences. Professionals need to be mindful of that and ensure that academic aspects are geared towards continuity of curriculum and learners are provided more flexibility and small steps when they first move, especially in terms of the new rules, expectations of staff and difficulty level of the task.

FURTHER READING

Jindal-Snape, D. (2013). Primary-secondary transition. In S. Capel, M. Leask, & T. Turner, *Learning to teach in the secondary school: A companion to school experience* (6th edn.). New York: Routledge, 186–198.

Jindal-Snape, D. & Ingram, R. (2013). Understanding and supporting triple transitions of international doctoral students: ELT and SuReCom models. *Journal of Perspectives in Applied Academic Practice*, 1(1), 17–24.

emotional intelligence

Emotional intelligence is considered to consist of an individual's ability to be aware of their own emotional response to particular stimuli and the ability to manage that response (Mayer, DiPaulo, & Salovey, 1990; Salovey & Mayer, 1990). Goleman (1995) identified five 'domains' of emotional intelligence, namely (i) knowing your emotions, (ii) managing your emotions, (iii) motivating yourself,

(iv) recognising and understanding other people's emotions, and (v) managing relationships.

Emotional intelligence is considered to play a significant role in academic achievement and retention. Fredrickson (2004) suggested that positive emotions enable an individual to build a variety of resources including social resources such as friendships, intellectual resources such as ability to work on complex tasks, and psychological resources such as resilience. Görgens-Ekermans, Delport and Du Preez (2015) used Fredrickson's hypothesis to argue, and found evidence from their study, that people with higher emotional intelligence tend to experience more and frequent positive emotions than negative emotions, which then had an impact on success due to the acquisition and maintenance of higher self-efficacy and lower stress. A study with young adults making transition from secondary school to university also found that students who persisted in their studies and moved to the second year of university had scored significantly higher on a broad range of emotional and social competencies as compared to those who withdrew from university (Parker, Hogan, Eastabrook, Oke, & Wood, 2006). Others emphasise the importance of not only the service user but also the professional using their emotional intelligence (e.g. Colverd & Hodgkin, 2011). Colverd and Hodgkin suggest that those children who have secure attachment with primary carers will be able to navigate transition to primary school easily. However, some looked-after children might find this difficult, as their emotional intelligence might be negatively affected by trauma and lack of secure attachments, and therefore the professionals need to use their own emotional intelligence to build sound and positive relationships with them to facilitate the child's learning and effective transition, and over time their resilience and emotional intelligence. Research conducted in China found that emotional intelligence can significantly influence job satisfaction of employees (Ouyang, Sang, Li, & Peng, 2015). The researchers also suggested that employees' job satisfaction can be improved by developing their abilities to control and manage their emotions and cope with stress.

Adaptation to any significant change requires the ability to use and regulate emotion to facilitate thinking, control impulsive behaviour, perform effectively under stress, and nurture intrinsic motivation (Adeyemo, 2005, 2010). Researchers have used emotional intelligence interventions to enhance academic achievement, self-efficacy and self-esteem, resilience and ability to adjust to the new academic environment during transitions, well-being, and socialisation (Adeyemo, 2007, 2010; Qualter, Whiteley, Hutchinson, & Pope, 2007). Adeyemo (2010) suggests this might be due to the acquisition of intrapersonal and interpersonal skills that would help individuals deal with their own and others' emotions. Similar to Goleman's (1995) and Bar-On's (2006) classification, he highlights that these skills include, amongst others, the ability to recognise, understand, express, manage, and control emotions of self and others; and the ability to manage change, problem-solve, and adapt. As mentioned earlier, Fredrickson (2004) suggests that this is due to the development of social, intellectual, physical, and psychological resources.

Several scales have been developed to measure emotional intelligence in line with the change in conceptualisation and models. Amongst others, these include the *Schutte Self Report Emotional Intelligence Test* (SSEIT) developed by Schutte and colleagues (1998), which is a 33-item self-report measure of emotional intelligence. Bar-On developed *Emotional Quotient Inventory,* a self-report measure of a number of personality traits that make up emotional intelligence. The *Mayer–Salovey–Caruso Emotional Intelligence Test (MSCEIT)* was developed by Mayer, Salovey, and Caruso (2002a, b) based on the theory developed by Salovey and Mayer (1990). These scales can be used to identify an individual's emotional intelligence to create interventions and provide support during transitions.

Implications for practice

1. Professionals can facilitate the development of others' emotional intelligence (see Adeyemo, 2010, and Görgens-Ekermans, Delport, & Du Preez, 2015 for examples of interventions). It is also important for professionals to regulate their own emotions when supporting someone else's transitions. The first step, of course, is being aware of one's own transitions and how the transitions of those they are supporting can have an impact on them (see entry on **multiple and multi-dimensional transitions**).

FURTHER READING

Adeyemo, D. A. (2010). 'Educational transition and emotional intelligence'. In D. Jindal-Snape (Ed.), *Educational transitions: Moving stories from around the world*. New York: Routledge, pp. 33–47.

Goleman, D. (1995). *Emotional intelligence: Why it can matter more than IQ for character, health and lifelong achievement*. New York: Bantam Press.

Mayer, J. D., Salovey, P., & Caruso, D. R. (2002a). *Mayer–Salovey–Caruso Emotional Intelligence Test (MSCEIT) item booklet*. Toronto, Ontario, Canada: MHS Publishers.

Mayer, J. D., Salovey, P., & Caruso, D. R. (2002b). *Mayer–Salovey–Caruso Emotional Intelligence Test (MSCEIT) user's manual*. Toronto, Ontario, Canada: MHS Publishers.

employment transitions

SEE ALSO **bereavement, Nicholson's theory of work role transitions, person-centred planning**

Job transition is a process that starts with considering one's skills, interests, and aspirations; scoping availability of roles/jobs, managing matches/mismatches and one's reaction to them, and entry into the job market (Rudisill, Edwards, Hershberger, Jadwin, & McKee, 2010). Nicholson (1987) envisaged work-role transitions as four stages of Preparation, Encounters, Adjustment, and Stabilisation (see entry on *Nicholson's theory of work role transitions*).

Given the current rapid change in organisations, economy, potential for mobilisation, and job markets, individuals will most likely not stay in the same job for the entire duration of their employment life course. Even within the same job, the role will change substantially over time (which one could argue would be required for staying motivated and job satisfaction anyway). Based on their study exploring the impact of organisational change on scientists' transitions, Snape and Jindal-Snape (2009) presented a matrix of motivation and job satisfaction that can be used to understand what the chances of employees staying in the same job and organisation or moving away might be, or what might be unhealthy behaviour patterns (see Figure 4). According to this matrix, employees with high motivation and high job satisfaction will perform well (called Performers) and stay with the organisation. However, those with high motivation and low job satisfaction due to organisational change

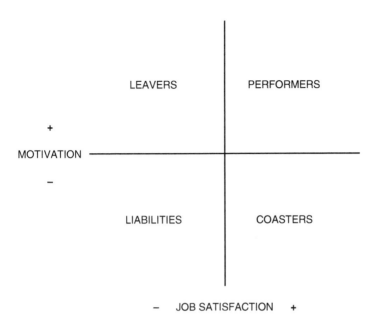

FIGURE 4   *Job Satisfaction and Motivation Matrix (based on Snape & Jindal-Snape, 2009)*

will look for opportunities to leave the organisation (Leavers), with the other two categories (Liabilities and Coasters) preferring to stay even though they might not be productive for the organisation and therefore might risk losing their job.

Currently, the number of young people being recruited after leaving any educational stage is falling and many reasons have been proposed for this in the literature, such as structural shifts in the labour market, with employers preferring older and experienced employees, employer dissatisfaction with the outcome of the educational system, economic immigration, skills mismatch, issues with job quantity and quality, and need for employees who can manage multiple jobs and locations (Keep, 2012; Rubery, Grimshaw, & Marchington, 2010). According to the OECD's data for 15–19 year olds and 20–24 year olds, there has been an increase in the not in employment, education or training (NEET) rate in the majority of OECD countries. Further, recent data show long-term unemployment to be very high and has raised concern that many in the NEET group are becoming disengaged (OECD, 2015). Some of the characteristics of young people who are in the NEET group have been identified as low grades at secondary school level, exclusions or suspensions from school, low socio-economic background, having a child, and disability (e.g. see data from The Longitudinal Study of Young People in England) (Delebarre, 2015).

Other research also suggests that young people and adults with disabilities and additional support needs find it difficult to get employment with substantial differences in employment rates as compared with others of their age and stage world-wide, despite specific policies and legislations to promote their employment rights (Riddell, Edward, Weedon, & Ahlgren, 2010; Yaeda, 2010). Along with problems of entering the job market, those who do enter might find it difficult to retain their employment. This can be due to the mismatch between their aspirations and needs, and the job. Yaeda suggests that job retention can be improved through *supported employment* from a *job coach*. In Japan, for instance, *Individual Transition Plans* (ITP) are created that are linked with Individual Educational Plans (IEP), Individual Vocational Rehabilitation Plans (IVRP) and Individual Support Plans (ISP), to provide support with transitions in the context of education, social welfare, community living, medical services, and employment. The supported employment approach emerged from the USA and is now used in other countries as well. It is seen to be a personalised approach (see entry on *person-centred planning*) to supporting people with disabilities into jobs that are meaningful and can fulfil their aspirations. The UK Government has identified several guiding principles for supported employment, including choice and control, partnership, inclusion, natural and long term support that fades over time, use of assistive technology, and protection from abuse (HM Government, 2011). Key stages of supported employment are considered to be Vocational Profiling, Job Finding, Job Analysis and placement, Job Training and Follow-along services (Beyer & Robinson, 2009). According to Beyer and Robinson, research suggests that supported employment can lead to better success in the number of jobs obtained and retained over time, with psycho-social-economic benefits to the individual.

Similar to other transitions, a sense of control and agency is important for employment transitions. For example, in an empirical study, Brewington, Nassar-McMillan, Flowers, and Furr (2004) found that involuntary job loss was associated with despair, sense of loss of control, and feelings of powerlessness to move on for some people in their study (see entry on *agency*). They reported that this might particularly be the case for those who had been unemployed for a long time, had dependents, and were not given enough notice for termination of their jobs. They suggest that these individuals' psychosocial well-being might be affected substantially, with symptoms of grief (see entry on **bereavement**).

Retirement from employment was historically seen as linked with age and as a specific time point or event, with cultural connotations and stereotyping of someone being an older employee, and potential negative impact on their sense of worth (see entry on *ageing*). However, now it is considered to be a gradual process which has unique phases that individuals need to adapt to over time (Holcomb, 2010). According to Atchley (1988), there are eight retirement phases, although not everyone will go through all of these; pre-retirement and preparation, honeymoon, retirement routine, rest and relaxation, disenchantment, reorientation, routine, termination of retirement phase, with the potential for retiree to move back and forth between full and partial employment. This can be an enjoyable life transition that most people look forward to. However, for some this can be stressful, depending on how it links with other life changes such as ill health. Others suggest that it can be stressful for those who enjoyed work and gained most of their self-esteem messages through it, with some studies finding that people reported being depressed at the prospect of, and after, stopping work due to uncertainty of life after work, financial hardships, relationship problems with partners, and isolation (Holcomb, 2010).

Implications for practice

1. As can be seen, transition related to employment starts during schooling and can go through various phases prior to reaching its long-term termination. There can be inequality in access to employment, and even when there is access, retention can be difficult. Supported employment becomes important for people who are affected by health conditions and disabilities. Most

importantly, early planning and preparation for all phases and situations, whether entry into employment, retirement, job loss, changing jobs, is vital. Ongoing support is required by different people; guidance teachers, career counsellors, social workers, occupational health professionals, and job coaches playing an important role. This highlights the need for effective interprofessional and multi-agency collaboration.

FURTHER READING

Atchley, R. C. (1989). A continuity theory of normal aging. *Gerontologist*, 29(2), 183–190.

Beyer, S., & Robinson, C. (2009). *A review of the research literature on supported employment: A report for the cross-Government learning disability employment strategy team.* London: Department of Health.

Ebberwein, C. A., Krieshok, T. S., Ulven, J. C., & Prosser, E. C. (2004). Voices in transition: Lessons on career adaptability. *The Career Development Quarterly, 52*, 292–308.

Rudisill, J. R., Edwards, J. M., Hershberger, P. J., Jadwin, J. E., & McKee, J. M. (2010). Coping with job transitions over the work life. In T. W. Miller (Ed.), *Handbook of stressful transitions across the lifespan.* New York: Springer, pp. 111–131.

expectancy-value-cost theory

SEE ALSO ecological systems theory, resilience, self-esteem

Several theories have been proposed to understand individuals' motivations, one of them being the Expectancy-Value Theory. According to this theory, motivation is influenced by an individual's beliefs about their ability, expectancies for success, and subjective values assigned by them to a task (Atkinson, 1957; Eccles, Midgley, Wigfield, Buchanan, Reuman, Flanagan et al., 1983; Wigfield & Eccles, 1992; Wigfield & Eccles, 2000). Further, it has been suggested that this is also weighed up against the cost of doing that task, such as doing homework might mean giving up on playing with friends. Similarly, a learner might decide not to go to university based on their expectancy of ability to succeed on the basis of their perception on their perception of higher academic work required, whether they perceive that university education is valuable to their aspirations, and realities of cost attached in carrying on with studies as compared to exiting and getting a job. Therefore, it can be argued that an individual's willingness to be in a learning environment and to apply themselves to the learning task is influenced by the value attached to learning, expectancy of success, and balancing the cost of the alternative given up to engage in learning (Expectancy-Value-Cost theory, Kosovich, Hulleman, Barron, & Getty, 2015).

It is possible to explain any dip in motivation to learn during transitions based on the judgements an individual makes about expectancy-value-cost. If we use this theory to understand what might be happening during times of educational transition, any 'horror stories' or negative language might have an influence on the learner's expectancy of their ability to achieve and succeed; if the new learning is not seen to be 'useful' they might not value it and, for example, costs against making new friends and form-ing relationships might seem too high when their focus during the move might be on social and emotional factors rather than academic attainment. There is also a marked decline in such val-ues and expectations as children progress through school (Jacobs, Lanza, Osgood, Eccles, & Wigfield, 2002); even those perform-ing well in primary and middle school with high aspirations can decide not to continue on to secondary school. Research shows a dip in academic attainment and motivation to learn due to vari-ous changes and transitions, some contextual and others related to relationships, e.g. changes in the organisational culture of mid-dle and secondary schools (Galton, 2010; Jindal-Snape & Foggie, 2008). In some developing countries, this could be due to age and development stage (e.g. start of menstruation for girls and lack of facilities in schools), gendered stereotypes, lack of positive desti-nations, low educational outcomes, changes in opportunities to learn in schools and home, changes in school level policy, rela-tionships, changing parental expectations to undertake household work/supplement family income, or distance to school (Beutel & Axinn, 2002; Rothchild, 2005; Stash & Hannum, 2001), all of which contribute to changes in perceptions of expectancy-value-cost. It is also likely that the judgements a learner might be asked to make in terms of their own ability and value might be limited, as they might be unsure of the accuracy of their assessment in the new educational context, as well as in relation to others (see Wigfield & Eccles, 2000 for an explanation of judgements about self, and how they are relative to different subjects and peers), as several aspects will be in a state of flux including their knowledge of the ability levels of their peers and difficulty level of the work in the new context.

Wigfield and Tonks (2002) also highlighted the role of significant others' attitudes, beliefs, and behaviours in the development of children's expectancies and values. Research suggests that such expectancies and values are shaped over time by individual and contextual factors, including personal and family demographics (e.g., gender, culture), past experiences of success and failure, an individual's aspirations and self-competence/worth, and the influence of interactions with significant others (e.g., parents, teachers, peers, community) (see entries on *ecological systems theory, self-esteem* and *resilience*).

Research in challenging contexts suggests young people are expected to look after siblings when parents go to work, have to supplement household income, and face several gender- and disability-specific cultural and social challenges (Helmet & Marcotte, 2013; Jain, 2006; LeVine, 2006; Rothchild, 2005; Suh & Suh, 2006; Tsujita, 2009). A study of Delhi slums, for example, shows that most children dropped out of primary/secondary school for financial reasons (34.1%), followed by parents' negative perception of education (13.6%); providing further evidence of the impact of value-cost calculations on decisions to continue (Tsujita, 2009).

Although this theory was developed in the context of adolescence and education, it can be applied to other ages, context and settings, and motivation during other life transitions. For example, motivation to do well at work would follow the same weighing up of expectancy-value-cost.

Implications for practice

1. This theory provides an important insight into issues of motivation as learners progress from one educational stage to another. It also highlights the importance of designing a curriculum that has some continuity, small steps to success, and educators are able to make explicit the usefulness of it, along with being mindful of the opportunity costs for the learner.

FURTHER READING

Eccles, J. S., Midgley, C., Wigfield, A., Buchanan, C. M., Reuman, D., Flanagan, C., & MacIver, D. (1993). Development during adolescence: The impact of stage-environment fit in young adolescents' experiences in schools and families. *American Psychologist, 48*, 90–101.

Kosovich, J. J., Hulleman, C. S., Barron, K. E., & Getty, S. (2015). A practical measure of student motivation: Establishing validity evidence for the expectancy-value-cost scale in middle school. *Journal of Early Adolescence, 35*(5–6), 790–816.

Wigfield, A., & Eccles, J. S. (2000). Expectancy–value theory of achievement motivation. *Contemporary educational psychology, 25*(1), 68–81. doi: 10.1006/ceps.1999.1015.

expectations and reality

SEE ALSO educational and life transitions (ELT) model

Prior to any change, it is natural for an individual to start thinking about what the new context or relationships might be like. These expectations can be both positive and negative, making them excited or concerned. These expectations can be diverse and, for example, in the case of educational transitions link to academic or daily life aspects (see entry on *educational and life transitions (ELT) theory*). Research suggests that expectations have an impact on successful transition, and therefore it is important to understand the individual's expectations and their consequence in order to intervene accordingly (Alexson & Kemnitz, 2004; James, 2002).

Once an individual is in the new context they might find that the reality is either similar or different to what they had expected. Research also suggests that during transitions there can be a mismatch in expectations and reality (Krause, Hartley, James & McInnis, 2005; Zhou, Topping, Todman, & Jindal-Snape, 2010), sometimes for the better, such as concerns about bullying that did not happen in the new context (Delamont, 1991; Jindal-Snape, 2013), or negative in terms of socialisation being less positive than expected (Keup, 2007; Rienties, Helliot, & Jindal-Snape, 2013) and myths of expectations of adjustment that do not materialise fully for everyone (Baker, McNeil, & Siryk, 1985), or what might be seen as positive or negative by different individuals, such as expectations of higher level academic work, which when lesser than expected can leave some learners happy and others disappointed (Jindal-Snape & Ingram, 2013). Nelson, Kift and Clarke (2008) reported interesting findings from their study with university students from two distinct disciplines. They found that expectations of students were diverse, with complex match and mismatch of expectations and reality but with an overall positive experience; aspects students had not expected emerged as challenges but they were able to meet them successfully (positive), challenges they had expected did not emerge (positive), and some expected challenges emerged but they were not able to overcome them (negative).

In the context of employment, Marso and Pigge (1987) found a mismatch between expectations and reality (with 'reality shock') of teachers from a range of contexts, which had a negative impact on their transition experience. Oxenbridge and Evesson (2012) suggest that career guidance staff and educators should provide a clear understanding of what jobs entail in order to minimise the anxiety faced by young people when starting work for the first time.

Even in the cases where the reality of the new context is more positive than expectations, it is important to remember that the stress accompanying their prior perceptions might have already had a detrimental impact on the individual (Jindal-Snape, 2013). This can be illustrated through a medical empirical study with women undergoing genetic amniocentesis, in which Ferber, Onyeije, Zelop, Oõreilly-Green, and Divon (2002) found that women's perception of pain and anxiety before the procedure was moderate; however, their experiences of pain during the procedure were significantly lower. They argue that this demonstrates that perceptions of pain and anxiety are highly and positively correlated with each other (both at the expectation and reality stage) and fear of pain led to anxiety. They suggest that counselling prior to the procedure could have changed their perception about the expectation of pain, which would have led to lesser anxiety and pain.

Although in the context of university students, James (2002) has suggested that a mismatch between student expectations and the university experience is not necessarily detrimental and can be an important part of their learning, other research suggests that the closer the match between expectations and reality, the smoother the transition will be (Zhou et al., 2010). Therefore, accurate and detailed information should be provided to bridge the gap between expectations and reality. This can be done through familiarisation with the new context, physical and human, through open days, induction, reciprocal visits, with *first-hand experience* prior to the move being of utmost importance.

Implications for practice
1. It is important to provide as accurate information of the new context as possible to ensure that there is no mismatch between expectations and reality.
2. It might be useful to provide this from various perspectives (e.g. from that of peers or those who have experienced the same transition, professionals) as well as in various forms (e.g. information packs, visuals such as virtual tours, video case studies of others who have experienced that transition, online chat, reciprocal visits).

FURTHER READING

James, R. (2002). Students' changing expectations of higher education and the consequences of mismatches with the reality. In P. Coaldrake & L. Stedman (Eds.), *Responding to student expectation*. Paris: OECD, pp. 71–83. www1.oecd.org/publications/e-book/8902041E.PDF

Keup, J. R. (2007). Great expectations and the ultimate reality check: Voices of students during the transition from high school to college. *NASPA Journal*, 44(1), 3–31.

Nelson, K. J., Kift, S. M., & Clarke, J. A. (2008). Expectations and realities for first year students at an Australian university, 11th Pacific Rim First Year in Higher Education Conference 2008, 30 June–2 July 2008, Hobart.

f

familiarisation

SEE ALSO **creative approaches, games-based approach**

Transition involves change in context and relationships. This implies that individuals experiencing transitions will work with new people in new contexts. For some people, this lack of familiarity can be overwhelming and stressful. In the context of international students, Kashima and Sadewo (2016), for example, suggest that people with high Need for Cognitive Closure (NCC) are more likely to want to have all the relevant information before going into a new situation or environment in order to reduce their sense of confusion, uncertainty, and ambiguity.

Familiarisation can take the form of actual or virtual exploration of the new context and people in that context. For example, in an education as well as in an employment context, there is a period of induction to familiarise the person with the new environment (see entry on *induction*). Organisations also organise Open Days, reciprocal visits, virtual tours of campuses, videos and podcasts of others talking about their experiences, and photographs in order to facilitate and provide familiarisation and knowledge of the new context. These attempts have been found to be fairly successful. However, they have been found to be most successful when this happens over a long period of time, e.g. children starting to use the swimming pool in the secondary school a couple of years prior to the actual move or using the gym at a university from early years such as through summer camps.

Research suggests that most learners want to move to the new educational institution with familiar peers, perhaps so that they have someone familiar to them continuing in the new context. It might especially be the case for those who have high NCC, as they prefer in-groups (Kashima & Sadewo, 2016), and studying together over a number of years might satisfy this need. However, it is important to remember that moving with friends alone cannot guarantee successful transition. Further, the link is unclear, as some learners who moved with friends have reported difficulties, and some of those who did not reported no difficulties with transitions (Jindal-Snape, 2010). Nevertheless, professionals have to be mindful of the impact of the learner's perception as separating from friends can cause anxiety for some learners.

Several examples of effective familiarisation activities are available in literature, especially in the context of school transitions, including open days, induction events and residentials, information packs including photographs of significant people in the new environment, hunts around the new school to help children navigate the physical environment (Galton, 2010) and provide opportunities to work with other students they do not know (see entries on *creative approaches* and *games-based approach,* QR Whodunnit), assignment of buddies, and online links between children from different levels of schools and further and higher education. Individuals may be assigned buddies or mentors and, in the age of technology, this can also involve online links between the new and existing students or staff. In other contexts, such as hospitalisation, as a norm, hospitals send out an information booklet explaining the appointment and what to expect, videos, especially in the case of in-patient appointments, information about learning opportunities that can be accessed in the hospital or palliative care setting in case of interrupted education, etc.

Implications for practice

1. It is important to consider the environment of one's organisation, both physical and human, from the perspective of a newcomer. With this as a starting point, it is important to consider what information needs to be disseminated and when. For example, a school took photographs around the school building of significant areas and people to send to children, so that parents could familiarise their children with them several months prior to starting school. In another case, first-year primary school children were asked to take photographs they considered to be important and these were sent to the new children – they captured what was most significant to them as children as well

as capturing the actual perspective from the size/height of a child rather than an adult! This applies to all ages, of course. In a university context, when existing international students' video case studies were created, some of the information was unfathomable to the local people, and it was evident that they could not have thought from that perspective.

2. The sooner the familiarisation process can start the better it will be for the individual. Considering transition as an ongoing process, this implies not waiting until close to the move or change but starting, at least in terms of normative transitions, as soon as the person has started thinking of a move or change that is to come.

FURTHER READING

Kashima, E. S., & Sadewo, G. R. P. (2016). Need for cognitive closure and acculturation of international students: Recent Findings and Implications. In D. Jindal-Snape and B. Rienties, *Multi-dimensional transitions of international students to higher education*. London: Routledge, pp. 37–52.

friendships

SEE ALSO **group identification, relationships**

Friendships are important to human beings. During transitions, friendships can be in a state of flux, and individuals can be very concerned about making new friends. Previous research suggests that friends act as a support network during transitions, thereby enhancing one's resilience to challenges related to change. Research with children and young people in the context of educational transitions indicates that they perceive moving with friends to the new context to be important for a successful transition (Jindal-Snape, 2013). They strive to stay with existing friends and find any changes in the friendship group as cause for concern. However, making new friends is important for them too; it excites some and worries others.

The importance of friendships is not limited to any particular age group. People form friendship groups in different contexts, whether short term, such as a new parent through a 'mother and toddler' group, or long term, such as childhood friendships carrying on until old age. There is evidence from group identification literature that supports the impact of friendships on mental health (e.g. reduction in depression and stress) (see entries on **group identification** and **relationships**; Miller, Wakefield, & Sani, 2015; Sani, Herrera, Wakefield, Boroch, & Gulyas, 2012).

Implications for practice

1. Professionals are well placed to provide opportunities for forming friendships, e.g. through groupwork (see entry on **groupwork**). They can use Social Network Analysis to identify where strong networks exist as well as identifying areas of risk of isolation (see entry on **social network analysis**).

FURTHER READING

Miller, K., Wakefield, J. R. H., & Sani, F. (2015). Identification with social groups is associated with mental health in adolescents: Evidence from a Scottish community sample. *Psychiatry Research, 228*(3), 340–346. 10.1016/j.psychres.2015.05.088

Sani, F., Herrera, M., Wakefield, J. R. H., Boroch, O., & Gulyas, C. (2012). Comparing social contact and group identification as predictors of mental health. *British Journal of Social Psychology, 51*(4), 781–790. 10.1111/j.2044-8309.2012.02101.x.

g

games-based approaches

SEE ALSO agency, collaboration, self-determination theory

Games-based approaches are seen to support creativity at *all* ages (Cremin, Burnard, & Craft 2006; Cumming, 2007; Miller, Hudson, Shimi, & Robertson, 2010), sustained and shared thinking (Davies, Jindal-Snape, Collier, Digby, Hay, & Howe, 2013), faster processing of information, high levels of engagement and interest, global self-esteem (Miller & Robertson, 2011), improvement in attitude towards learning (Miller & Robertson, 2010; Vogel, Vogel, Cannon-Bowers, Bowers, Muse, & Wright, 2006), significant knowledge gains compared to traditional methods (Wolfe, 1997), and engagement of cognitive and affective processes (Sitzmann, 2011). Also, gaming is fun irrespective of age group (Kapp, 2012). They are also effective in providing opportunities for agency, self-determination, social learning, social networking and collaboration, competitiveness, and immersion (Kapp, 2012) (see entries on *agency, self-determination theory* and *collaboration*). They can be tapped into for different reasons, including facilitating transitions.

Several examples of games-based approaches to transition planning and preparation exist, including the use of board games, whodunnit mystery activities (paper and online), and use of commercial-off-the-shelf computer (COTS) games (Jindal-Snape, 2012). For example, in some schools in a local authority in Scotland, children started using a computer game in primary school to familiarise themselves with different aspects of it. The game 'Guitar Hero' was embedded and explicit links made with different aspects of the curriculum such as English, Maths, Arts, and Computing. When the children from different primary schools came to the secondary school for induction days, they were put in teams with children from other schools who they did not know. The computer game required teams of four to five children working together with explicit roles such as lead singer, drummer or guitarist. To this were added the roles of band manager, public relations officer, and marketing people. Based on their interests and skills, children were asked to choose roles, with auditions for the lead singer within the band. Ultimately, the aim was for the bands to compete against each other. After the children started secondary school, they carried on working within their bands and again the work was embedded within different subjects (e.g. producing posters, badges, keyrings, and t-shirts for their bands based on the work they had started during induction days) as well as the first meeting with the guidance teacher being about the material they had produced. After a few weeks the 'Battle of Bands' took place. This games-based project was seen to be very effective in ensuring a smooth transition by children, staff, and parents (Jindal-Snape, Baird, & Miller, 2011). The study participants highlighted how the project, spanning primary school, induction days, and the first few months of secondary school, had helped them in several ways; it was a leveller for all children, gave them something positive to talk about with new peers and staff, was fun, children at times knew more than their teachers and were able to show them how to use the console, and it was a project where they were slowly increasing their repertoire of skills and subject knowledge. Along with curricular continuity, there was a sense of progression towards a specific and clear goal. Games-based learning provided a common pedagogical approach to build from, as well as primary and secondary school teachers needing to collaborate and communicate frequently over a period of time as songs were chosen and exchanged, consoles were shared, pedagogical approaches were discussed (especially as not all teachers were familiar with games-based learning).

Jindal-Snape, Baird, and Miller (2011) used a board game specifically designed to listen to children's voices around primary and secondary transitions. Children were later asked to provide feedback on the use of the board game for generating discussion during the focus group, where the adult researcher did not ask any direct questions. Children reported that they preferred this games-based method as it was more natural to them, and when playing the game they were more at ease about sharing their views; it also meant that they did not have to respond to adult-posed questions. The audio recording of the session captured continuous laughter during the focus group as children played the game.

Tonner and Jindal-Snape (2015) used mobile technology and strategically placed QR codes for a Whodunnit, small group games-based activity to familiarise university students with the new environment, peers, and staff in a fun way, as well as helping students to get to know each other through this small group activity that involved problem solving using some clues. Most students were positive about how the activity had helped develop their social networking skills with their tutor group and with familiarisation, although the latter was limited due to the short time assigned to the activity in the overall time allocated within the induction week. Further, not all students that were required to complete the task had smart phones and due consideration needs to be given to their availability when working with different groups. On the basis of these findings, changes were made, resulting in even more positive feedback from the next cohort of students. Therefore, when using games-based approaches it is important to be mindful of them being age and stage appropriate, and to ensure that the required resources (e.g. skillset, time, technology) are available.

Implications for practice

1. Games-based approaches have been found to be effective in facilitating transitions. As their basis is in self-determination and learner agency, professionals have to be mindful of letting go of control and for the learner to take the lead (see entries on *self-determination* and *agency*).
2. Research suggests that when using games-based approaches it is important that the professionals and the participants are clear of the objectives behind their use. It is also important to be mindful of the resources required, whether in terms of time, staffing, or equipment, so that games-based approaches do not become a barrier for any participant (for instance, when using smart phones or games consoles).

FURTHER READING

Miller, D. J, Hudson, A., Shimi, J., & Robertson, D. (2012). Signature pedagogy in early years education: A role for COTS game-based learning. *Computers in the Schools, 29*(1–2), 227–247.

Miller, D. J., & Robertson, D. P. (2010). Using a games console in the primary classroom: Effects of 'Brain Training' programme on computation and self-esteem. *British Journal of Educational Technology*, 41(2), 242–255.

group identification

SEE ALSO Abcs of acculturation, international students' transitions

Group identification is the feeling of identity and sense of belonging that an individual might have for a group. It is more than being part of a group; it is the subjective feeling of attachment, belonging, and feeling of commonality. This could be a national group, family, club, or school. Sani and colleagues have provided evidence to demonstrate the positive effect of group identification for adults and adolescents (e.g. with army, family) on mental health (Miller, Wakefield, & Sani, 2015; Sani, Herrera, Wakefield, Boroch, & Gulyas, 2012). (It is important to note that they highlight it is not about just being a member of a group; it is actually identifying with it that has a positive impact.)

At times of transitions, the groups the person belongs to might be in a state of flux and they might themselves be struggling to renegotiate their self-identity. For example, a child who is part of a set peer group at nursery might end up losing that group, and therefore related sense of identity with it, as they, and peers, move to different primary schools. They lose the support network they might have had in the form of this group. Therefore, it is important that a sense of identity and belongingness with the new group is generated. It might be possible to proactively promote group identity and sense of belonging through symbols and sharing the values and beliefs of the group explicitly. For example, schools try to generate a sense of group identity through the school uniform or the university through clothing with their crest on it or motto. Even the lanyards worn by employees can start generating a sense of identity and belonging to the organisation.

Group identification in this way has been seen to be beneficial during transitions. In a higher education context, reporting on two longitudinal studies Iyer, Jetten, Tsivrikos, Postmes, and Haslam (2009) found that although transition to university had a detrimental impact on students' well-being, identification with the university improved it. Further, identification with multiple groups increased the chances of identifying with the new group and provided a buffer against negative impact of significant change (see also Sani, Madhok, Norbury, Dugard, & Wakefield, 2015a, b). The predictive relationship found by Iyer and colleagues remained statistically reliable even when they controlled for other factors relevant to the transition to university.

It is possible that well-being and transition experience improved due to the individual, who can identify with multiple groups, having the resources (and experience) to easily participate in a new group environment. Alternatively, it might be that the other groups that are not in a state of flux are providing them with the much sought after stability or continuation of familiar contexts. For instance, a child who only identifies strongly with their primary school group might face problems when moving to secondary school due to it being in a state of flux. However, a child who has a strong sense of belonging to other groups as well, such as scouts, sports teams, or drama clubs, will have groups that will stay constant despite the change in the primary school group. This ongoing support network in the form of unchanged groups might then make them more resilient to changes in the other group/s. Iyer et al. (2009) also suggested that life transitions can be difficult due to change in group membership, and hence changes in feelings of group identification, highlighting the need for multiple group memberships. However, it is also worth reminding ourselves that it is not just the multiplicity of group membership but the quality of each one that might have an impact on strong identification with a group.

It is interesting when group identification and well-being are considered in the context of literature around acculturation and international students' transitions (see entries on *ABCs of acculturation* and *international students' transitions*). Research highlights problems with acculturation and adaptation due to the lack of interaction between the international and host national students, with students (whether international or host) preferring to set up or stay in the co-national groupings. Although it is seen as a problem from a multi-cultural perspective, Beech (2016) found that some students in her study on purpose chose 'not to be acculturated' and appeared to benefit psychologically and socially from their decision to form co-national groups. Therefore, the identification with the national grouping perhaps acted as a buffer to transition issues related to moving to a new country and educational system. Also, any perceived or actual power differentials in groups, especially when two groups come together with one being (or seen to be) more dominant than the other, as can be seen in the case of international and host students, can actually lead to schisms with members not identifying with the group. Further, Mittelmeier and Kennedy (2016) reported that international students were able to form a strong identity with the university and had a sense of belonging and acceptance despite relatively low levels of interaction and involvement with host national students and social clubs. They demonstrated that their feelings of acceptance and sense of belonging were best developed through immersion in the local language and culture, irrespective of individual group membership. The students reported, for example, that the sense of group identity was generated due to being at that university and in the country, and one reported that it was generated by simple things such as the wearing of clothing with the university symbol. Skyrme (2016), in her study, found that international students looked for other types of groups that they might have affinity with in the new environment. They went beyond the university community and joined religious groups that generated a sense of belonging within the local community. She also found that when those same groups were not in line with the beliefs of the individual, they left them. Therefore, irrespective of the type of group a person chooses to become a member of, as long as they have the freedom to choose and a sense of control, it seems they would benefit from the sense of identity and belongingness it could generate.

Interestingly, these groups do not always have to be long term, as was seen in a study by Jindal-Snape, Baird, and Miller (2011), where a sense of group identity was generated for children coming together to form bands for two days, or as observed in the case of Olympics volunteers who came together for only two to three weeks but felt a strong sense of group identity (Jindal-Snape & Fernando, 2013). This might be contrary to the view that group identity is linked to long-term membership of a group and might be explained by the idea of 'perceived cultural continuity', which has been defined as the perceived continuity of norms, values, and traditions that transcend time (Sani, Bowe, Herrera, Manna, Cossa, Miao et al., 2007); for Jindal-Snape and Fernando's (2013) participants this might be the values behind volunteering per se rather than at that particular event, especially as most volunteers indicated that they had volunteered in the past and all indicated they would volunteer in the future.

To measure group identification, researchers such as the aforementioned Sani have used the Group Identification Scale (GIS), focusing on four items based on sense of belonging (e.g. I have a sense of belonging to...), and sense of commonality (e.g. I have a lot in common with the members of...) (Sani, Madhok, Norbury, Dugard, & Wakefield, 2015a, b). Professionals could use this to identify the nature and number of groups a person is part of and ascertain the support systems available to them, as well as to understand any risks to an individual's well-being during transitions.

Implications for practice
1. Group identity can play an important role in enhancing well-being and acts as a buffer during transitions. However, as group/s can be in transition, it is important that individuals have membership of more than one group at a time, so that the stable group/s can act as the support system for the individual experiencing change.
2. Children and adults should be encouraged to join multiple groups. However, as noted earlier, it is not participation but its quality and the sense of identity and belongingness that is important.

FURTHER READING

Miller, K., Wakefield, J. R. H., & Sani, F. (2015). Identification with social groups is associated with mental health in adolescents: Evidence from a Scottish community sample. *Psychiatry Research, 228*(3), 340–346.

Sani, F., Herrera, M., Wakefield, J. R. H., Boroch, O., & Gulyas, C. (2012). Comparing social contact and group identification as predictors of mental health. *British Journal of Social Psychology, 51*(4), 781–790.

Sani, F., Madhok, V. B., Norbury, M., Dugard, P., & Wakefield, J. R. H. (2015a). Greater number of group identifications is associated with lower odds of being depressed: Evidence from a Scottish community sample. *Social Psychiatry and Psychiatric Epidemiology, 50*(9), 1389–1397.

Sani, F., Madhok, V., Norbury, M., Dugard, P., & Wakefield, J. R. H. (2015b). Greater number of group identifications is associated with healthier behaviour: Evidence from a Scottish community sample. *British Journal of Health Psychology, 20*(3), 466–481.

groupwork

Groupwork refers to collaborative work undertaken in a small group for a specific purpose (Doel & Kelly, 2014). It is seen to have many advantages, including sharing of good practice and learning, scaffolding the learning provided by the professional, social and emotional support, and enhancing one's own learning when supporting others and by developing higher order skills. Groupwork has been used extensively in different disciplines and professions, such as education, social work, and psychology, for various reasons, such as learning Maths, developing a voice, and group therapy. Groupwork has also been used to enhance the transition experience and to facilitate smooth transitions.

There are examples of use of groupwork for facilitating transitions at school level. For instance, Jindal-Snape, Baird, and Miller (2011) reported on the use of groupwork for primary–secondary transitions. Professionals put children from different primary schools in mixed groups of six to eight children and followed good principles of groupwork by clarifying the purpose of the groupwork, tasks, and resources. Further, children were asked to take roles within the group according to their strengths, thereby emphasising that every child had something positive to bring to the group. The work required thinking and creative skills. The subsequent research suggested that the schools in which the groupwork had been structured well were child-led rather than teacher-led, enough time was made available to the group to work through their dynamics, and led to smoother transitions which children, teachers and parents highlighted had played a major part in smooth transitions through getting to know others in a positive and collaborative environment. Researchers observed that even during break time children stayed in these new small groups rather than reverting to mixing with children from their primary schools.

Similarly, other researchers have used groupwork for enhancing the transitions of higher education students, specifically to encourage cross-cultural learning and social networks (Rienties, Alcott, & Jindal-Snape, 2014; Rienties, Johan, & Jindal-Snape, 2014, 2015). Rienties, Alcott, and Jindal-Snape (2014) concluded that teachers can actively encourage students to learn with students from different cultural backgrounds. In two studies, one where students chose group members and another where the teacher allocated group members, it was found that when students were assigned to a group by the teacher and were 'forced' to work in multi-national groups for a sustained period of time on *authentic* and complex group products, contrary to popular thinking, the students developed stronger learning and social networks (with knowledge spill overs across groups). However, it is important to note that similar to research in school education, when students are put into groups where they already know one or two others, building of trust might be easier and quicker (Krackhardt & Stern, 1988; Hernandez Nanclares, Rienties, & Van den Bossche, 2012), as long as cliques are not allowed to develop. Also, it was found that not all students were motivated to undertake groupwork, especially when it was not assessed and seen as an authentic task, or members felt that they were having to work for everyone as 'others were not pulling their weight' (Rienties, Heliot, & Jindal-Snape, 2013).

Groupwork has also been used to support parents going through transitions when their children moved to secondary school (Jindal-Snape & Hannah, 2014c), for families dealing with bereavement, or those moving from inpatient to outpatient care. Small groupwork can also be used to discuss issues related to transitions, what might be exciting and/or worrying someone, how did or would they resolve any issues, and it can provide a support system for those experiencing transitions.

Implications for practice

1. As with any work, it is important to be mindful of whether any task is better done individually, in small groups, or in large groups. For example, although people can learn a lot from each other, there might be issues of confidentiality or ease when discussing aspects that might be worrying someone.
2. Group dynamics play an important part in successful groupwork, and professionals might need to intervene or move themselves out of the groups accordingly. Development of trust

and mutual respect can be very important for groupwork to be meaningful.

3. The purpose of the groupwork needs to be clear to the professional and participants for it to be effective.

FURTHER READING

Doel, M., & Kelly, T. B. (2014). *A-Z of groups and groupwork* (Professional keywords). Basingstoke: Palgrave Macmillan.

Rienties, B., Alcott, P., & Jindal-Snape, D. (2014). To let students self-select or not: that is the question for teachers of culturally diverse groups. *Journal of Studies in International Education*, 18(1), 64–83.

Rienties, B., Hernandez Nanclares, N., Jindal-Snape, D., & Alcott, P. (2013). The role of cultural background and team divisions in developing social learning relations in the classroom. *Journal of Studies in International Education*, 17(4), 322–353. doi: 10.1177/1028315312463826.

h

health transitions

SEE ALSO bereavement, multiple and multi-dimensional transitions theory, resilience

The term 'health transition' in literature normally refers to the shifts that have taken place in the patterns and causes of death in many countries and covers demographic and epidemiological transition. However, in this book it is used in the context of changes related to individuals' health and the impact they have on their other life transitions.

Health transitions might have different dimensions. They can start from the time of diagnosis of a condition, if not before, and dealing with the change in the health condition. It can have an impact on other transitions such as developmental, educational, or work-related. For example, if a child has a health condition that requires hospitalisation or specific administration of medication, it will have an impact on their schooling, friendships, and relationships, and, in terms of long-term health conditions, on what support might be required for independently undertaking daily activities. Similarly, an adult might have to give up particular employment or older people might have to leave home to move into a nursing home or adult care.

Therefore, the age and onset of health condition might affect individuals and those supporting them differently. For example, many children are surviving longer with conditions that were previously unique to childhood (Beresford & Stuttard, 2014; Doug, Adi, Williams, Paul, Kelly, Petchey et al., 2011). However, the needs of young adults with life-limiting conditions are different from younger children and adults in the context of their physical and psychological development (ACT, 2007), and they would have transitions related to their clinical trajectory as well as those from adolescence to adulthood, educational transitions, changes in identity, and change in the nature and type of relationships (Jindal-Snape, Johnston et al., 2015). These needs are of further concern as they leave children's services and move to adult services (Beresford & Stuttard, 2014). Depending on the time of diagnosis, they might have to reconceptualise their life and aspirations. The biographical uncertainty faced by these young adults can impact on their ability to engage in the psychosocial transitions required to deal with adulthood (Parkes, 1971). Previous assumptions about the way life will be spent in the future, or even in the short term in some cases, may be challenged and changed by many different types of sudden, unexpected situations. When children with life-limiting illnesses are not expected to live to adulthood, little preparation for these transitions might have been made (Jindal-Snape, Johnston et al., 2015).

How someone might be able to deal with health conditions might depend on the support networks they have, as, like with any other transitions, they might enhance their resilience (see entry on *resilience*). Bandura (2004) used Social Cognitive Theory to explain how someone might deal with matters related to health and well-being. He posits that health is not only an individual but also a social matter, and that a person's belief in their self-efficacy and ability to achieve their goals despite the impediment of their health condition might influence how they are able to deal with a change in their health condition or bring about a change in their health when related to behaviours leading to particular health conditions, where there is control over it, such as smoking. Professionals have been using interventions based on similar theories and models; for example, in the case of adults with arthritis and dealing with chronic pain through community self-help.

Transition to hospital for an inpatient referral can lead to support needs that are similar to transition to any new and unfamiliar context. These days, hospitals are aware of these transition needs and make information packs and videos explaining the procedures available – some even provide a virtual tour of the new setting. Similarly, information is available for moving out of hospital into care at home.

Health transitions impact not only the person who is ill but also others (see entry on *Multiple and Multidimensional transitions (MMT)*). For example, Jindal-Snape, Johnston, and colleagues (2015) found that families and professionals were affected in various ways; parents and siblings had put their life on hold, with siblings choosing not to move away from home and being limited in terms of employment, social life, and financial situation, as well as living with the emotional burden. There was also an unwillingness to 'let go' and lack of acknowledgement of the young person's evolving identity due to their care focus over several years. Families and professionals working with them seemed to have trauma-like symptoms and had support needs that were often unmet. There can be a lack of honest and open communication about death, with lack of preparation for palliative care (see entry on **bereavement**).

Implications for practice

1. Age/stage-related holistic service provision is required for all those affected by health transitions. This provision needs to take into account not only medical but also psychological and social needs of the patient as well as their family. As transition is a process, early transition planning and preparation along with support is required. Families form the immediate support network of the patient; therefore it is important that they are provided with training and recognise their own transition needs, and start preparing early in the context of the impact of significant others' health-related transitions.
2. It is also important that the professionals receive appropriate training to work with patients and their families to enable them to support their transition needs beyond medical needs. Further, professionals are also affected by the patients' and families' transitions in various ways, with some experiencing stress-like symptoms and requiring support.

FURTHER READING

Bandura, A. (2004). Health promotion by social cognitive means. *Health Education & Behavior, 31*(2), 143–164.

Kirk. S., & Fraser, C. (2014). Hospice support and the transition to adult services and adulthood for young people with life–limiting conditions and their families: a qualitative study. *Palliative Medicine, 28*(4), 342–352.

holistic approach

SEE **Multiple and Multidimensional transitions (MMT); Educational and Life transitions (ELT) model**

horror stories

SEE expectations and reality

home-nursery/day care transitions

SEE ALSO attachment, parental participation

Young children make several transitions, and the first normative one might involve separation from the regular carer to another carer, whether paid and professional carer or extended family and friends. Some of these changes might happen in the familiar home environment with the other carer coming to them, while others involve moving to a new and unfamiliar environment. Going to nursery or day care involves the latter. This transition can be difficult for both the child and parents.

Jovanovic (2011) talks about the 'transitional process of separation'. The separation from parents when dropped off at day care or nursery can be difficult for the young child, who might see absence as non-existence at that developmental stage, with effective communication with carers, consistent patterns and rituals (for example, saying goodbye) reducing some stress, for which the parents and carers have to be mindful of the child's needs (Gunnar, Kryzer, Phillips, & van Ryzin, 2010; Jovanovic, 2011; Klein, Kraft, & Shohet, 2010). There is a large body of research in early years that focuses on the young child's attachments with the primary and secondary care givers (see entry on *attachment*). There are clear links between transitions to secondary care provision and attachments, as can be seen by Ainsworth's stranger experiments. Children with secure attachments might find it easier to make these transitions. Lack of familiarity in the new environment can be the main concern for the young child, whether with the physical or social environment, or in terms of forming relationships. Therefore, 'objects' of attachment, such as a favourite stuffed toy, are sometimes used to make these transitions smoother.

The parent and carer relationship becomes important for the child and parent making this transition successfully, with the opportunity to establish daily communication, both verbal and written, and rapport becoming key to this relationship (Reedy & McGrath, 2010; see entry on *parental participation*). Drugli and Undheim (2012), in their study, found that parents had a high level of satisfaction with the overall relationship despite not having much knowledge of what was happening in the day care. Similarly, although good parent–carer relationships were noted, professionals did not seem to, or consider it important to, know what the child's experiences were at home.

Implications for practice
1. Professionals working with young children will become providers of secure attachment in that environment. It is important that they are aware of the importance of their behaviour and cues that the child will use to form that attachment. However, close parental participation is also very important, as the child's first understanding of interaction and response to particular adult behaviour will emerge from that interaction. When working with looked-after-children, ongoing observation would be required to understand the child's support needs. The importance of a good parent–professional relationship, with appropriate (two-way) information sharing, cannot be emphasised enough for successful transition.

hospitalisation

SEE **health transitions**

i

identity

SEE ALSO ABCs of acculturation, multiple and multi-dimensional transition theory, transition from offending and reintegration

Simply put, identity is a set of characteristics, values, and beliefs that makes someone who they are. However, the constructs of identity and identity development can be quite complex, and there are several different definitions based on the discipline they come from. Erikson (1968) took a life course approach to identity development and suggested eight stages, starting in infancy, with substantial changes during adolescence (13–19 years) marked according to him by identity versus role confusion and identity crisis due to developmental and contextual changes, and changing throughout later life. Similarly, Archer (2007) suggests that the formulation of identity is an ongoing process that involves continuous revision, evaluation, and reformulation of self over time. According to Vignoles, Schwartz, and Luyckx (2011), identity is not only *who one thinks they are* but also *who that person acts as being*, in particular *interactions with others*, and the *social recognition* of that from others. Identity is contingent upon relations with other social actors and the challenges of social structures that the individual might face (Archer, 2000, 2003). Therefore, identity is formed within a psychosocial context.

Most individuals belong to several social groups and therefore can have multiple identities, including ones as learners, professionals, colleagues, parents, and siblings (Jindal-Snape & Hannah, 2014a, b). Therefore, identity can be fluid, dynamic, and multi-dimensional, with an individual operating within multiple identities in different contexts, with some considered to come to the fore in one context and others in another. Research on multiple identities suggests that people can have up to seven significant identities and can function with several at the same time (Roccas & Brewer, 2002).

Some researchers see transition as a change from one identity to another (Lam & Pollard, 2006). This suggests that transition is not only a change in contexts but also a change in who the person thinks they are or are seen to be by others. Ecclestone and colleagues suggest that transitions lead to complex processes of 'becoming somebody' but also 'unbecoming' (Ecclestone, 2007; Ecclestone, Biesta, & Hughes, 2010). It is worth considering that this process will therefore be fraught with uncertainties and grieving, as becoming can take time to deal with and adapt, and unbecoming can lead to a sense of loss.

Others see transitions as times of identity crisis, when one is coming to terms with changing identities. For example, Jindal-Snape and Foggie (2008) found that when children moved from primary school to secondary school, professionals' perceptions of 'who' the children were changed, with accompanying change in their expectations of them. The child might still be adapting to their new identity of being a secondary school child or, as some teachers put it, 'more grown up', but the society and professionals' perception of that change might be immediate. Jindal-Snape, Johnston et al. (2015) found that the young adults with life-limiting conditions were developing a new identity of an adult and wanted to move in to their own house with a partner, but this identity did not reconcile with the identity others had given them of someone who was a 'patient', 'needing to be cared for', or 'too young'.

Transitions are also opportunities that people use to change their identity. For example, a child moving to a secondary school might not want to carry on with old friends and choose to make new friends so that they can explore who they want to be and create a new identity for themselves. A professional on a training programme might want to relinquish their professional identity in that context and take the identity of a learner or higher education student. A teacher might choose to be seen as a parent when they go to their child's school. So some might carry on with multiple identities and move from one to the other in particular contexts; others might struggle to adapt to changing identity, particularly when imposed by others. Consider, for example, an international student who moves from a country where racially he was in majority to a new country where they are told that they are a member of the minority ethnic community. Cross-cultural transition might also involve changes in one's cultural identity and inter-group relations (Zhou, Jindal-Snape, Topping, &

Todman, 2008) (see **ABC**). Or consider an individual who wants to see themselves as an able university student but others see their identity as that of a disabled student. This mismatch in identities can lead to, what Erikson called, identity crisis. What has also been found is that there is an interaction in different people's identities, as they can be in transition due to someone else's transitions (see entry on *multiple and multi-dimensional transition theory*). A parent whose child has moved from nursery to primary school might find that they now have a new identity of a primary school parent.

See entry on *transition from offending and reintegration* for the role of change in identity.

Implications for practice

1. Contextual transitions lead to change in identity. But change in identity itself is a transition. Both transition and change in identity are ongoing processes. It is important to be mindful of the changing identities and what messages an individual is receiving from their environment, what impact it might have on their identity (potentially identity crisis), and its psychosocial impact on the individual's well-being.

FURTHER READING

Erikson, E. (1968). *Identity: Youth and crisis.* New York: Norton.

Schwartz, S. J., Luyckx, K., Vignoles, V. L. (Eds.) (2011). *Handbook of identity theory and research.* New York: Springer.

induction

SEE ALSO **familiarisation, Nicholson's theory of work role transitions**

Induction involves familiarisation with a new environment and people, systems and structures, expectations and role, policy and procedure of an organisation, group, or programme (see entry on *familiarisation*). The purpose of induction is to help a person adjust to the new context. It usually takes place in the first week of starting in a new organisation or environment, and can be limited to a couple of days to a couple of weeks. In some cases, such as in educational contexts, induction can start prior to starting in a new school, for example.

Richardson and Tate (2013), in a higher education context, argue for a longer induction and one that includes the voices of the existing students through peer mentoring. The latter would involve bringing students on the same programme together, with existing students sharing experiences of transition to university and providing insights on the basis of that. Participants of Richardson and Tate's (2013) 'Extended Induction' pilot positively evaluated the programme, which ran over a period of five weeks and included lectures, seminars, workshops, tutorials and mentor meetings, and a residential. This induction programme has some similarities with what is provided, for example, to children starting primary or secondary school in terms of peer mentoring or peer buddies and residentials (Jindal-Snape et al., 2011; Jindal-Snape, 2013). Similarly, in the context of employment, mentors are assigned to the new employee or probationer. In the context of moving into the unknown environment of health and social care, professionals and organisations provide valuable insights through videos and leaflets, for example what surgery or a procedure might involve.

Induction in general starts when the person has arrived in the new context, whether educational, employment, or other such as health or social care related. However, it is worth considering whether this is sufficient. The familiarisation aspect of induction should ideally start prior to the move, when the individual is still in a familiar and known context. Research suggests that individuals are most stressed prior to the move due to the uncertainty of the new environment and people. There is also evidence of 'horror stories' that are often found to be baseless once the person experiences the new context first hand. The lack of adequate exposure to the new context, especially for those with high Need for Cognitive Disclosure (Kashima & Sadewo, 2016), could be detrimental to the adaptation process and well-being. Some professionals have provided some of the familiarisation and peer mentoring aspects of induction effectively through online induction, sending of information packs, virtual tours of campuses, videos and podcasts of others talking about their experiences, photographs and setting up online communities with new and existing students prior to the move (Jindal-Snape & Booth, 2010). Jindal-Snape and Booth (2010) used video case studies of existing international and home students in a higher education context that focused from the stage of researching which university to attend and why, and scholarships and other funding options, to daily life in a new city, academic life in a new educational environment and system, arriving in the new country and what to do once in the new environment, and provision of first-hand experience throughout this period to the current situation of the student (in some case the first and in others the final year of the programme of study). They also reported on online chats between staff and old and new students, and creation of webpages and email accounts for students from the stage of application to induct them and to facilitate a sense of belonging amongst the new applicants. Similarly in the transition to primary school context, Gorton (2012) reported the use of photographs that the existing first-year children took to send to the nursery children to familiarise them with significant people and places. The Open Day or Induction days held prior to starting a new organisation also aim to help with that. In the context of employment and Nicholson's Theory of Work Role Transitions (1987), of the four stages of Preparation, Encounters, Adjustment, and Stabilisation of work-role transitions, this is seen to be part of the 'Preparation' stage, where the individual can be provided with the opportunity for familiarisation and a discussion of what is exciting or worrying them (see entry on *Nicholson's theory of work role transitions*).

It is important to be mindful that induction, whether starting prior to the move or once the move has happened, is only one aspect of the formal support process. As transition is an ongoing process, support needs to be provided beyond the formal 'induction period'. An evaluation of any induction programme is important as well (Akos, 2010).

Implications for practice

1. Induction plays an important role in providing support for transition. As with familiarisation, the induction process should ideally start prior to the move to a new context or relationship, as this can minimise stress for individuals.
2. It is important to remember that transition is an ongoing process and that formal support should not be stopped at induction.
3. Induction should include the voice of those who already have experienced similar transitions in the past, as they can have unique insights to offer to others in terms of their own experiences but also suggest what should be included in an effective induction programme.

4. With advancements in technology and availability of social media, it is worth considering how induction can happen virtually, through online communities. There are good examples of these being set up through organisations, especially, increasingly, universities' Facebook and Twitter accounts.

FURTHER READING

Jindal-Snape, D., & Booth, H. (2010). *International doctoral students' experience of transitions: examples of video case studies to facilitate transitions*. S-ICT Conference, Student mobility and ICT: World in transition, 1–2 November 2010, The Hague, Netherlands. Access proceedings from www.fdewb.unimaas.nl/educ_v2/STEP/Documents/Proceedings_S_ICT2010_Final.PDF.

Nicholson, N. (1987). The transition cycle: a conceptual framework for the analysis of change and human resources management. *Research in Personnel and Human Resources Management, 5,* 167–222.

Richardson, M. J., & Tate, S. (2013). Improving the transition to university: Introducing student voices into the formal induction process for new geography undergraduates. *Journal of Geography in Higher Education, 37*(4), 611–618.

information packs

SEE familiarisation

information sharing

SEE collaboration

interactionist approach

SEE readiness

international students' transitions to higher education

SEE ALSO ABCs of acculturation, educational and life transitions, groupwork, multiple and multi-dimensional transitions, social network analysis

The numbers of international students are increasing, with 4.3 million studying overseas in 2011 (OECD, 2013). International students bring several benefits to the host country and university academically, culturally, and economically, as well as gaining a lot themselves from this experience (Jindal-Snape & Rienties, 2016). Although sometimes grouped together as a homogeneous group of 'international students', there are several categories and character-istics of international students. Apart from the lone international student who may go to another country for a year or longer, there are others, for example, coming as a cohort from one institution to another due to agreements between two universities or countries, distance education international students who rarely physically are in the other country, short-term exchange students, from offshore campuses, and staff making in-country visits (Jindal-Snape & Rien-ties, 2016). Depending on educational stage they can be very young or mature. Some might be coming for undergraduate studies and leaving home for the first time (let alone country) and others might be postgraduate students who have studied overseas for an under-graduate degree before coming to another new country. Exchange students with frequent exchange of staff and students between the two universities might be more familiar with some of the people involved, more prepared, and have been working towards the trip for a long time. Further, whether they come on their own or with families will also change the dynamics for them in terms of transi-tions. Depending on similarity between mother tongue and host nation's language and cultural distance, again their experiences will be very different.

They face multiple challenges, such as learning to live in a new country and community, studying in their second language (or even third), working in a different educational system with quite different norms and expectations, and forming and/or losing rela-tionships (see *ABCs of acculturation, educational and life transitions, multiple and multi-dimensional transitions* and *social network analysis* for more information) (Jindal-Snape & Ingram, 2013). The issues they face when they arrive in a new country will be different based on their age, stage, location, individual/group, exchange, life experi-ences, family dynamics, culture, and language. Research suggests that there are substantial differences in academic and social adjust-ment of international students from different regions; the lesser the cultural difference between own nation and host-nation, the easier it is to adjust and students have fewer transition problems (Rienties, Beausaert, Grohnert, Niemantsverdriet, & Kommers, 2012; Rienties & Tempelaar, 2013). Similarly, research suggests that when students come as a cohort, they face fewer problems on arrival; however, their academic and social integration in the new context and acculturation might be limited. International students interact not only with staff and students but also the local communities. Their well-being and academic success are reliant on positive interactions and learning experiences. It is worth noting that not all students are motivated to study abroad for academic purposes; some see it as a great opportunity for self-development (Jindal-Snape & Ingram, 2013).

For successful adaptation and academic progress, international students have to learn to not only adapt to a new educational system but also to adapt to the host country's culture. ABCs of acculturation is a framework that has been used to understand the cultural adaptation of international students during their transition to higher education institutions in a new country (Ward, Bochner, & Furnham, 2001; Zhou, Jindal-Snape, Topping, & Todman, 2008; see entry on *ABCs of acculturation*). It is also worth remembering that international students *actively* choose to go to a new environment and educational system. They pay high fees and have a menu of options available to them. Therefore, it stands to reason that their adaptation might follow a different path from that of other migrants who have entered the host country for other reasons, whether economic or political. Further, due to technological changes, the international students are more aware of what is happening in another country and educational system than some might have been even 20 years ago. Also, it has meant that they are more able to keep in touch with friends and family back home.

In terms of international students' effective transitions, Bethel, Szabo, and Ward (2016) assert that integration, engagement with both co-nationals and host nationals, provide the individual with a better range of resources for inter-cultural adaptation. However, empirical studies indicate the lack of close interaction between host and international students (Rienties, Heliot, & Jindal-Snape, 2013), leading to lack of acculturation, isolation, and difficulty in pedagogical adaptation (Rienties, Heliot et al., 2013; Rienties, Hernandez

Nanclares, Jindal-Snape, & Alcott, 2013). This lack of interaction should not be seen as a failure on the part of international students as has often been asserted in the past. International students have reported that host national students have closed pre-existing networks that are difficult to enter. Also, some host national students are found to have low motivation towards acculturation and prefer to focus on getting good grades that are sometimes perceived to be more achievable by forming learning and social networks with other host national students (Rienties, Johan, & Jindal-Snape, 2014, 2015). Further, it is worth noting that in reality there are not just two groups, co-national and host national, but also a third one, i.e. multi-national, with substantial interaction between this group, perhaps due to smaller numbers and having the same purpose. 'Multi-national' in this context implies other international students with whom an international student would form networks, and indeed research suggests that after forming networks with co-nationals, international students found it easier to form networks with international students from a different country and culture compared to with host nationals (Rienties, Heliot et al., 2013).

Rienties and colleagues have used Social Network Analysis (SNA) to determine international and host student networks in higher education, followed by small mixed group tasks to encourage acculturation (Rienties, Heliot et al., 2013; Rienties, Hernandez Nanclares et al., 2013; Rienties & Jindal-Snape, 2016; Rienties, Johan et al., 2014; see entry on *social network analysis*). They found that mixed groups provided opportunities to develop more and stronger cross-cultural ties, with some students becoming bridge builders between different cultures (see entry on *groupwork*). The key characteristics of bridge builders, which increased the possibility of better pedagogical and cultural adaptation, included cultural sensitivity, motivation to do well, positive attitude towards sharing and learning from others, accepting of differences in experience and expertise, accepting of different learning styles, good conflict resolution strategies, good leadership skills, adaptability, respecting people's choices, good communication skills and willingness to communicate, and academic ability (Rienties, Johan, & Jindal-Snape, 2015). These characteristics are reflective of all three aspects of Affect-Behaviour-Cognition (see entry on *ABCs of acculturation*).

Rienties and Jindal-Snape (2016) and Bethel et al. (2016) suggest that internationalisation literature should broaden the focus of ABC to a holistic understanding of the ecosystems of host national and international students (e.g. dynamic SN-ABC model, Social Network-Affective-Behaviour-Cognition, Rienties & Jindal-Snape 2016). The SN-ABC model is based on the premise that transition is an ongoing process, with adaptation over time, and is multiple and multi-dimensional (Jindal-Snape & Rienties, 2016). It highlights the agency of the student to adapt or otherwise in particular ways for 'cultural or pedagogical adaptation', highlighting the importance of self-determination (Deci & Ryan, 2000).

Not surprisingly, more is known about international students' transitions to countries such as the USA, UK, Australia, New Zealand, and mainland Europe, as these used to be the main destinations for a large number of students from across the world. However, there has been a change, with an increasing number of students going to Asian universities, for instance.

Jindal-Snape and Rienties' (2016) suggestions for enhancing successful transition include, amongst others:

1. Information related to the academic and daily life in the host country should be provided prior to the move.
2. Creation and use of intercultural training resources for all students and staff.
3. Allow time for adjusting to the daily life prior to focusing on academic life.
4. Creation of opportunities to interact with co-national students and community, and host and other international students and communities.
5. Support the multiple transitions of *all* students and significant others, such as spouse and children, in their lives.

Please see entries on **groupwork** and **social network analysis** for some suggestions of methods that have been found to be useful with international students.

Implications for practice
1. It is important to consider the holistic transitions of international students who go through multiple transitions at the

same time. There is a lot of good research in this area as well as examples of good practice that can be found from different university websites.

2. Along with international students, host university staff, students, and community have to adapt and learn to work and interact with them. Proactive learning about other cultures and acculturation is as important for these groups as for the international students.

3. Professionals should also consider familiarising the host nationals with the culture of different international students. This could be facilitated through development of intercultural educational resources for students and staff, both international and host national. The intercultural training should start as early as possible and ideally be incorporated in the curriculum.

4. It is advisable to set up a peer pairing or buddy system that starts prior to international students moving to the new environment.

FURTHER READING

Bethel, A., Szabo, A., & Ward, C. (2016). Parallel lives? Predicting and enhancing connectedness between international and domestic students. In D. Jindal-Snape & B. Rienties, *Multi-dimensional transitions of international students to Higher Education*. New York: Routledge pp. 21–35.

Jindal-Snape, D., & Rienties, B. (Eds.) (2016). *Multi-dimensional transitions of international students to Higher Education*. New York: Routledge.

interrupted education

SEE hospitalisation

j

job coach

<small>SEE</small> employment

k

key worker

SEE special educational needs, transition meetings

1

language used

SEE ALSO **big-fish-little-pond effect, rite of passage, virtual backpack approach**

Transitions, educational transitions in particular, can be surrounded by a lot of myths and negative language, based on an individual's own perceptions of what it might be like or lived experience of professionals or parents at that stage (Jindal-Snape & Foggie, 2008). The language used can be very worrying for those going through or preparing for particular transition phases. For example, teachers, and indeed children and parents, talk about high school being 'bigger' with concerns of 'getting lost', which would lead to high school teachers punishing the child, as they are a 'lot stricter' than the primary school teachers, along with, of course, concerns of 'head flushed down the toilet by bigger kids', 'a lot of home work', and the need to 'work harder'. Professionals and parents talk about the child being 'not ready' to start school or indeed a young person being 'not ready' to start university or move to the 'big unknown real world' or 'wait till you are older' or 'when you have to work'. There is the use of 'big-fish-little-pond' in the literature, with parallel imagery of 'little-fish-big-pond', which invokes thoughts of individuals being overwhelmed in the new 'big pond' environment. There is some positive language, albeit limited, used as well when describing it as a 'rite of passage' and that 'virtual backpacks' should be opened (see entries on *rite of passage* and *virtual backpack approach*).

Transitions research also seems to focus on the dip in attainment, self-esteem, and anxieties. It is not surprising that this is the case as the research itself perhaps emerged from the concerns in practice and the focus was on trying to 'resolve the issues'. However, this was perhaps done to the detriment of the positive narratives of transitions. When individuals are asked about their views of transition after a significant move, they express surprise at the stories and languages not matching their experience (Jindal-Snape & Foggie, 2008), and they comment on the unfounded nature of the 'horror stories' (Lucey & Reay, 2010). This negative language tends to focus on the anxieties related to transition as well as potentially increasing them. In fact, several studies indicate that individuals are also excited at the prospect of moving on with increased choices and opportunities (Graham & Hill, 2003; Jindal-Snape, Douglas, Topping, Kerr, & Smith, 2006; Jindal-Snape & Foggie, 2008; Lucey & Reay, 2000; Zeedyk, Gallaher, Henderson, Hope, Husband, & Lindsay, 2003). These studies reported that transition leads to anxiety but children/young people also positively anticipate the new opportunities. Indeed Jindal-Snape (2013) and Muszynski and Jindal-Snape (2015) reported that the same aspects worried and excited people making transitions. These included the excitement of making new friends but concerns about not being able to make friends and losing old friends, the bigger organisation offering more opportunities but also concerns of being lost, losing previous relationships but gaining several new ones, and so on. Further, the same aspects that worried some were seen to be positive, but challenging, by others. For example, in the Jindal-Snape and Ingram (2013) study an international doctoral student reported that,

> The very challenging academic structure and the ability to structure my own time because I had previously been a full time carer for my children and now I am in a full time PhD, which has required adjustment for everyone but I am thoroughly enjoying it and wouldn't want anything else. (p. 20)

Further, people's positive and negative views also shift over time. It is to be noted that some life transitions do not lead to such positive outcomes, such as death of a significant other, but over time the adaptation process takes place, as the person deals with their bereavement and grief.

Implications for practice
1. It is important to be mindful of the language used so that it does not lead to unnecessary concerns for the person experiencing transitions. A critical reflection of the language and discourse in the context of transitions might change the way others unrealistically expect transitions to go.

2. Jindal-Snape (2011) created board games that captured the key themes that were found in literature to worry or excite learners during educational transitions in a value-neutral manner. These could be used to discuss how the learners (appropriate for children) are feeling about particular transitions without using any language that indicates the adult's perceptions of what might worry or excite them.

FURTHER READING

Lucey, H., & Reay, R. (2000). Identities in transition: Anxiety and excitement in the move to secondary school. *Oxford Review of Education*, *26*, 191–205.

West, P., Sweeting, H., & Young, R. (2010). Transition matters: pupils' experiences of the primary–secondary school transition in the West of Scotland and consequences for well-being and attainment. *Research Papers in Education*, *25*(1), 21–50.

life course theory

Each transition is part of a social trajectory of education, work, and family; Life Course Theory (LCT) can be used to understand transitions across the life course (Elder, 1998). The life course framework is used extensively in several disciplines such as health and social work (Braveman & Barclay, 2009; Wise, 2003). LCT focuses on biological factors as well as psychosocial and physical environment as determinants of life trajectory, such as in the case of health, over time (Lynch & Smith, 2005). It has been used in health to understand how early life experiences influence adult health. LCT includes concepts such as critical or sensitive periods, cumulative effect over time, trajectories or pathways, and intergenerational models (Braveman & Barclay, 2009). Similarly, Zaidi (2014) has used LCT to look at well-being outcomes in old age based on age and developmental changes over time and space, including family and work history, healthy living, access to education, health, and social care; recognising individuals as active agents, making choices and affected by them, within the opportunities and constraints of their contexts.

LCT usually views human development chronologically, starting from infancy to old age, with certain phases in the life of every individual. The advantage of using LCT is that it reminds us that transitions are a journey: with individuals following a trajectory. It highlights the need to ensure that early transitions are positive so that there is a positive trajectory for all transitions over time. However, there are some disadvantages of using LCT for this, namely it seems fatalistic in that if one transition has gone wrong early on, others would have the same outcome, and it also therefore overemphasises early intervention, and the value of later interventions is not considered in changing the life trajectory (Wise, 2003).

Implications for practice

1. Life course theory can provide important insights into understanding transitions as a processes and how one particular transition can have (or has had) an impact on other transitions. However, the significance of effective intervention at any time in life cannot be overemphasised.

FURTHER READING

Elder, Jr., G. H. (1998). The life course as developmental theory. *Child Development, 69*(1), 1–12.

Zaidi, A. (2014). *Life cycle transitions and vulnerabilities in old age: A review*. Occasional Paper, UNDP Human Development Report Office, http:// hdr.undp.org/en/content/life-cycle-transitions-and-vulnerabilities-old-age-review.

life transitions

SEE ALSO **border crossing, educational and life transitions theory, multiple and multi-dimensional transitions theory, parental participation**

There are several life transitions that start from birth and carry on until one dies. The term 'life transitions' in this book refers to not only the normative transitions an individual might expect but also the non-normative and unplanned for transitions that might take place over time. These would include changes that an individual, family, organisation or group might experience across the life course, e.g. ageing and developmental changes, educational, employment, marriage or divorce, health-related, changing house, bereavement of significant others, trauma, growing up with a disability, moving to a new environment with different language and culture, and birth of a child. These then lead to changes in appearance, identity, status, interactions and relationships, beliefs and values, self-esteem; requiring substantial psychosocial and cultural adaptation (Miller, 2010; Vogler, Crivello, & Woodhead, 2008).

Life transitions require multiple lenses. It would be a mistake to see transitions as linear, either chronologically or developmentally. Rather, the purpose of the life transitions approach is to understand that any particular transition is only one part of what an individual might be experiencing in their life. They will be working across several domains of their life and cross several borders within the same day (see entry on *border crossing*). So if we take the case of a young adult with a life-limiting condition, their life transitions would include their clinical needs but also other needs due to becoming a young adult, education, changes in identity (including sexual identity), and change in the nature and type of relationships (Jindal-Snape, Johnston et al., 2015). It is imperative that professionals in the caring professions understand the multiple transitions of that individual even though they might be primarily supporting them through a specific transition. For example, a teacher cannot support a child with their educational transition if they do not put it in the context of other life transitions that the child is experiencing, such as parents separating, birth of a sibling, death of a pet (see entries on *Educational and Life transitions (ELT) model* and *Multiple and Multidimensional transitions (MMT)*).

Implications for practice

1. It is perhaps very difficult for a professional to be able to get information about all aspects of the life of an individual they are caring for or supporting. However, it is important to be open to other reasons for a particular behaviour they might be observing, especially if there is a remarkable change in behaviour. This can become difficult for a professional working with an individual for the first time. Therefore, it is important to have proper sharing of information from one context to another, which involves a range of information. For example, a nursery school teacher should pass information about all aspects of a child's life to the primary school teacher, namely academic, social, and emotional. This is where, for instance in this example, parental

participation or involvement of significant others also becomes crucial to find out the other transitions the child and family might be experiencing (see entry on ***parental participation***).

FURTHER READING

Miller, T. W. (Ed.) (2010). *Handbook of stressful transitions across the lifespan*. New York: Springer.

Vogler, P., Crivello, G., & Woodhead, M. (2008). *Early childhood transitions research: A review of concepts, theory, and practice*. Working Paper No. 48. The Hague, The Netherlands: Bernard van Leer Foundation.

longitudinal studies

In a longitudinal study, one would follow participants over time with continuous or repeated data collection. They can involve retrospective and prospective studies, and use of primary or secondary data. Longitudinal studies can help understand change over time and the factors that might have led to that change, along with understanding the impact of those changes on an individual (and others). To be effective, data is collected over at least a few months and ideally over a year to a few years. Further, they are most effective when data collection is continuous rather than at particular time points. Due to the nature of long-term participation, attrition rates can be very high. There are several examples of longitudinal studies at national level over decades with large samples such as the Millennium Study in the USA and Growing Up in Scotland.

If we conceptualise transitions as a process with changes and adaptation over time, it is evident that any research related to transitions has to happen over a period of time. For example, it is possible that a child who was looking forward to starting secondary school might find it quite difficult once they arrive there. Another child who might be concerned prior to the move might find that their transition was actually smooth. However, for both of them the picture might change 6 months later, and again a few months later or when they are in the second year of secondary school. Several transition researchers have tended to collect data either at one time point or immediately before and after the move. This could lead to misinterpretation of what might be happening for an individual or a group, with the focus being on an 'event', such as moving to secondary school, without understanding the subtle changes over time. This transition research literature can also be misguiding for professionals who might focus transition practice on supporting an individual immediately before and after the 'big' and/or 'tangible' move. Longitudinal studies can help us understand the transition and adaptation process better. This also applies to evaluation of transition practices or any research that aims to look at the impact of any practice.

Longitudinal studies can follow an individual or a group during transitions. They can help understand not only what is happening but also why it might be happening. That will then be helpful information for providing support to that individual or group as well as for modifying future practice.

One form of longitudinal studies is cohort studies that follow the same cohort of people over a period of time as part of a longitudinal study. A cohort is a group of people who share some characteristics, for example year of birth, medical condition, starting university at the same. They can be part of comparative designs, for example when a sample from the general population of that cohort can become a comparison group for the sample that might have been chosen for an intervention. Cohort studies take a life history approach, and can be prospective (capturing data in the future) or retrospective (using data captured in the past). One example of a famous cohort study is the birth cohort studies from Britain that include four long-term studies carried out over the lives of the participants from birth, including two that have continued over 50 years. Cohort studies can also be useful in understanding life course transitions.

Implications for practice
1. Professionals should consider using a longitudinal study design to effectively collect data about transitions and/or the impact of transition practice. To better understand what variables might be playing a part in certain outcomes, cohort studies can be a good way forward.
2. When undertaking longitudinal studies, it is important to develop strong relationships with the participants that would motivate them to participate in a study over a long period. This also involves ongoing contact with the participants.

3. Longitudinal studies can be resource intensive so it is important to consider what is most feasible within the constraints of available resources. Some researchers use audio or written diaries that can be completed by the participants themselves. However, it is still important for the researcher to be in constant contact to encourage the continuation of recording.

FURTHER READING

Holland, J., & Edwards, R. (Eds.) (2014). *Understanding families over time.* Basingstoke: Palgrave Macmillan.

maturational approach

SEE readiness

migration (international transitions) of children

SEE ALSO ABCs of acculturation, additional support needs, attachment, creative approaches, friendships, identity, multiple and multi-dimensional transitions theory, resilience, transition planning and preparation, voice, virtual backpack approach

Children experience international transitions for various reasons. Some transitions are related to accompanying parents when they move to another country for education or employment (see entry on *multiple and multi-dimensional transitions theory*). (Please note there are substantial transitions also for those whose parent/s move overseas but the child stays back in the home country, see Cebotari & Mazzucato, 2016.) Other children are forced to leave their country for political, economic, and/or social reasons. In the latter case, some might move to another country on their own. Each type of transition has various psychosocial (Bronstein & Montgomery, 2011) and educational consequences (Cebotari & Mazzucato, 2015; McKenzie & Rapoport, 2011), and are identified as additional support needs (see entry on *additional support needs*), with some being particularly traumatic for children, which increase exponentially for those already affected by trauma in their country and then making another move, for example when leaving war affected areas (even when migrating *within* the country, such as Barron & Abdallah, 2012, 2015; Barron, Abdallah, & Smith, 2013; Barron, Dyregrov, Abdallah, & Jindal-Snape, 2015). Referring back to the ABC framework, children's international transition has affective, behavioural, and cognitive dimensions (see entry on *ABCs of acculturation*). Children will leave behind familiar places and relationships, and would need to familiarise themselves with the new environment and form new friendships. Further, whether the child had any choice in the decision-making (see entries on *self-determination* and *voice*) and whom/what they are leaving behind could have a big impact on their ability to cope with the change (Bhugra, 2004). Age and stage again become important factors in determination of the impact on their psychosocial well-being (Vathi & Duci, 2015). However, others have argued that this migration can have positive benefits, such as educational and economic, and in some cases will enhance their psychosocial well-being, with closer bonds being formed with the immediate family.

The adaptation process will not only be affected by what is happening to the child and family, but also the degree to which the host country and immediate community are welcoming and open to them. Terms like 'refugees' and 'migrants' can become stigmatising labels that have implications for the communities' perception, legal aspects, and service provision. The media perception and handling of the situation for refugees and migrants can play a part in either sensationalising their arrival or raising empathy of the community – neither might be perceived as helpful for a child who has arrived after traumatic experiences in the previous country, with significant consequences of how others see them on their self-perception and identity. Children separated from parents, who are forced to leave and seek 'refuge' in another country, are not always recognised as refugees with accompanying rights and protection and instead are allowed to stay until they are 18 years old on a discretionary humanitarian basis and are then expected to return (Crawley, 2011). Crawley argues that therefore their voices might not be heard in the same way as those of adults, and they are usually constructed as passive and vulnerable victims. In general, return to the 'homeland' is viewed as a positive thing. However, Vathi and Duci (2015) highlight the double racism experienced by some of the children who return to their parents' 'homeland' even when parents had moved overseas voluntarily for economic or educational purposes. This might be worse for those who are forced to leave due to reaching a particular age, irrespective of whether they would feel safe once they return. The sense of belonging to the 'new' country would make adaptation to the 'homeland' difficult, as would the potential lack of language and the sense of displacement.

It is important to remember, however, that children and young people will not passively experience 'culture shock'; they will proactively look for strategies to adapt to the new environment, whether it is in terms of first-time migration or return migration (see *ABCs of acculturation*). The cultural adaptation would require a strong support network to enhance their resilience as well as early planning and preparation for this transition (see entries on *resilience, transition planning and preparation*). For example, in Vathi and Duci's (2015) study children who had experienced return migration reported that after the initial feelings of loss they started employing strategies such as learning the language of their parents' country of origin, proactively making new friends and developing their support networks, consciously stopping themselves from letting it negatively affect their psychosocial well-being, and maintaining transnational ties. Similar strategies would apply to those moving to a 'new' country from their parents' country.

As can be seen, similar to other transitions, relationships and social networks become immensely important in dealing with this move. Transition support for children and young people would need to start prior to leaving the home country and be involved in the decision-making process. These days, with advances in technologies, it is important that previous relationships are maintained even at a distance. Further, preparation of communities, whether schools or neighbourhoods, can play a big part in building positive relationships in the new environment.

Implications for practice
1. Children and young people will be affected differently based on the circumstances of their international transitions. It is important that an assumption is not made about its impact on them and that they have a voice in narrating what their transition experience and support needs are. As there might be language difficulties at the start, creative approaches could be used to give them an opportunity to express themselves (see entries on *voice* and *creative approaches*). Support networks and friendships are important for most people, and therefore preparing the receiving organisations, peers, and communities would facilitate transitions and enhance their resilience (see entry on *friendships*). The *virtual backpack approach* can also be used to nurture their

sense of identity, attachment, and belonging with the old environment and to enhance the understanding of others about the
social and cultural capital these children and young people will
bring to the new contexts (see entries on *attachment, identity*
and *virtual backpack approach*).

FURTHER READING

Barron, I. G., Abdallah, G., & Smith, P. (2013). Randomized control trial
of a CBT trauma recovery program in Palestinian schools. *Journal of
Loss and Trauma, 18*(4), 306–321.

Bronstein, I., & Montgomery, P. (2011). Psychological distress in refugee
children: A systematic review. *Clinical Child and Family Psychology
Review, 14*(1), 44–56.

Bushin, N. (2009). Researching family migration decision-making:
A children-in-families approach. *Population Space and Place, 15*(5),
429–443.

Cebotari, V., & Mazzucato, V. (2015). Educational performance of children
of migrant parents in Ghana, Nigeria and Angola. *Journal of Ethnic and
Migration Studies., 42*(5), 834–856. doi: 10.1080/1369183X.2015.1125777.

Vathi, Z., & Duci, V. (2015). Making other dreams: The impact of
migration on the psychosocial wellbeing of Albanian-origin children
and young people upon their families' return to Albania. *Childhood,*
1–16. doi: 10.1177/0907568214566078.

motivation

SEE dip in attainment, expectancy-value-cost theory, self-determination

multiple and multi-dimensional transitions (MMT) theory

SEE ALSO ecological systems theory

In transitions research there is a tendency for professionals and
researchers to focus on the transition of *one* individual (even when
done as a group) and one type of transition. For example, if a person
is starting university, the research focuses on the single transition
of a person or group of persons independent of how their transitions might be interacting with each other's. This then does not

take into account that there are multiple students going through transitions at the same time, and therefore one person's issues might exacerbate another student's problems, or that the first student is actually experiencing other transitions apart from, or due to, starting university.

This is also done to the exclusion of other significant others around them, such as family and professionals, despite a clear case for one person's transitions affecting someone else's. Bronfenbrenner's (1979) ecological systems theory, for example, highlights the interaction between an individual's systems, such as family and school (see entry on *ecological systems theory*). It has been used in conceptualising and understanding educational and life transitions (Fabian & Dunlop, 2002; Hannah, Gorton, & Jindal-Snape, 2010; Jindal-Snape, Johnston, Pringle, Gold, Grant, Scott et al., 2015), and this interaction between systems enabling or hindering successful transition for that individual is acknowledged. However, what it seems to fail to take into account is that these systems, and individuals within these systems, are also in transition, albeit not necessarily the one that the researcher or professional might be focusing on. In fact, one can argue that because of one individual's transitions, significant others will also experience a change. For example, what we might see as 'one transition' for an old person moving into a care home is embedded within their other life transitions as well as being influenced by the interaction of significant others' transitions such as their partner being hospitalised or their son/daughter moving away from the city for employment purposes.

Similarly, a parent might experience transition due to their child's developmental stage such as their ability and time to go back to full-time employment after the chid starts primary school, change in identity from nursery school child's parent to that of primary school child's parent, along with any changes independent from their child's transitions in their personal, social, professional life, and so on. Further, that child will be affected by the changes in their parents' life. So parents and children will experience transitions as a result of each other's transitions as well as their own concurrent transitions. The ecosystems of the child and parents will not be entirely the same, so there will be interaction between them as well.

Further, one child and parents' transitions will interact with the transitions of other children, their parents, and professionals. For example, a primary school teacher who might have developed relations with 25 sets of children and parents over a year might find that she has to let go of them and develop relationships with another 25 sets of children and parents. This teacher might be experiencing other transitions at the same time, such as getting married, pregnancy, moving house, starting part-time study, etc.

The Multiple and Multi-dimensional Transitions (MMT) model highlights these multiple layers of transitions and their interactions (see Jindal-Snape & Hannah, 2014c). To understand it better, it can be visualised as multi-dimensional on a Rubik's cube style base.

Each individual and their interactions with others can be seen as one colour. If one set of interaction or aspect of life changes, it can lead to changes across the spectrum. The changes might be similar to a small ripple effect or much more significant like a domino effect. Therefore, it is important to understand the multiple layers and complexities of these multiple transitions. Further, these transitions for individuals are happening within the context of wider changes in the policy, legislation, socio-economic environment, and cultural context.

According to the MMT model, for example, if we look at the child's educational transition from a narrow perspective (e.g. focusing solely on the changing curriculum), we might miss out on several key psychosocial aspects that might lead to transition not working as expected. For example, in Jindal-Snape (2009) a parent highlighted that the planning and preparation was going well for their child starting school. However, after the sudden death of her father two weeks prior to the child going to school, the mother felt unable to support her child at the time of starting school, which then led to her son experiencing problems, as she was not able to support him fully whilst dealing with her own transition related to the bereavement. Therefore, alongside starting school, the child was coming to terms with a life transition, i.e. bereavement of a grandparent, along with the transition of the mother dealing with her bereavement.

Similarly, Jindal-Snape and Ingram (2013) found that when international students moved to the UK, they had to deal with a new country, culture, educational system, level of study, and life style, along with supporting their families who had accompanied them and were experiencing their own transitions. For example, their children had similar experiences which included starting a new school, at times without having the same English language skills as the adult learner, and spouses had to reorganise their professional life. The entire family was going through multiple transitions as a result of one person's decision to make a move; therefore, one person's transitions can trigger others' transitions and vice versa.

Recent research suggests that professionals, as well as some families, feel that they should not express their transition support needs despite acknowledging that children starting secondary school led to their own transition (Jindal-Snape & Mitchell, 2015). In other studies, a similar reluctance was found on the part of health care professionals to acknowledge trauma-like symptoms resulting from supporting young adults and families with life-limiting conditions (Jindal-Snape, Johnston et al., 2015) and of police officers supporting children affected by sexual abuse (MacEachern, Miles, & Jindal-Snape, 2014). This can be at times due to a lack of awareness of one's own transition needs but at others due to the socially imposed expectations voiced by parents as 'I am an adult and it is about my child' or by professionals as 'I am a professional I am used to dealing with this'.

Implications for practice
1. It is important that professionals consider their own transition support needs. If they are not supported with their transitions, they might find it difficult to support others with their transitions. It is also vital that organisations are geared to support and provide appropriate transition-support training to professionals. Being mindful of the MMT theory would help them understand the complexity of transitions and support all the relevant people.

FURTHER READING

Jindal-Snape, D., & Hannah, E. F. S. (2014c). Promoting resilience for primary-secondary transitions: supporting children, parents and professionals. In A. B. Liegmann, I. Mammes, & K. Racherbäumer (Eds.), *Facetten von übergängen im bildungssystem: nationale und internationale ergebnisse empirischer forschung.* Munster: Waxmann, pp. 265–277.

n

Nicholson's theory of work role transitions

SEE ALSO employment

Nicholson (1987) suggested transition cycles and stages, specifically in the context of work-role transitions (see entry on *employment*). The stages are:

a. Preparation: This is the stage before the move or change and involves processes of anticipation. Individuals can face certain issues such as concerns, lack of readiness, and expectations that are unrealistic (So, 2010).

b. Encounters: This happens in the first few days of the change and involves emotional response and sense making about the change. Individuals can face problems related to sense of denial, shock and regret at the change or loss.

c. Adjustment: This is the next stage and involves finding one's feet, making sense of one's place in the new context, and working out one's role or identity.

d. Stabilisation: This comes from an expectation that after the change an individual will experience a sense of stability when they will have adapted to the new context. Continuous adjustments are however required within this stage in line with any environmental change.

These stages can be applied to any educational transition or, in the case of normative transitions, to life transitions. For example, Galton (2010) used Nicholson's theory to suggest that primary and secondary schools need to think longer term and plan accordingly. Considering the four stages and potential issues arising during these stages, one can consider an effective transition support programme to support an individual.

During *Preparation* stage, the individual can be supported through induction weeks and open days, discussion of concerns and excitement, and visits from peers and professionals from the new context. For instance, in the case of a terminal illness of a family member, this could include conversations around life and death. In the *Encounters* stage, an individual would need to be supported through exploration of their role in the new context and this could involve support with understanding their emotions and managing them, and meetings with guidance staff in the case of schools. During the *Adjustment* stage regular and immediate feedback would have to be provided on both success and failure, and strategies for identifying and correcting mistakes discussed. It is important to ensure that individuals get a sense of achievement through small steps to success. The *Stabilisation* stage would involve future goal setting and appraisal of how the individual might be developing, such as in the end of year reviews. This could look at those aspects of the individual's adjustment (whether social, personal, or academic) where improvement is required as well as setting of future goals for the following year, with preparation for the next change.

The final stage proposed by Nicholson points out the limitations of the transition programmes that conceptualise transition as a ***one-off event*** and put activities in place immediately before and after the move, ignoring the continuous changes experienced by the individual.

Implications for practice
1. This theory reminds us of the nature of transition and the different stages an individual might experience.
2. The different stages can be used as a guide for transition planning and preparation, whilst being mindful that even in the stabilisation stage there is a need to plan for the next change, and that everyone might not experience the stages in this manner.

FURTHER READING

Galton, M. (2010). Moving to secondary school: What do pupils in England say about the experience? In D. Jindal-Snape (Ed.), *Educational transitions: Moving stories from around the world*. New York: Routledge, pp. 107–124.

Nicholson, N. (1987). The transition cycle: a conceptual framework for the analysis of change and human resources management. *Research in Personnel and Human Resources Management, 5*, 167–222.

nursery–primary school transitions

SEE ALSO attachment, big-fish-little-pond, creative approaches, relationships, virtual backpack approach, voice

Starting school can be a significant event for the entire family, with new identities of a 'school child' and the 'parent of a school child' (Deckert-Peaceman, 2006; Niesel & Griebel, 2001), and unspoken rules and new roles to be navigated. Children's patterns of interaction with parents and other adults might change, with children learning to be independent and more aware of their peers' responses to their physical interaction, for example a hug with the parent dropping off a child at nursery might have been initiated and desired by the child, but in primary school the child might resist this as they adopt the new identity of being 'grown up' as a school child. Similarly, schools expect parents to know the norms and behaviour. After the open and accessible environment of the nursery, parents can find the primary school not accessible; they may also find it frustrating to wait for a few months before speaking with the teacher to find out how their child is settling in. This, therefore, is not only a transition for the child but also for the parents, and they require transition support as well (Jindal-Snape & Hannah, 2013). Interestingly, although the difference within the small sample was not large, Jindal-Snape and Hannah found that more parents reported that preparation from nursery was better for their child than for them as parents. A mother in their study highlighted the importance of developing trusting relations with the new primary school teacher.

> ...I meet a teacher once in a large group and I'm supposed to trust her with my child, why? Because it's socially accepted? This seems weird. (Jindal-Snape & Hannah, 2013, p. 129)

Most nursery–primary transitions research is dominated by the readiness debate, primarily a child's readiness to start school (see entry on *maturational approach*), with some highlighting the need for the school to be ready (Pianta & Cox, 1999) and others the need for both child and school readiness (see entry on *interactionist approach*). The research focusing on a child's readiness usually focuses on the age for starting school. However, such research has been inconclusive in demonstrating age as an appropriate predictor of school readiness (Ford & Gledhill, 2002; Stipek, 2002), with variations around the world finding no optimum starting school age. Others have also highlighted the social and emotional readiness of the child: again a *maturational approach* with children being retained in nursery if staff and parents did not see them as ready to start school (Hannah et al., 2010).

Researchers have highlighted that smooth transition to school depends on the quality of pre-school experience (Hannah et al., 2010; Peters, 2010; Mayer, Amendum, & Vernon-Feagans, 2010), whether through formal pre-school systems or through a supportive family and community (Jindal-Snape, 2010c). Children who receive good support from family and teachers during the transition to primary school were found to perform better on standardised literacy measures (Mayer et al., 2010; Ramey & Ramey, 1999), and have better school trajectory (Alexander & Entwisle, 1988), and vice versa (Coyner, Reynolds, & Ou, 2003).

Although a mismatch in expectations of teachers and difference in organisational culture has been found at various educational stages, it is most evident when children start school. It is not uncommon to see discrepancies in pre-school and primary school teachers' assessments of children, with the former rating the children's abilities higher than the latter, and focusing on their ability to 'do school' (Dunlop, 2002; Peters, 2010; Robinson, Timperley, & Bullard, 2000), with a move from Big Fish Little Pond to a Big Pond Small Fish (see entry on *big-fish-little-pond*). Children move from a flexible, autonomous and playful environment to a more structured, timetabled and conformity-to-school-norm environment, with a longer school day (Dunlop & Fabian, 2002, 2006; Fortune-Wood, 2002; Jindal-Snape & Miller, 2010), and substantial change in staff–child ratio (Jindal-Snape & Miller, 2010). Dockett, Perry, and Howard (2000) have provided guidelines for effective transition-to-school programmes, which they have emphasised are not prescriptive, including establishment of positive relationships based on trust and respect between all stakeholders; involvement of a range of stakeholders and good communication; well planned and continuous evaluation; flexible and responsive to the context and take into account the context of the child, family, and communities; and facilitate the development of every child as capable learners.

Despite the obvious secure attachments and meaningful relationships formed by a child with their nursery school teacher, and over the year with their new primary school teacher, there is little, if any, focus on transitions of the professionals in this context (see entries on **attachment** and **relationships**). With a small staff–pupil ratio, professionals might feel a sense of letting go of the relations they had created with the child and parent, and having to start the process again with new children and parents.

These highlight gaps in research as well as transition support. Similarly, only a few researchers have made an effort to listen to the voice of young children going through this transition (e.g. Dockett & Perry, 2003; Gorton, 2012; Jadue-Roa & Whitebread, 2012; Niesel & Griebel, 2001). used photographs to explore children's perspectives on They transitions as well as interviews and focus groups. Jindal-Snape designed storybooks (Jindal-Snape, Snape, & Snape, 2011a, 2011b) and a board game (see Jindal-Snape, 2012 for an example) with children to provide meaningful ways of supporting their transition to primary schools. These methods were chosen as they are seen to be meaningful to young children (see entries on **creative approaches** and **voice**). They focused on scenarios related to forming friendships, expectations of adults in primary school, reason for wearing a uniform, learning rules of the new environment, as well as to exploring their concerns and providing them with an opportunity to explore the consequence of their actions in the guise of the characters. These storybooks and board game were also designed to collect data and explore children's views about starting school as well as progression through primary school. Another study found that photographs of significant others and places in the new environment were used by the school to enhance their familiarity (Jindal-Snape, 2012) as well as parents organising 'play dates' over the summer prior to the start of school, and school organising a summer fair for new and old children and families to meet in a fun environment (Jindal-Snape & Hannah, 2013).

Implications for practice
1. It is important to be mindful of the various transitions that take place as a child starts school, for them, their families, and professionals. This highlights the importance of transition support for all stakeholders.

2. A focus on the readiness of the child is a very narrow perspective, with a focus on skills and behaviours of the child to 'fit' into the new environment. Assessment and checklists that identify gaps that need to be met are not helpful. It is important for schools to be ready to receive children with all their differences and adopt a virtual backpack approach with a focus on positives and understanding that each child might have a different developmental trajectory (see entry on *virtual backpack approach*).

3. The child's voice is very important to understand their perspectives as well as to give them a forum to discuss their concerns (see entry on *voice*). Professionals working with them on a day to day basis are well placed to listen to their voice to improve their practice.

FURTHER READING

Dockett, S., & Perry B. (2003). Children's views and children's voices in starting school. *Australian Journal of Early Childhood, 28*(1), 12–17.

Fabian, H., & Dunlop, A. -W. (Eds.) (2002). *Transitions in the early years. Debating continuity and progression for children in early education.* London: Routledge Falmer.

Gorton, H. (2012). *"Are they ready? Will they cope?" An exploration of the journey from pre-school to school for children with additional support needs who had their school entry delayed.* Dundee: Doctoral thesis. http://discovery.dundee.ac.uk/portal/files/2112743/Gorton_dedpsych_2012.pdf.

Jadue-Roa, D. S., & Whitebread, D. (2011). Young children's experiences through transition between Kindergarten and First Grade in Chile and its relation with their Developing Learning Agency. *Educational and Child Psychology, 29*(1), 32–46.

O

offending and reintegration

SEE ALSO agency, expectancy-value-cost theory, identity, rites of passage, self-determination

There are several links with transitions within the literature on offending behaviour: transition as a change in identity from offending to desistance, transition from prison to community, and life transitions that may lead to offending behaviour or desistance. Desistance has been defined as cessation from offending; however, this is not an abrupt change or end, rather an ongoing process of change as the individual transitions from offending to desistance and vice versa through primary desistance with the journey ending in long term or secondary desistance (King, 2013; Maruna, Immarigeon, & LeBel, 2004).

According to King there is evidence to demonstrate that desistance leads to a change in identity from that of 'offender' to 'non-offender' or as some have put it 'ex-offender'. This change in identity relates to change in perception of one's own identity and perception of others regarding that person's changed identity (see entry on *identity*). He also highlights that individuals' narratives need to change for desistance to happen and found early narratives of desistance that can lead to transition to long-term desistance. He argues that individuals need to have autonomy, self-determination, and agency, and professionals can support them by identifying and building on the positive narratives to support their transition (see entries on *agency* and *self-determination*). Healy (2014), concurs with the required agency and self-determination but argues that this change will only happen when the desired identity is highly valued by the individual and is perceived to be attainable. Similar to King's (2013) suggestion of changed narratives, Healy suggests that it is the individual's ability to imagine a meaningful and credible new self that is important for agentic action. It seems that self-concept and sense of self-competence play an important role in making this transition (Lloyd & Serin, 2012) and sustains motivation during primary desistance to enable a move to secondary desistance (Giordano, Cernkovich, & Rudolph, 2002).

Barry (2009) suggests that a meaningful relationship between the professional and service user that is built on trust, good listening, is motivating and encourages them to change is required for this transition to happen and sustain in the long term. Young people in her studies highlighted push and pull factors. Push factors were negative consequences of offending that discouraged them from offending, such as loss of liberty, and decline in well-being. Pull factors were the positive factors that encouraged them to desist, such as supportive new relationships, change in life style, and new opportunities (Barry, 2006; Cruickshank & Barry, 2008).

Related to these push and pull factors is the discourse about the impact of life course transitions and significant and transformative life events on desistance, for example marriage or employment. Several researchers have provided evidence for change in offending behaviour after marriage, with the link being seen to be related to attachment, development of risk averseness, change in perception of the cost of crime, change in friendships and social networks, and change in identity (Laub & Sampson, 2003; Maruna, 2001; Maume, Ousey, & Beaver, 2005; Skardhamar, Monsbakken, & Lyngstad, 2014), whereas some are more cautious and have suggested the role of self-control in the link between marriage and desistance (Forrest & Hay, 2011).

Some of these discussions also resonate with the concept of expectancy-value-cost (see entry on *expectancy-value-cost theory*). The individual's intention to desist seems to be based on their expectancy of success, the value they attach to this change, and the comparative cost of making this change. For example, if the cost of desistance is too high, such as losing the perceived support networks and friendships one might have formed with others who are offending, and the value ascribed to a changed life style is low, a person might not be motivated to desist.

In terms of reintegration into the community, Maruna (2011) uses Van Gennep's (1960) 'rites of passage' to argue the case that, similar to the ritualistic nature of trial, punishment, and imprisonment, there should be clear rituals to support the reintegration, de-labelling, and de-stigmatisation (see entry on **rites of passage**). He suggests that these reintegration rituals should be symbolic and emotive, repeated as necessary, involve community (natural community of care, or voluntarily set up community groups for support), and should focus on challenge and achievement rather than risk.

Implications for practice

1. There are clear links between life course, desistance, and change in identity. Professionals can work with individuals in generating positive narratives of a new self that is considered to be worthwhile and attainable. Further, there is an emphasis on reintegration that is inclusive and de-stigmatising if it is to work in the long term. Some studies that have shown patterns of desistance over time and also those that have explored narratives of primary desistance emphasise the importance of positive distractionary activities related to leisure and employment.

2. As with other types of transition, for it to be successful desistance requires the individual to have agency, feel in control, and have a positive self-concept, sense of self-competence, and self-determination.

FURTHER READING

Barry, M. (2006). *Youth offending in transition: the search for social recognition*. Abingdon: Routledge.

Barry, M. (2007). Listening and learning: The reciprocal relationship between worker and client. *Probation Journal*, 54(4), 407–422.

Forrest, W., & Hay, C. (2011). Life-course transitions, self-control and desistance from crime. *Criminology & Criminal Justice*, 11(5), 487–513.

King, S. (2013). Early desistance narratives: A qualitative analysis of probationers' transitions towards desistance. *Punishment & Society*, 15(2), 147–165.

Maruna, S. (2001). *Making good: How ex-convicts reform and rebuild their lives*. Washington, DC: American Psychological Association Books.

one-off event

SEE **ongoing process**

ongoing process

Transition is an ongoing process, with individuals adapting over time. However, some see transitions as significant *one-off events*. It seems that the biggest problem with planning and preparation comes from transition being seen by some as a *one-off event* rather than a process where children have to make sense of everyday changes and relationships (Jindal-Snape, 2011). When conceptualised as a one-off event, practice focuses on supporting the individual *prior* to and *after* the move. This means that, first, transition planning and preparation is happening only in terms of a big change and, second, it is for visible, tangible, and physical transitions. For example, when children are about to move to secondary school, school visits, induction days, and week-long residentials are organised in the final year of primary school. After the child has moved to secondary school there might be a few days of getting to know each other and 'settling-in' activities.

However, research clearly shows that there is no single pattern in how long individuals might take to adapt to the move or any change. According to a longitudinal study, some children who had reported transition to be difficult immediately after moving to secondary schools reported that they had no problems two months later, and those who had found transition not to be a problem immediately after the move reported problems by the end of the first term, and for one child problems emerged at the end of the second term (Jindal-Snape, Baird, & Miller, 2011). However, how many organisations would still be looking at any issues with adaptation at that stage?

Implications for practice

1. To support individuals according to their support needs it is important to conceptualise transition as a process of adaptation rather than a one-off-event. Similarly, in research it is important to conduct longitudinal studies to understand this process over time.

FURTHER READING

Jindal-Snape, D. (2013). Primary-secondary transition. In S. Capel, M. Leask, & T. Turner, *Learning to teach in the secondary school: A companion to school experience* (6th edn.). New York: Routledge, 186–198.

opportunities for secure attachment

SEE attachment

P

parental involvement/parental participation

SEE ALSO ecological systems theory, resilience

Parental involvement has been defined as the involvement of parents in their child's education. Previous research suggests that parental involvement can have a significant impact on the child's performance regardless of ethnicity, socio-economic background, and maternal educational background (Jeynes, 2007). There is a view amongst some professionals that, despite this, some parents do not want to be involved in their child's education. However, a previous meta-analysis of literature found that the term 'parental involvement' has not been defined clearly and it has been used across a range of behaviours, such as parent–child interaction at home and involvement in school activities (Fan & Chen, 2001). It is possible that professionals take a narrow view of parental involvement, i.e. parental involvement is limited to parents' presence in the school, ignoring the wider perspective that includes involvement with the child at home or within the community (Desforges & Abouchaar, 2003; Jindal-Snape, Roberts, & Venditozzi, 2012). This is despite the fact that research suggests that daily activities at home and in the community can lead to positive learning outcomes (Tizard & Hughes, 2002). Further, several benefits have been reported for the parents themselves, such as enhancement of their learning, confidence, self-esteem, and relationships with their child (Clark, 2007).

As parental involvement has sometimes been interpreted as a one-way process, with schools deciding when to involve parents, Jindal-Snape et al. (2012) suggested moving the focus to '*parental participation*', where an equal relationship can be formed with responsibilities on both the school and parents to work towards an effective home–school partnership. They proposed a Multi-dimensional Parental Participation (MPP) model that includes parent–child interaction, parent–school interaction, and parent–parent interaction. The latter was evidenced in the context of transitions, with parents finding each other to be the best source of support and information. It was also found that this is the least tapped source of parental participation at times of transition.

Parental participation and home–school partnerships have been the focus of several transition studies, especially in the case of early years transitions (Dunlop, Lee, Fee, Hughes, Grieve, & Marwick, 2008; Fabian, 2000; Griebel & Niesel, 2000; Mayer, Vernon-Feagan, & Amendum, 2010), with positive partnership and parental participation seen to facilitate transitions (Hannah, Gorton & Jindal-Snape, 2010). This is not surprising as parents and family can be the most important support network of any child, and the secure base needs to be attended to by a home–school–child relationship (Jindal-Snape et al., 2012, see entries on *ecological systems theory* and *resilience*).

Jindal-Snape et al. (2012) suggest that during transitions, parental participation can take the form of setting up parent buddy pairings similar to pupil buddies that several organisations set up. In fact, they argue that this could be extended to family buddies that could lead to increased interaction for children at school and also through parent–parent interaction at home and community. This would lead to effective transition support networks for children and parents.

Parental participation is also important from the perspective of supporting parents with their own transitions as well. Unless the home–school partnership is effective, professionals will not be able to support parents, who in turn might not be able to support their own child. For example, it was found that even good interaction between parent and professional can have an impact on how the child copes with separation from their parent, even as an infant, when making transition to a day care environment (Jovanovic, 2011); however, this participation can be limited with gaps in knowledge of what is happening for the child in each other's context (Drugli & Undheim, 2012).

Implications for practice
1. Parental involvement and parental participation can include several dimensions such as parent–child, parent–school and parent–parent interaction and it is important that professionals and policy makers are aware of this.

2. Previous research tends to focus on the impact of parental involvement and participation on a child's academic achievement. However, it is important to understand that the impact goes beyond educational achievement and is crucial in their emotional and social development. As mentioned elsewhere, the emotional and social dimensions are crucial during transition.

3. It is important to tap into the unused potential of parental participation during transitions not only in terms of supporting their own child and planning and preparation for transition, but also to support other parents and children who are experiencing transitions. The practice of providing peer buddies to children when they move to new schools has been seen to be effective. Professionals could also consider providing parent buddies, or indeed family buddies, to enhance the child's and parent's transition experience.

FURTHER READING

Desforges, C., & Abouchaar, A. (2003). *The impact of parental involvement, parental support and family education on pupil achievement and adjustment: a literature review.* www.dcsf.gov.uk/research/data/uploadfiles/RR433.pdf.

Jindal-Snape, D., Roberts, G., & Venditozzi, D. (2012). Parental involvement, participation and home-school partnership: Using the Scottish lens to explore parental participation in the context of transitions. In M. Soininen & T. Merisuo-Storm (Eds.), *Home-school partnership in a multicultural society.* Publications of Turku University Faculty of Education B80, 73–101.

Tizard, B., & Hughes, M. (2002). *Young children learning* (2nd edn.). Oxford: Blackwell.

pedagogical adaptation

SEE ABCs (affective, behaviour, and cognitive) of acculturation

person-centred planning

SEE ALSO creative approaches, post-school transitions, self-determination theory, voice

Person-centred planning is an approach that places the person at the centre of the plan and assists them to plan their life and support, with a focus on strengths and capacities. Person-centred planning involves listening and learning about what an individual wants; helping them to think about what they want now and in the future; and significant others such as family, friends, professionals, and services working together with the person to make sure their aspirations are met (O'Brien, 2004; Rasheed, 2006). Person-centred planning has been used extensively with people with disabilities, for example during post-school transitions of young people with disabilities (see entry on *post-school transitions*). Coyle and Lunt (2010) have highlighted four core tools that help with person-centred planning, namely Essential Lifestyle Plans (ELP) to elicit information about what a person needs; Planning Alternative Tomorrows with Hope (PATH) to plan for the next few years and ensuring that support systems are available; Making Action Plans (MAPs) to find out the person's history and aspirations; and Personal Futures Planning (PFP) to ascertain where the person wants to be and what might hinder that. Person-centred planning leads to self-determination, empowerment, and ensuring that an individual has a voice (see entries on *self-determination theory* and *voice*).

Research suggests that person-centred planning for transitions has been seen to be effective by different stakeholders, for example young people, families, and professionals (Wertheimer, 2007), and is widely accepted as the most effective way of transition planning for those with disabilities (Kaehne, 2010). It is seen to be beneficial due to choice, community involvement, contact with friends, contact with family, social network, and scheduled activities (Robertson, Emerson, Hatton, Elliot, McIntosh, Swift et al., 2005; Sanderson, Thompson, & Kilbane, 2006). However, there is also suggestion from these studies that it works differently for different people and that the evidence base for its effectiveness is limited, for example in the context of employment. This might be due to it not being used effectively at present despite great potential for its use (Aziz, 2014; Richardson, 2015).

Implications for practice
1. Person-centred planning can be important in providing voice and choice to a person during transition planning and preparation if used effectively with buy-in from all stakeholders. Creative approaches could be used to ensure that the person with a

disability can express their wishes, needs, and aspirations in a way that is meaningful and empowering for them (see entry on *creative approaches*).

FURTHER READING

Kaehne, A. (2010). Multiagency protocols in intellectual disabilities transition partnerships: a survey of local authorities in Wales. *Journal of Policy and Practice in Intellectual Disabilities, 7*(3), 182–188.

O'Brien, J. (2004). If Person-centred Planning did not exist, valuing people would require its invention. *Journal of Applied Research in Intellectual Disabilities, 17*, 11–15.

Rasheed, S. A. (2006). Person-centered Planning: Practices, promises and provisos. *The Journal for Vocational Special Needs Education, 28*(3), 47–59.

portfolios

SEE **virtual backpack approach**

post-school transitions

SEE ALSO **additional support needs, collaboration, educational and life transitions, employment, parental participation, person-centred planning, special educational needs, voice**

Post-school transition refers to a period after completing formal schooling and moving to a new phase in life, with a variety of transitions based on the destination and pathways of the individual who leaves compulsory/school education. These destinations can include a gap year to travel around the world, university, college, employment, volunteering, and/or adult services for those with special educational needs (see entries on *additional support needs* and *special educational needs*). This is a time when the continuous service provided by children's services and education department comes to an end, and some individuals have been found to fall through the gap due to change in state-level services, such as for those who are looked after or have additional support needs (Topping & Foggie, 2010).

This also comes at a time of developmental and identity changes as an individual progresses through young adulthood. These changes can lead to a desire for independence, moving out of the family house, and sexual relationships, with ensuing changes and transitions for families as they adapt to these changes, with some parents finding it difficult to 'let go' (Jindal-Snape, Johnston et al., 2015). The environment around the young people and school experiences would play a role in their outcomes and destinations. They will have transition needs similar to those they experienced at other educational stages along with the changed expectation from others due to their developmental stage, and assertion from them of independence and aspirations of starting on a positive pathway. A young adult moving from the structured and guided environment of the school might find it difficult to adapt to the *relatively* unstructured, and self-determined, environment, for example, of the university. This could be in the context of academic experiences where they would have moved away from regular homework and classwork to self-directed learning, change in the nature of relationships with staff and peers as well as parents. This is the first time many will have left home and would find themselves managing a budget, accommodation, public utilities, and transport. The adaptation process will involve moving between educational and daily life aspects (see entry on *Educational and Life transitions (ELT) model*). See also entry on *employment* for transition to employment.

Some interventions to support positive destinations have involved individual and group projects. One such project, that deployed key workers to support the post-school transition of young people at the risk of social exclusion, aimed at enhancing their independence and employability. This project was rated highly by young people who reported an enhancement or maintenance of their self-confidence, self-esteem and sense of independence. However, the observation of related behaviours showed little correlation with the perceptions of the young people or their key workers (Topping & Foggie, 2010).

In the case of young people with disabilities or other additional support needs, several issues have been highlighted, such as lack of information and options, lack of transition plans for all, difficulties in forming friends and relationships, and problems with multi-agency collaboration (see entry on *collaboration*). It seems that those with complex needs have limited options (or are made aware of limited options) for moving on from school, with the most often-mentioned destination being further education college, where they go on to do life skills courses and/or adult services. However, whether those young people who move to further education eventually move from college to other positive destinations, such as employment, is not known and further research and reporting are required. Person-centred planning has been seen as a good way to help plan positive pathways for young people with complex needs (see entry on *person-centred planning*).

This is the stage where collaboration between professionals from children's services and adult services becomes crucial. This can be problematic due to tensions related to interprofessional collaboration (see entry on *collaboration*) and lack of clear responsibilities, handing over of responsibilities and a feedback loop to see what worked. Again, similar issues emerge in the context of the young person's voice and parental participation (see entries on *parental participation* and *voice*). The post-school transition meetings involve several professionals from different agencies, and the young people and families can find those meetings to be overwhelming. The power dynamics can be such that not only the young person but also the parents can find it difficult to express their views. Of course, that is if a young person is present at those meetings in the first place. There are several reports of young people being invited by the teacher but declining to participate (Aziz, 2014). Very few reports have been found of young people being involved in meaningful ways, such as through the use of pre-prepared PowerPoint presentations by the young person, the young person taking a friend with them, and using other visual and creative ways of expressing themselves (Richardson, 2015). The power dynamics at the meeting can also be changed subtly by deciding on a venue of the young person's choice, the layout of the venue being more relaxed, control of the meeting by the young person or family, etc.

As with any other transition, this is a time when relationships are in a state of flux, with the person leaving secure networks developed with secondary school teachers, for example, and developing them with staff at college or adult services, or employers. For others, there are issues of moving, for example, from paediatric to adult health care, where the professionals might not have been trained previously in some childhood conditions that are now prevalent during young adulthood. There is a change in expectations of others. For example, it has been often reported that behaviours that were seen as additional support-related during childhood and adolescence can be seen as troublesome and troubling in young adults. In a Japanese context, Yaeda (2010) found that many employees with disabilities left employment due to interpersonal difficulties, and emphasised the role of job coaches, vocational rehabilitation services, and social workers in supporting long-term continuation of employment (see entry on *employment*).

As mentioned earlier, the young people will also be exerting independence in developing adult relationships and moving out of the family home to live in accommodation shared with their partner. For those with complex needs, such as serious health problems, this might involve adaptation of the living space before this can happen. Also, with some growing up in a relatively protected environment as children due to their complex needs, independent living might require gradual psychological adaptation; both for the young person and significant others in their life (Jindal-Snape, Johnston et al., 2015).

Several countries have adopted policies and legislation to support young people with complex needs when making this transition. For example, in the USA, the IDEA Act mandates that transition goals and services should be in the student's Individual Education Program (IEP) beginning in the year they turn 16 or earlier if considered appropriate, with annual transition planning thereafter (US Department of Education, 2004). Within this legislation, the transition services are a coordinated set of transition activities that promote the move from school to post-school activities, such as vocational training, employment, continuing and adult education, adult services, independent living, and/or community participation. Further, it is stipulated that these should be based on the student's needs and take account of their interests and preferences. The IEP should include their transition plans with clear statement of goals and services (see entry on *special educational needs*). Similarly, in Australia in 2009, the Council of Australian Governments agreed to the National Partnership on Youth Attainment and Transitions to improve educational outcomes and post-school transitions to further education, training, or employment. It focused on 15–24-year-olds, specifically young people at risk, and was found to have had mixed impact, with participation and attainment rates increasing (Dandalo Partners, 2014).

Implications for practice

1. As can be seen, successful post-school transition is crucial but fraught with difficulties. The need for interprofessional collaboration, and effective collaboration with young people and families, cannot be underestimated. There are clear legislative requirements in several countries to ensure this happens; however, the interpretation of the law and its appropriate implementation depends on the professionals.
2. Transition planning and preparation should start as early as possible, and taking a life course approach should carry on for as long as required by the young person.

FURTHER READING

Dandolo Partners. (2012). *Evaluation of the national partnership on youth attainment and transitions*. A report for the Department of Education. Melbourne: Dandolo Partners.

The Scottish Government. (2009). Education (Additional Support for Learning) Act (Amendment). Edinburgh: The Scottish Government.

US Department of Education. (2004). Individuals with Disabilities Education Act (IDEA) http://idea.ed.gov.

primary to secondary school transitions

SEE ALSO **collaboration, parental participation, transition planning and preparation**

This is one of the educational stages which has been the subject of extensive research internationally especially in the developed countries. Similarly, it has concerned policy makers and practitioners for some time, with several countries adapting their curriculum and educational stages to minimise disruptions and discontinuities. Usually, this research has been in the context of *physically* moving from one school to another, between the ages of 10 and 12, and from a smaller school to a bigger school. However, some countries with change in their educational policy have tried to minimise disruption at this age by staging the transitions to make the move/change smaller. For example, in the USA there were junior highs (age 11–14 years) at the start of the century, with a shift in the last 35 years to middle schools (age 10–13 years) that are seen to be more in line with developmental stages (Akos, 2010). Even in the same country, there can be various configurations. There are even more variations across the world; examples include primary/secondary, primary/secondary/senior secondary, elementary/middle/high school, junior high school. Most studies have taken place in the USA, the UK and a few other European countries, Australia, and New Zealand. There are very few studies from elsewhere in the world; hence we have little knowledge about how these transitions are experienced or dealt with elsewhere. Here we discuss the primary-secondary transition more generally.

Although moving to secondary school signals progression and 'moving up', suggesting that most children would find primary-secondary transition to be satisfying and fulfilling (Galton, 2010; Jindal-Snape & Foggie, 2008; Lucey & Reay, 2000), some find this move to be stressful and challenging (Jindal-Snape & Miller, 2008). Several children have reported that they are excited about increased choice of subjects, sports, and meals; opportunities to make new friends and indeed leave some behind; working with a range of teachers rather than one for example in primary schools in Scotland; re-badging themselves or developing and asserting new identities; and increased independence and travelling to the new school (Akos, 2010; Jindal-Snape, 2010b; Jindal-Snape & Foggie, 2008). Others have found the same aspects worrying (Hannah & Topping, 2012; Jindal-Snape & Mitchell, 2015). Jindal-Snape and Foggie (2008) reported that several factors contributed to the concerns that children had, including bigger size, location, and structure of the school, losing old and making new friends, expectations of teachers in terms of independence, bullying, and discipline. There were some other factors that were not directly related to the educational transition, but to other aspects of life transitions such as puberty, family circumstances including bereavement, parental experiences of secondary education, and the community's aspirations. Hannah and Topping (2012) found that transitions caused anxiety to children with autism that in turn had a substantial negative impact on their well-being.

Similarly, it can lead to anxiety for families while they and the child adjust to a new educational environment, different organisational culture, and unspoken rules and expectations (Jindal-Snape, 2013; Jindal-Snape & Foggie, 2008; Jindal-Snape & Hannah, 2014). Teachers working with these children and families have to modify their strategies based on the varying needs of children they work with every year, whilst experiencing their own loss of relationships with children and families, as well as establishing new relationships, hence experiencing transitions themselves.

In the literature, as in practice, the importance for early primary–secondary transition planning has been highlighted, with emphasis on high quality activities (e.g. Akos, 2010; Galton, 2010). In some schools the norm is for children to start visiting the secondary school once a week two years prior to finishing primary school, for example, to use the swimming pool or science labs. This can help with familiarisation with the physical environment and learning the layout of the building, as getting lost and being late for a class is one of the major concerns children report. If the secondary school staff, such as the sports instructor, are involved with them during those visits, it can also give them opportunities to get to know some staff.

As transition is a dynamic process, it is vital that transition activities are carried on *across* the educational lifespan rather than at a particular point. In practice, however, most schools see transition as a one-off event with activities put in place immediately before and after the move (Jindal-Snape, 2013). This can be problematic due to the short nature of the activities and children who might start worrying about the move earlier or taking longer to adapt (or indeed experiencing difficulties after the first couple of months of starting secondary school) not being supported effectively.

Jindal-Snape (2010c) summarised some examples of effective transition practice from around the world, these included (see entry on **transition planning and preparation**):

- Induction days
- Portfolios from previous school
- Opportunities to create friendship networks
- Information passed should focus on educational, social, and emotional aspects
- Opportunities for secure attachment with teachers and guidance staff
- Involving child as an active participant
- Creation of transition teams
- Sharing pedagogy across schools
- Parental involvement
- Information packs

Jindal-Snape, Baird, and Miller (2011) found that primary schools in Scotland were preparing children in the following ways:

- Conversations with the children
  - Discussions about what to expect
  - Giving opportunities for them to talk about any concerns
  - Asking them about what they are looking forward to
- Sharing of information between schools
  - Passing academic information about each pupil to the Secondary School teachers and Secondary School Guidance staff
  - Passing social-emotional information about each pupil to the Secondary School teachers and School Guidance staff
- Reciprocal visits of staff and children
  - Visits to Secondary School with the children
  - Inviting Secondary School staff to the primary class
  - Taking children to Induction Day
- Organising residential trips where they could meet children from other Primary Schools
- Meeting with the parents and other professionals, especially for children with Additional Support Needs (see entry on *collaboration*).

Similar components were included in a primary–secondary transition programme developed to support children with ASD (Hannah & Topping, 2012). Prior to starting secondary school, children participated in six 2-hour group sessions with other primary school children who were going to the same secondary school. The sessions included information about secondary school), discussion of expectations of secondary school, understanding of ASD, improving social communication, and organisational and emotional regulation skills.

In other contexts, professionals have been seen to work in each other's class for a few days to ensure curricular and pedagogical continuity. However, these require time, good will, and structural flexibility. Some local authorities also favour through-schools where children stay in the same physical location for their entire school career. There is no evidence to suggest that transitions are easier in through-schools compared to when children have to move to different locations.

As mentioned elsewhere, parents and professionals also require support during these transitions. The biggest cause of concern for them seems to be the lack of timely communication, including incomplete information being passed on or information not being acted upon, and lack of a feedback loop to see which transition practices worked or not.

Implications for practice

1. There are several examples of good practice available. However, there seems to be no consistency in its application across even the same school from one year to the other. Also, we need to be aware of individual differences when children experience transitions.
2. Reciprocal visits of staff might be as important as those of children. This would enhance the understanding of pedagogical approaches and curriculum focus at different stages of schooling, with a smoother transition being planned for children. Please note that this does not imply no change; it suggests that there is gradual progression that is age and stage relevant and can be dealt with by all children.

FURTHER READING

Akos, P. (2010). Moving through elementary, middle, and high schools: the primary to secondary shifts in the United States. In D. Jindal-Snape (Ed.), *Educational transitions: Moving stories from around the world*. New York: Routledge, pp. 125–142.

Evangelou, M., Taggart, B., Sylva, K., Melhuish, E., Sammons, P. & Siraj-Blatchford, I. (2008). *Effective pre-school, primary and secondary education 3-14 project (EPPSE 3-14). What makes a successful transition from primary to secondary school?* Nottingham: DCSF Publications.

Galton, M. (2010). Moving to secondary school: what do pupils in England say about the experience? In D. Jindal-Snape (Ed.), *Educational transitions: Moving stories from around the world*. New York: Routledge, pp. 107–124.

r

readiness

There is a debate regarding school readiness. In some countries, there is continuing focus on optimal school starting age, taking a maturational approach. Research has been inconclusive about the appropriateness of age as a predictor for readiness to start school (Ford & Gledhill, 2002; Stipek, 2002). Elsewhere the focus seems to have moved to readiness to learn as well as social and emotional readiness. However, the overarching debate is whether it is about the child being ready or is about the schools being ready to work with every child as an individual recognising his/her unique differences and building on his/her strengths. Vernon-Feagans, Odom, Panscofar, and Kainz (2008) highlight that readiness is the interaction and fit between the child and his/her family, and the readiness of the school to teach that child. Mayer, Amendum, and Vernon-Feagans (2010) suggest that readiness is at levels beyond the child, and includes the community, school, and family. Whether in the context of educational transitions or other life transitions, it is important to remember that readiness is the fit between the individual and organisation, with the individual being ready and willing to adapt to the new environment and organisations working with each individual according to their specific needs.

Implications for practice
1. Although the term 'readiness' is usually used in early years and starting school, it is important to consider the implications for any transition. This would imply professionals being ready to understand the stage the individuals are at and adapting their services and support (as well as advising the receiving organisations) to meet their needs.

FURTHER READING
Booth, A., & Crouter, A. C. (Eds.) (2008). *Disparities in school readiness.* New York: Lawrence Earlbaum Associates.

relationships

<small>SEE ALSO</small> ageing, attachments, creative approaches, health transitions, resilience, self-determination theory, self-esteem, social network analysis, stage-environment fit theory

Relationship is a connection between two people related to each other or who have dealings with each other. Relationships, specifically those that lead to secure attachments, are crucial for an individual's well-being (see entry on **attachments**). According to self-determination theory, individuals have a need for relatedness, i.e. the need for development and creation of close personal relationships with others (see entry on **self-determination theory**). Similarly, the Stage–Environment Fit theory highlights the importance of developmentally appropriate social environments with relationships that promote them (see entry on **stage-environment fit theory**). However, it is important to remember that the freedom to choose relationships, and their nature, might have an impact on their effectiveness or perceived importance for an individual. For children in Emond's (2014) study who were in state care, peer relationships took specific meaning, as they saw them as peers *choosing* to interact with them rather than those they had with adults, whom they saw as having *no choice* but to interact with them either due to their employment/professional role (e.g. social workers, teachers) or through predetermined family/carer roles, which were usually under professional scrutiny.

Transition itself is defined as a *change* in context and *interpersonal relationships*. During times of change, relationships can be in a state of flux. There is ample research suggesting, for instance, that during transition from primary to secondary school, children are worried about losing known teachers and peers, and worried about making new friends and forming relationships (Jindal-Snape & Foggie, 2008). Indeed, relationships seem to be the top most priority for learners and families during *any* educational transition, with concerns about forming new relationships, bullying, or being isolated, as well as 'letting go' of old relationships, especially those who might have been the most stable support networks in the previous environment (Jindal-Snape & Ingram, 2013; Jindal-Snape & Rienties, 2016). There are also concerns about the ability to form relationships and being worthy of others wanting to form meaningful relationships with them (see entry on *self-esteem*). During school transitions, it is not only the teacher–child relationship that is changing. It is also the case for teachers and parents, with old relationships coming to an end and new ones being formed. Again the quality of these relationships will have an impact not only on them but also the transition experience of the child.

In the case of developmental transitions and ageing, the nature of relationships changes. For example, when a child grows into an adolescent and then an adult, they are keen to move away from dependence on the caregiver and strive for independence leading to change in what they seek to gain from the relationships. Similarly, if the old person moves into supported care, especially away from home, they may be concerned about leaving known people and building relationships with new people in the new environment. They might also move from independence to dependence with feelings of frustration about their health transitions and leaving home (see entries on *ageing* and *health transitions*).

As relationships change but are crucial during transitions, it is important that opportunities are provided for establishing new and meaningful relationships. These opportunities might help ensure that the individual's sense of self-worth is kept intact and even enhanced, and leads to creation of strong external protective factors (see entries on *resilience* and *self-esteem*).

Implications for practice

1. Professionals can provide opportunities for building relationships through interaction with staff, families, and peers prior to the move, reciprocal visits, familiarisation activities, small groupwork, buddying. They can tap into existing networks and monitor the creation of new ones by using Social Network Analysis and build on the social capital at their disposal (see entry on *social network analysis*). Creative approaches such as creative drama can be used to rehearse formation of new relationships in a safe environment (see entry on *creative approaches*).

FURTHER READING
Emond, R. (2014). Longing to belong: children in residential care and their experiences of peer relationships at school and in the children's home. *Child and Family Social Work, 19*, 194–202.

Rienties, B., Hernandez Nanclares, N., Jindal-Snape, D., & Alcott, P. (2013). The role of cultural background and team divisions in developing social learning relations in the classroom. *Journal of Studies in International Education, 18*(1), 64–83.

resilience

SEE ALSO **creative approaches, educational and life transitions model, risk, self-esteem**

Resilience is a process of relative positive adaptation despite substantial adversity (Luthar, 2006), i.e. adaptation is better than expected given the circumstances. Resilience studies led to the identification of factors that seemed to be common amongst individuals who were able to deal with adversity, such as social charisma, and affectionate and strong ties with family and the wider community. Rutter (1987) suggested four main protective processes that seemed to mediate risk at key life-turning points: (i) lessening the impact of risk (by either changing the experience or exposure to the risk), (ii) decreasing the number of risk factors and avoiding an accumulation of unmanageable risks, (iii) increasing self-esteem, and (iv) providing opportunities to develop confidence and necessary life skills (see entry on *self-esteem*). Similarly, Gilligan (2000) suggested that resilience could be developed by: (i) decreasing the number of problems in the person's life, (ii) seeing their life course as a developmental pathway that can be altered at any point, (iii) providing them with a secure base with opportunities to examine and explore the external environment, (iv) providing opportunities for development of their self-esteem, and (v) involving them in planning and preparation for any changes. Positive experiences were seen to work as protective factors, and he argued that the individual could move in and out of risk situations. In the past, although some saw resilience as static, i.e. either an individual is resilient or not, recent research suggests that resilience is dynamic and changes across context and over time (Jindal-Snape & Miller, 2008). Further, resilience should not be seen as inherent in the individual. The environment plays a major role in giving messages that lead to development of self-esteem as well as in providing support to the individual. It is worth noting that the same individual might be seen to be resilient in one context but not in the other (Newman & Blackburn, 2002).

Despite differing views in literature on many aspects of resilience, there seems to be a consensus on the importance of internal protective factors (for example, self-esteem) and external protective factors (such as support networks at home, school, community, or university) (Newman & Blackburn, 2002), with these protective factors being available across the individual's social and ecological environment (Daniel & Wassell, 2002). Some researchers have used resilience theory to understand what is happening during transitions and how individuals can be supported.

As is obvious from Luthar's (2006) definition earlier, resilience research sees two conditions to be critical: (i) exposure to significant adversity or threat, and (ii) achievement of relative positive adaptation *despite* that significant adversity or threat. Jindal-Snape and Miller (2008) have argued that transitions can be seen as times of substantial adversity, as what might be seen as everyday minor hassles by some can be seen as major critical incidents by others, especially when they are numerous, repeated in quick succession, and accumulate without little resolution. Further, it has been argued that and long-term problems can be more stressful than acute problems (Newman & Blackburn, 2002). There are several aspects of transitions that can lead to feeling this adversity, namely concerns about the ability to adapt to the new environment, forming new relationships and potential for bullying or being isolated, and 'letting go' of old relationships, especially those which might have been the most stable support networks in the old environment (Jindal-Snape & Ingram, 2013; Jindal-Snape & Rienties, 2016). In the context of international students, for example, Lee, Koeske, and Sales (2004) found that stress related to acculturation led to mental health problems during transitions and that support available to them acted as a protective factor and a buffer against the effect of stress. Similarly, Wang (2009) found that resilience had the biggest impact on international students' adaptation.

In transitions research, several external support networks have been highlighted as enhancing resilience and facilitating transition, namely support from family and extended family, local community, various professionals in the same organisation, and peers

(Jindal-Snape & Foggie, 2008; Rienties, Johan, & Jindal-Snape, 2014; Skyrme, 2016; Zhou et al., 2008).

Further, research suggests that if the primary support networks such as parents are absent for any reason, other external networks can provide the individual with secure attachments and make them more resilient (Luthar, 2006). This would suggest that multiple support networks could negate the impact of the risk factors, leading to the development and maintenance of resilience to any change in their life (see entries on *educational and life transitions model, risk*).

However, it is worth remembering that these same external 'support' networks can become both protective and risk factors (Jindal-Snape & Miller, 2008; Newman & Blackburn, 2002.). Newman and Blackburn (2002) have suggested that a supportive family is a protective factor but a chaotic family is a risk factor. Also, it is important to recognise that protection does not lie in avoiding the risk but in developing appropriate strategies to manage and deal with the risk in a healthy manner (Rutter, 1979). Therefore, it is important to provide the individuals with skill sets and strategies that can help them deal with any stressors.

According to Masten (1994), resilience intervention strategies include reduction of vulnerability and risk as well as the number of stressors and 'pile-up', increase in resources available to the individual in different aspects of their life and through significant others, mobilisation of protective processes and developing resilience strings with an improvement in one domain, leading to a knock on effect on another. It is important to ensure that the individuals do not feel bombarded by new and difficult situations, that there is a gradual increase in the difficulty level of tasks, and that they have time to resolve a problem before being confronted with another. Professionals can build small steps to success to enhance the resilience of individuals.

Resilience during transitions can be enhanced through creative approaches, providing a safe environment to rehearse concerns and potential solutions, and by working closely with the individual and significant others (see entry on *creative approaches*). For example, creative drama can be used in which a possible real life scenario can be 'tried out', in which the actors can depersonalise their actions and responses in the guise of 'playing the character' to address the individual's concerns and prepare them for real life situations as they move to a new context or environment (Jindal-Snape, Vettraino, Lowson, & McDuff, 2011). Individuals can find this safer by moving from 'my concerns' to 'Helen's concerns' – a fictional character on whom everybody is comfortable projecting their own concerns and trying out solutions that might not work without fear of being ridiculed. This could lead to active participation as well as feeling in control by resolving any problems. It also gives them an armoury of strategies and responses that they can use in similar real life situations along with feeling more competent in dealing with change.

Implications for practice

1. It is important to be mindful that resilience is dynamic and professionals can play a part in enhancing it for successful transitions. Reduction in multiple stressors and increasing difficulty level gradually can enhance an individual's resilience. Professionals can enhance an individual's resilience in two ways, giving positive messages to increase their self-esteem and by being their support network.

2. It is important to be mindful that at times protective systems can also be risk factors. For example, a supportive family can act as a protective system but a chaotic family life could heighten risk.

FURTHER READING

Daniel, B., & Wassell, S. (2002). *Adolescence: Assessing and promoting resilience in vulnerable children*. London: Jessica Kingsley.

Jindal-Snape, D., & Miller, D. J. (2008). A challenge of living? Understanding the psycho-social processes of the child during primary-secondary transition through resilience and self-esteem theories. *Educational Psychology Review, 20,* 217–236.

retirement

SEE **employment**

risk

SEE ALSO **creative approaches, ecological systems theory, resilience**

According to Tilleczek and Ferguson (2007) risk is systemic, assessment-based, grounded in actual practices, and fluctuates over time.

A risk factor is anything related to the individual or the environment that increases the probability of the person suffering harm; however, it only increases the probability of a negative outcome; it is not necessarily the cause of it (Office of the Surgeon General (US), 2001). Transitions are seen to be times of increased risk as individuals have to adapt to a new situation, context, or identity (Newman & Blackburn, 2002) (see entry on *resilience*).

Some professionals also identify particular individuals to be more likely to experience problems during transitions, such as children with autism (Schoon, 2006). This then signals to them what types of additional support systems need to be put in place for those individuals. However, it is important to recognise that there can be considerable individual variability, for example, in the anxiety levels of children with autism (Hannah & Topping, 2012). There might be other risk factors that the professionals might have lesser information about such as those emerging in terms of family problems, bereavement, etc. Further, professionals might focus on one transition, whereas the individuals might be experiencing multiple transitions, e.g. puberty and moving from primary to secondary school would be concurrent factors leading to stress for some individuals.

It is not only important to know whether and when an individual might experience risk but also to identify how many risk factors there might be. For instance, an individual with only one risk factor might have similar outcomes as those with no risk factors (Rutter, 1985). Further, if the number of risk factors increases, the outcomes are negative not as a summation of number of risk factors but exponentially. Rutter (1985) found that this could be four times for those with two risk factors and ten times for those with four risk factors.

Based on previous research, it is argued that the risk factors do not have a strong biological basis and they are either a result of social learning or the combination of social learning and biological processes (Office of the Surgeon General (US), 2001). Some researchers have likewise suggested that risk should not be seen as within a person and we should move from 'at-risk youth', for example, to 'youth in at-risk situations' (Smink & Schargel, 2004; Tilleczek & Ferguson, 2007).

Literature has categorised the risk factors across the domain, namely, individual, family, peers, school and community

(Jindal-Snape & Foggie, 2008; Office of the Surgeon General (US), 2001). On the basis of a review of literature in the context of primary–secondary transitions, Tilleczek and Ferguson (2007) categorised risk factors as school-related risk factors and risks beyond the school. They further summarised them according to the ecological systems as risks factors that were found at three levels (see entry on *ecological systems theory*):

a. Micro (at the individual level):
   a. Identity issues
   b. Mental health
   c. Dip in achievement leading to disengagement
   d. Isolation
b. Meso (related to families, friends, and classroom):
   a. Losing and forming friendships
   b. Change in family relationships and lack of support
   c. Teacher–student relationships in flux with increase in distance as compared to primary school
   d. Quality of school provision and some learning pathways being better than others
   e. Changes in curriculum, pedagogy, and nature of assessment
c. Macro (related to culture and school structure):
   a. Ethnicity
   b. Social class and poverty
   c. Gender
   d. Differences in the culture of organisations

These examples of risk factors are not only true for primary–secondary transition; they can apply to several contexts. Also, if the individual is not able to deal with risk factors appropriately, they might lead to problems during other transitions and over time.

As can be seen some of these risk factors cannot be changed such as ethnicity or gender, and others cannot be changed at least in the short term such as poverty. Other risk factors can be reduced, especially the compilation of several unresolved risk factors at the same time (Jindal-Snape & Miller, 2008). Protective factors can also act as a buffer to circumvent any negative outcomes (see entry on *resilience*).

Some have cautioned that too much focus on identifying risk factors could cause more harm than benefit, and have suggested a better balance between protecting from risk and providing better development opportunities (Newman & Blackburn, 2002). Indeed, Rutter (1979) suggested that protection lies not in avoiding the risk but developing strategies to manage it (see entry on *resilience*). Therefore, some of the risk factors mentioned earlier that cannot be changed, namely ethnicity and gender, should not be a cause of concern. Instead, if there are negative outcomes arising from these, it is important to develop the appropriate coping strategies (see entries on *resilience* and *creative approaches*).

Implications for practice

1. Although an awareness of potential risk factors for individuals about to experience or experiencing substantial change is important, we also need to be aware of all the other factors that might be interacting with a particular risk factor. Further, every individual is likely to be affected by a risk factor differently as well as having different ways of dealing with risks. Any risk factors attached to particular groupings in literature such as autism should not be seen to mean that it applies to every person with autism.

2. Resilience is a more positive way of considering what can be proactively done to deal with risk factors. In transitions, some of the risk factors, such as lack of friends, negative relationships with teachers, massive change in curriculum, or pedagogical approach, can be minimised and professionals should make an effort to do so. However, it is important to realise that individuals will not develop resilience unless they have experience of dealing with some risks. It is important to support individuals to learn to deal with risks in a safe and supportive environment. For example, creating a safe space to discuss or role play how children might deal with bullying in primary school would help them deal with similar potential risk in all aspects of their life at that time and in the future.

FURTHER READING

Newman, T., & Blackburn, S. (2002). *Transitions in the lives of children and young people: Resilience factors.* Edinburgh: Scottish Executive Education Department.

Office of the Surgeon General (US). (2001). *Youth violence: a report of the surgeon general.* Rockville (MD): Center for Mental Health Services (US).

rites of passage

SEE ALSO border crossing, ongoing process

Arnold van Gennep (1960) used the phrase 'rite of passage' to describe the celebration of the passage that occurs when an individual leaves one group to enter another, within the context of significant life transition events. He describes this as having three sequential stages:

(i)   Preliminal rites: Rites of separation from their previous group
(ii) Liminal rites: When the person has not fully left the previous group and has not entered the new group
(iii) Postliminal rites: Rites related to incorporation into the new group

These rites usually involve a public ceremony and mark a change in status (primarily social) and identities, and indicate readiness to move on and take new responsibilities (Vogler, Crivello, & Woodhead, 2008). According to Vogler et al. this starts at an age when the individual might not even be aware of this change in status, such as baby shower, naming, and religious initiation. They also highlight that these ceremonious aspects might be delayed due to socio-economic and cultural factors.

The term 'rite of passage' has been used for other types of transitions such as organisational transitions. Voger et al. provide examples of how this has been used to explain the transition process in several studies. One such study was undertaken by Lam & Pollard (2006) in the context of starting nursery. They suggest that the preliminal stage involves leaving home care-givers, liminal stage involves experiencing the transition programmes put in place by the nursery, and the postliminal involves them settling in and feeling a part of the nursery. This involves change in identity from that of a child to nursery pupil. Other aspects of this rite of passage can include buying uniform, stationery, or lunch box when starting primary school, for instance (Fabian & Dunlop, 2007). Rites of passage are seen as significant learning points in the life of any individual, even when they are stressful or might appear negative, such as the prison experience, with Visher and Travis (2003) suggesting that going to prison is a beneficial departure from a prior life of antisocial behaviour which can help the individual change their life for the better.

Although some authors have suggested that the middle stage, liminal, is a transitional stage, from the perspective of transitions being an ongoing process, some would argue that all three stages are part of the transition process (see entry on *ongoing process*). Rites of passage are seen as life course transitions that are vertical in nature, i.e. moving in a particular direction forever. This is in contrast to border crossing as horizontal transition (see entry on *border crossing*).

Implications for practice

1. 'Rites of passage' provides a sound framework to understand transitions and on the whole provides a positive and celebratory perspective on change. However, the loss of identity or relationships as described by stage one can also lead to anxiety.

FURTHER READING

Van Gennep, A. (1960). *The rites of passage.* Chicago: University of Chicago Press.

Vogler, P., Crivello, G., & Woodhead, M. (2008). *Early childhood transitions research: A review of concepts, theory, and practice.* Working Paper No. 48. The Hague, The Netherlands: Bernard van Leer Foundation.

S

self-determination theory

SEE ALSO person-centred planning, relationships, self-esteem, special educational needs, transition planning and preparation

Self-determination Theory (SDT) emerged from the study of human motivation, in particular intrinsic motivation. According to SDT, human beings have three innate psychological needs, namely competence, autonomy, and relatedness (Ryan & Deci, 2000). Competence relates to the need for mastery and feeling skilled and competent in controlling the environment. Autonomy is the extent to which one has control over one's actions and choices. Related-ness refers to the need for development and creation of close per-sonal relationships with others. The satisfaction of these needs is key to the enhancement of motivation and well-being. Social contextual factors can either enhance or thwart the fulfilment of these needs. According to Wehmeyer and colleagues (Wehmeyer, 2005; Williams-Diehm, Wehmeyer, Soukup, & Garner, 2008), self-determination refers to actions where an individual makes conscious choices or has the autonomy to make conscious choices. These actions, called volitional actions, have four characteristics: *autonomous action* by an individual, including *self-regulation* of their behaviour and *psychologically empowered response* to the event or environment, for the *improvement of their quality of life* (Wehmeyer, Abery, Mithaug, & Stancliffe, 2003). There is increasing evidence regarding the impact of self-determination on different human behaviours and SDT being used to design interventions and under-stand behaviours, for instance health behaviours (Ng, Ntoumanis, Thøgersen-Ntoumani, Deci, Ryan, Duda et al., 2012; Ryan, Patrick, Deci, & Williams, 2008; Teixeira, Carraça, Markland, Silva, & Ryan, 2012).

During times of transitions when multiple and simultane-ous changes can feel overpowering and difficult to deal with, an individual might feel that they have no control over what is happening to them. Their relationships can be in a state of flux with leaving old friendships, for example, and having to make new friends (see entry on *relationships*). Similarly, the individual might feel that they are not competent enough to navigate through the changing context and relationships (see entry on *self-esteem*). This implies that the three needs mentioned above are not being satisfied, with a detrimental impact on the individual's well-being. For example, an old person moving into residential care might find themselves leaving their known environment in terms of both their house and neighbours with concerns about building new relationships, and feel they will lose control over how they live their life from as simple an issue as when to have food. This is likely to have an impact on their self-esteem and well-being. However, if that person is involved in decisions made about all aspects, such as choosing the care home they want to move to, opportunity to interact with old neighbours and friends, along with opportunities to make new friends in the new environment, care provision in line with their wishes and felt needs, etc., they will feel more in control and their needs of relatedness and feeling competent are more likely to be satisfied. This can be seen from Williams-Diehm et al.'s (2008) study, where they found that those young people with disabilities who were more actively involved in transition planning were more self-determined. They recommended that professionals and carers should ensure their full participation in transition planning and Individual Education Plan (IEP) meetings along with developing skills such as problem solving and decision-making that can facilitate self-determination (see entries on *special educational needs* and *transition planning and preparation*). Although the direction of cause-effect was not clear from their study, it still highlights the importance of providing choice and control. This then provides support for person-centred transition planning (see entry on *person-centred planning*).

Implications for practice
1. For a sense of well-being, SDT raises the importance of an individual feeling in control of their environment, especially a rapidly changing one during transitions, changing relationships, and feeling competent in having that control over the environment and relationships. Individuals are more likely to

feel competent and in control if they are, first, fully aware of the changes that are going to take place and are familiar with the new environment. Therefore, it is crucial that they are involved fully in planning for their own transition and that transition planning is person-centred.

FURTHER READING

Deci, E. L., Connell, J. P., & Ryan, R. M. (1989). Self-determination in a work organization. *Journal of Applied Psychology, 74*, 580–590.

Deci, E. L., & Ryan, R. M. (2000). The "what" and "why" of goal pursuits: Human needs and the self-determination of behavior. *Psychological Inquiry, 11*, 227–268.

Ryan, R. M., & Deci, E. L. (2000). Self-determination theory and the facilitation of intrinsic motivation, social development, and well-being. *American Psychologist, 55*, 68–78.

self-esteem

SEE ALSO big fish little pond

There is little consensus regarding the definition of self-esteem, with it being equated with self-concept and various other self-related constructs (Tafarodi & Milne, 2002). After a phenomenological review, Mruk (1999) proposed a two-dimensional theory of self-esteem that he sees as including constructs from the main published work in this area. According to his two dimensional theory, self-esteem is the integrated sum of self-worth and self-competence (Jindal-Snape & Miller, 2008). He suggests that self-esteem is dependent not only on feeling competent (self-competence) but also on messages that individuals might get from others of their worth and value (self-worth). Deficiency in either of these could result in issues with self-esteem and lead to what he terms as *defensive self-esteem*, when people appear to have higher self-esteem than they actually possess (see Mruk, 1999; Jindal-Snape & Miller, 2008 for details). Researchers have used various scales to measure self-esteem such as the Rosenberg (1989) Self-Esteem (RSE) and Single-Item Self-Esteem scale (SISE; Robins, Hendin, & Trzesniewski, 2001).

Research has suggested a decline in self-esteem during transitions (Eccles & Midgley 1989; Wigfield, Eccles, MacIver, Reuman,

& Midgley, 1991; Booth & Gerard, 2014), which can then have a negative impact on an individual's well-being and achievement (especially in the context of school transitions and academic achievement, see Baumeister, Campbell, Krueger, & Vohs, 2005; Ross & Broh, 2000). Transition research suggests that there are several instances when an individual's self-competence and self-worth might be shaken. For example, a child starting secondary school can be worried about their ability to do higher level work they expect to get at secondary school (self-competence) and/or about being liked by new teachers and peers, sustaining old friendships and making new friends (self-worth), as well as experiencing the **Big Fish Little Pond** to Little Fish Big Pond effect (Jindal-Snape & Miller). Similarly, an international student might worry about their ability to work in their second language (self-competence) and/or being accepted and respected by host nationals (self-worth).

So on one hand transitions can lead to decline in self-esteem, and on the other it is suggested that those with existing low self-esteem might respond more negatively to experiences of perceived or real 'failure' during transitions, whereas those with high self-esteem would persist in the face of difficulties (Tafarodi & Vu, 1997; Jindal-Snape & Miller, 2008). Although self-esteem can be seen as an inherent trait of an individual, on the basis of the two-dimensional model of self-esteem it can be argued that the role of significant others in the environment is crucial in enhancing self-esteem and ensuring it does not decline during transitions.

Implications for practice
1. Professionals can ensure that the individual going through transition receives positive messages on which their sense of self-worth and self-competence might be based. For example, primary and secondary school teachers can ensure (and make sure that the children are aware of it) that there is a gradual progression in difficulty level between primary and secondary school so that children can believe that they are competent to meet the demands of the new class. Similarly, by creating opportunities for forming positive peer and student–teacher relationships, their sense of self-worth might be kept intact and even enhanced.

FURTHER READING

Booth, M. Z., & Gerard, J. M. (2014). Adolescents' stage-environment fit in middle and high school: The relationship between students' perceptions of their schools and themselves. *Youth and Society, 46*(6), 735–755.

Jindal-Snape, D., & Miller, D. J. (2008). A challenge of living? Understanding the psycho-social processes of the child during primary-secondary transition through resilience and self-esteem theories. *Educational Psychology Review, 20*, 217–236.

social network analysis

SEE ALSO ABCs of acculturation, friendships, group identification, international students' transitions, relationships, resilience, self-esteem

Social Network Analysis (SNA) is used to map and measure relationships between entities (e.g. people, organisations), social structures, and social positions of groups within a network. It displays the individuals/entities as a set of nodes and the ties or relations between these nodes through lines with an aim to understand the social bi-directional interactions (Rienties & Jindal-Snape, 2016). SNA has received growing attention in recent years across a range of disciplines such as education, sociology, anthropology, business, economics, politics, psychology, mathematics, and physics (Freeman, 2004). It has been used both to quantify the social networks an individual has as well as to understand the quality and nature of the relationships. Although the quantitative methods in measuring SNA have become quite common in recent years, there is scope for a mixed-method approach 'to both map and measure network properties and to explore issues relating to the construction, reproduction, variability and dynamics of network ties, and crucially in most cases, the meaning that ties have for those involved' (Edwards, 2010, p. 6).

A simple questionnaire asking questions such as 'I learned the most from...' and 'I have worked a lot with ...' can help identify learning and social networks. Or data can be collected through interviews (Heath, Fuller, & Johnston, 2009) and observations of interactions over time (like ethnographic observations). Some have used questionnaires followed by interviews and focus groups to understand the nature of networks, why and how they developed, enablers and barriers, quality of relationships, and perceived advantages or disadvantages of those networks and also with case studies of those who were identified to be potential bridge builders (e.g. Rienties, Johan, & Jindal-Snape, 2015). These studies also noted the cognitive and affective aspects of the social networks through learning and social ties and spill overs.

In the context of transitions, SNA can be used for several reasons. As discussed elsewhere, transitions are a time when friendships are in a state of flux and individuals can be very concerned about making new friends (see entries on *friendships*, *relationships* and *self-esteem*). They can give us a better understanding of the quality of relationships that an individual has with their peers; for example, to ensure that when they are in the new environment some of the networks from the previous contexts are maintained. Social networks can also help identify the support systems someone might have around them and how active or passive these networks are. This is crucial, as the support networks can become protective factors during transitions (see entry on *resilience*). Also, professionals can identify whether someone is isolated with few ties within a network, as these could lead to lack of support systems. The SNA can also usefully indicate whether the transition support has helped in the development of new social networks or not, for instance by asking people about their support networks in an organisation during the first few weeks and then after a few months. The understanding of the quality of networks and ties might also explain the individual's sense of belongingness and attachment when we try to understand group identification (see entry on *group identification*).

SNA has also been used in higher education transitions to understand the relationships between students, especially between international and host national students, and to intervene with a view to enhancing cross-cultural interaction and acculturation (see entries on *ABCs of acculturation* and *international students' transitions*) (e.g. Rienties, Heliot, & Jindal-Snape, 2013; Rienties, Hernandez Nanclares, Jindal-Snape, & Alcott, 2013; Rienties, Johan, & Jindal-Snape, 2014).

Implications for practice
1. SNA can be used to understand the existing networks or lack of them (e.g. between children who have come together from the same primary school without making an assumption that there

will be existing friendships), to understand where there might be potential problems (e.g. limited connections or ties with others) and/or for assisting as a strategy to ensure that no one is left isolated and opportunities are available for everyone to form peer relationships (e.g. through small tutor groups, class groups, and organisational and departmental teams).

FURTHER READING

Edwards, G. (2010). *Mixed-method approaches to social network analysis.* ESRC National Centre for Research Methods Review paper. www.ncrm. co.uk: ESRC NCRM. eScholarID:78728.

Heath, S., Fuller, A, & Johnston, B. (2009). Chasing shadows: Defining network boundaries in qualitative social network analysis. *Qualitative Research, 9*(5), 645–661.

Rienties, B., Johan, N., & Jindal-Snape, D. (2015). Bridge building potential in cross-cultural learning: A mixed method study. *Asia Pacific Education Review, 16*(1), 37–48.

special educational needs

SEE ALSO **ageing, additional support needs, collaboration, employment, parental participation, primary–secondary transitions, post-school transitions, voice**

A wide range of terms is used around the world to refer to needs emerging due to disability or health. The terminology has developed over time, and the concept is socially constructed with changes based on the prevalent social, economic, and political concerns at that moment in time (Beveridge, 1999). For example, in the UK, the terminology that was in use until recent times emerged from the War-nock Committee report, which acknowledged it as a wider concept and defined it as any form of additional help irrespective of where it is provided (mainstream or special school). The term 'Special Educational Needs' (SEN) is used to indicate aspects that affect a child's ability to learn, such as behaviour or ability to socialise, reading and writing, ability to understand things and concentration levels, and physical needs or impairments. Scotland moved away from the use of this term to Additional Support Needs (see entry on *additional support needs*). In the USA, the Individuals with Disabilities Education Act (IDEA) led to the use of the term 'child with a disability'

(Bollmer, Cronin, Brauen, Howell, Fletcher, Gonin, & Jenkins, 2010) or 'students with exceptionalities' (Finn & Kohler, 2010). In Australia, a similar term 'special needs education' is used and includes children with physical and intellectual disabilities, and health conditions; whereas in New Zealand, the term 'special education' is used.

As can be seen from different entries on **ageing, additional support needs, primary-secondary transitions, post-school transitions, employment**, etc., children and young people can experience difficulties during transitions and might require additional support. To support the transitions of young people with disabilities there is legislative requirement in different countries that annual review transition meetings take place, although the timing might be different. These meetings provide information for the Transition Plan (TP) which is an action plan that captures what needs to be done to support the young person through their teenage years and into adulthood. For example, in England this TP by law should be drawn up when a young person is in Year 9 (around 14 years of age). The school has the responsibility for writing the TP and sharing it with everyone. The UK Government, for example, has highlighted that TPs should focus on meeting the hopes, aspirations, and potential of young people with disabilities and statements of special educational needs to maximise their life chances, choices, and independence, and lead to improved health outcomes and inclusive provision for education, leisure, training, and employment opportunities. This is the first formal opportunity for the young people and significant others such as parents and professionals to come together to start thinking about the young person's support needs as they move forward, with clear action points and people named against each of those action points (it is expected that there will be an ongoing review which might take place with 'formal' meetings).

A key worker or transition coordinator (or named person; different terms are used in different countries, such as liaison officer in Sweden) might be identified, who then becomes the main point of contact between the young person and family, and the professionals to provide continuity and support with decision-making. Please note that some children and young people, although not all, will already have key workers who would have been supporting them and their families for a long time before these transition meetings, as provision of key workers working across health, education, and social services has been recommended by policy and legislation for some time (Greco, Sloper, Webb, & Beecham, 2005). This key worker can be an education, social work, health care, school psychology, or careers professional depending on whoever is best placed to meet the needs of the child or young person, or indeed the key person/coordinator can be a family member. Research suggests that having a named 'key worker' who has a clearly defined role, and is appropriately managed, supported, trained, and supervised, results in better outcomes for the young person and families (Greco et al., 2005; Mitchell, 2012). The evidence base suggests that the outcomes include overall improvement in the quality of life for families; development of better relationships with services and quicker access to them; and reduction in stress levels (Liabo, Newman, Stephens, & Lowe, 2001). This might be due to families wanting a single, definitive and trusted source of information and guidance (Beyer, Kaehne, Grey, Sheppard, & Meek, 2008).

There are annual follow-up meetings until the young person leaves school. In line with person-centred planning (see entry on *person-centred planning*), at the meeting the young person is meant to be at the centre of the planning and their views are considered to be extremely important. In practice, however, not all young people attend these meetings, although an attempt might be made to capture their voice prior to the meeting taking place. In some cases, schools and professionals have found different ways of including the young people; for example, with support from a peer, a PowerPoint presentation could be made by the young person and then presented at the meeting (Aziz, 2014; see entry on *post-school transitions*, *voice*). Further, along with 'listening' to the young person's voice, *parental participation*, and interprofessional and interagency *collaboration* are seen to be crucial to effective transition planning (see entries on *collaboration* and *parental participation*).

Implications for practice
1. Early transition planning is crucial for effective transitions and service provision that meets the needs and aspirations of children and young people with SEN. To understand well what the aspirations and needs of children and young people are, it is important that their voice is heard and that they and families feel able to fully participate in the meetings.

2. The transition plans developed at school might not go beyond another educational context such as college. It is important to consider who should be the key worker who can carry on with the person beyond the educational context and support them post-school or post-college.

FURTHER READING

Beveridge, S. (1999). *Special educational needs in schools* (2nd edn.). New York & London: Routledge.

Beyer, S., Kaehne, A., Grey, J., Sheppard, K., & Meek, A. (2008). *What works? Good practice in transition to employment for young people with learning disabilities.* Cardiff University: Welsh Centre for Learning Disabilities.

Bollmer, J., Cronin, R., Brauen, M., Howell, B., Fletcher, P., Gonin, R., & Jenkins, F. (2010). *A study of State's monitoring and improvement practices under the Individuals with Disabilities Education Act.* US Department of Education: National Center for Special Education Research.

stage–environment fit theory

SEE ALSO **ageing, primary to secondary school transitions, self-determination**

Stage–Environment Fit Theory was proposed by Eccles and Midgley (1990), who highlighted that there can be a lack of fit between the developmental stage of adolescents and their needs and environment (Eccles, Lord, & Midgley, 1991; Wigfield, Eccles, MacIver, Reuman, & Midgley, 1991). Adolescence is marked with a need to assert autonomy, and therefore any mismatch with the adults, who might be perceived to be controlling, can lead to stress and strained relationships in different social environments, such as at home/care home or school (Gutman & Eccles, 2007). If the adolescent, for instance, is in a school environment that they perceive to have greater teacher control, to be less friendly and caring, with problematic relationships with secondary school teachers, it might lead to a change in their attitude towards learning, a dip in academic motivation, and negative self-image during transitions from primary to middle/secondary school (see entry on *primary to secondary school transitions*) (see entry Booth & Gerrard, 2014). According to this theory, the adolescents whose social environments change in developmentally regressive ways are more likely to experience difficulties, compared to those whose social environments respond to their changing needs (Gutman & Eccles, 2007). Therefore, developmentally appropriate or regressive shifts in the nature of social and learning environments, at home and school, may help in explaining individual differences in the quality and trajectory of their academic motivation, educational achievement, and social-emotional well-being during these years (Roeser, 2005) with impact on their future trajectories (Gutman & Eccles, 2007).

There is a link with self-determination, with optimum environment being one that meets the need for autonomy, relatedness, and competence (Deci & Ryan, 2000; Ryan & Deci, 2000; see entry on *self-determination*). In line with previous research with younger adolescents (12–14 years old), Zimmer-Gembeck, Chipuer, Hanisch, Creed, and McGregor (2006) provide evidence for this with older adolescents (15–16 years old) through their empirical research. Further, they found that the perception of environment (school in their case) fit partly depended on positive interactions and relationships with teachers and peers. This led them to conclude that school fit and engagement are mediators linking relationships with teacher and peers at school to students' academic achievement (Zimmer-Gembeck et al., 2006 for details). Although stage-environment fit has been conceptualised in the context of adolescence and primary–secondary transitions, it can be envisaged in the context of other transitions across the life course in line with Person–Environment fit, as this mismatch can be observed elsewhere: for example, professionals returning to education feeling de-skilled, or the old person in a care home experiencing a decrease in autonomy and sense of competence (see entry on *ageing*). If applied to the context of migration, for instance, involvement in decision-making regarding the move can provide a developmentally appropriate environment that will have a positive impact on well-being and dealing with the transition (Bushin, 2009).

Implications for practice

1. Since Stage–Environment fit can have a substantial impact on adolescents' motivation and achievement, it is important that the school and home environments are developmentally aligned. Providing them with more independence, autonomy,

and a clear role in any decision-making will lead to a developmentally appropriate environment. Similarly, creating opportunities for improved peer and staff relationships might support this. The structure of school and small class sizes might also help with the sense of belonging.

FURTHER READING

Eccles, J. S., & Midgley, C. (1990). Changes in academic motivation and self-perception during early adolescence. In R. Montemayor, G. R. Adams, & T. P. Gullotta (Eds.), *From childhood to adolescence: A transitional period?* London: SAGE, pp. 134–155.

Eccles, J. S., Lord, S., & Midgley, C. (1991). What are we doing to early adolescents? The impact of educational contexts on early adolescents. *American Journal of Education, 99*(4), 521–542.

Gutman, L. M., & Eccles, J. S. (2007). Stage–environment fit during adolescence: Trajectories of family relations and adolescent outcomes. *Developmental Psychology, 43*(2), 522–537.

strategies

SEE voice, induction, familiarisation, parental participation

successful transitions

In research as well as in practice, there is a lot of focus on successful transitions without clearly defining what one means by successful transitions. For example, there has been a tendency in the past in educational transitions, especially school-related, to focus on academic adjustment as successful transitions. This academic adjustment included aspects such as good attainment, attendance, and engagement at school/university (Rice, Frederickson, Shelton, McManus, Riglin, & Ng-Knight, n.d.). However, it is increasingly being recognised that we also need to look at social and emotional adjustment at school/university, i.e. the learner likes school/university and does not feel lonely, has a sense of belonging and well-being, and develops respectful and reciprocal relationships (Jindal-Snape & Rienties, 2016; Peters, 2010; Rice et al., n.d.). This is similar to the Affective-Behaviour-Cognitive (ABCs) of adaptation involving a sense of belonging, identification and group identity, and cultural and pedagogical adaptation (Jindal-Snape & Rienties, 2016).

Successful transitions might mean different things based on whose perspective we are looking at, and sometimes these perspectives might not match. Evangelou, Taggart, Sylva, Melhuish, Sammons, and Siraj-Blatchford (2008) reported that children and parents in their study identified five aspects of a successful primary to secondary school transition; making new friends; improvement in self-esteem and confidence; settling well in school (indicator was that parents had no concerns about them); an increased interest in school and school work compared to the previous school; adapting to new routines and school easily; and experiencing curricular continuity. They summarised these as social and institutional adjustment, and curriculum interest and continuity. However, according to a professional, a successful transition was one where there was timely receipt of parental choices and parents getting their first choice of school with few appeals. Therefore, it is important that the person who is most affected by a transition is asked what for them might be a successful transition.

Considering non-educational life transitions, similar aspects apply. For example, successful transition to work could include good attainment, attendance, and engagement with the organisation, as well as having a sense of belonging, identifying with the organisation, and having a sense of well-being. However, this might not be so clear cut for all transitions. For example, although not clearly defined, from Kirby, Broom, and Good's (2014) study on transitions to palliative care it seems that according to health care staff, effective transition would involve acceptance of medical futility, pain and symptom management, and well-being of patient and family both in a psycho-social and practical context.

Implications for practice
1. It is important to define successful transitions in one's own context, as otherwise it is difficult to know whether the transition practice was effective or not. As successful transitions can be different for various stakeholders, it is important to consult with them regarding what successful transition means to them. Also, not all transitions will be perceived as 'successful', e.g. by an individual who is moving into palliative care or their family who are experiencing grief.

2. Other terminology that has been used are 'smooth', 'seamless', and/or 'effective' transitions.

FURTHER READING

Evangelou, M., Taggart, B., Sylva, K., Melhuish, E., Sammons, P., & Siraj-Blatchford, I. (2008). *Effective Pre-school, Primary and Secondary Education 3-14 Project (EPPSE 3-14). What makes a successful transition from primary to secondary school?* Nottingham: DCSF Publications.

Kirby, E., Broom, A., & Good, P. (2014). The role and significance of nurses in managing transitions to palliative care: A qualitative study. *BMJ Open,* 4:e006026 doi: 10.1136/bmjopen-2014-006026.

supported employment

SEE employment

t

transfer

The term 'transition' has been conceptualised in different ways by researchers. Galton, Gray, and Ruddock (1999) differentiated between 'transition' as a process where children move between different classes in a school and 'transfer' as a move between different schools. Other researchers (Jindal-Snape, 2010b) have suggested the terms 'transition' and 'transfer' can be used interchangeably to describe any move that a child makes from one context and set of relationships to another. In this book, the term 'transition' has been used consistently and in line with Jindal-Snape's (2010a) conceptualisation, as this is the most commonly used term internationally.

Implications for practice
1. It is important to be mindful of the different terms used by authors, as they might indicate that their conceptualisation of transition is different to the professionals, especially across disciplines and professions.

FURTHER READING
Galton, M., Gray, J., & Rudduck, J. (2003). *Transfer and transition in the middle years of schooling (7-14): Continuities and discontinuities in learning*, Research Report 443, Annesley, Department of Education and Science.
Jindal-Snape, D. (2010b). Setting the scene: Educational transitions and moving stories. In D. Jindal-Snape (Ed.), *Educational transitions: Moving stories from around the world*. New York: Routledge, pp. 1–8.

transition

SEE ALSO educational and life transitions, identity, multiple and multi-dimensional transitions

There are several types of transition that an individual goes through from cradle to grave, such as educational transitions, bereavement, starting a family, ageing, etc. Although authors do not always define or operationalise transitions in their work, it is clear that they have been conceptualised in a variety of ways. Some have conceptualised transition as a single event at the end of, or the beginning of, one stage in life. Often those viewing transitions in this way are seeing it only as a significant change that is usually normative and focused on a particular moment in time. Viewed in this way transition can be a one-off event. Others believe that it is an ongoing process and involves several subtle as well as larger changes. There can be several such changes within the same day (e.g. Jovanovic, 2011) and in the same physical context (Pietarinen, Soini et al., 2010). Others have conceptualised it as vertical (from one stage to another) and horizontal transition (within the same stage but the constant adaptation and adjustment with peers and teachers) (see Pietarinen, Soini et al., 2010). Further, some see transition as a physical or visible change; others see it is a psychological process of experiencing change, for example, in one's identity. According to Wesley (2001) and Adeyemo (2010) transition is a change from one style, state, form, or location, with Fabian and Dunlop (2005) suggesting that transition involves a change in relationships, pedagogical approach, space, and/or context for learning. Whereas Zhou et al. (2010) have suggested that transition is a process of pedagogical, psychological, and cultural adaptation over time. Some researchers see transition as a change from one *identity* to another (Lam & Pollard, 2006), with it being more than a change in contexts but also processes of not only 'becoming somebody' but also 'unbecoming' (Ecclestone, 2007; Ecclestone, Biesta, & Hughes, 2010).

Therefore, there are various conceptualisations of transitions. These might be based on the disciplines and professional base of the authors. However, these can be very confusing for the reader. The common aspects of all these are change, whether visible or invisible; physical or psychological; one-off or ongoing. Some other key aspects are transformation of the individual and their identity, as well as adaptation to the change in different ways, and over time.

There is also difference in the focus of some, with some taking a life course approach, whereas others focus on a particular age and stage. Therefore, some might focus on one transition alone, whereas others would focus on multiple transitions someone might be experiencing at the same time (see entries on *educational and life transitions* and *multiple and multi-dimensional transitions*).

Further, along with conceptualising it differently in terms of what it is, it is conceptualised by some as a time of anxiety and concern, whereas others see it as an exciting time with a sense of achievement and progression. Some have referred to anxiety being part of the excitement and see it as positive (Lucey & Reay, 2000). Others have reported that the same aspects of transitions can worry or excite the same individual (Jindal-Snape, 2013). It is important to be aware of the context and conceptualisation of transition when considering whether it is positive or negative, and the discipline or professional discourse of the author; for example, transition related to death of a significant other or moving from a school would most likely have different consequences.

Implications for practice
1. As transition is conceptualised in so many different ways, it is not surprising that research findings and practices can be very different as well. Sometimes the term 'transition' is used very loosely, and it is important to understand the author's conceptualisation before drawing any conclusions from that study.
2. It is worth considering one's own practical experiences to further contextualise transitions.

FURTHER READING

Ecclestone, K., Biesta, G. J. J., & Hughes, M. (2010). Transitions in the lifecourse: The role of identity, agency and structure. In K. Ecclestone, G. J. J. Biesta & M. Hughes (Eds.), *Transitions and learning through the lifecourse*. London: Routledge, pp. 1–15.

Galton, M. (2010). Moving to secondary school: What do pupils in England say about the experience? In D. Jindal-Snape (Ed.), *Educational transitions: Moving stories from around the world*. New York: Routledge, pp. 107–124.

Jindal-Snape, D. (2010c). Moving on: Integrating the lessons learnt and the way ahead. In D. Jindal-Snape (Ed.), *Educational transitions: Moving stories from around the world*. New York & London: Routledge, pp. 223–244.

Transition meetings

SEE **special educational needs**

transition partnership

SEE collaboration

transition planning and preparation

SEE ALSO agency, attachment, multiple and multi-dimensional transitions theory, parental participation, emotional intelligence, familiarisation, resilience, self-esteem, virtual backpack approach, voice

Transition planning and preparation, especially for the normative transitions such as educational transitions, involves preparing the individual for the move to the new context and set of interpersonal relationships. Research suggests that those unprepared for transition were particularly vulnerable to poorer transitions, both organisational and social, and this is of concern, as this can have long-term consequences for mental health (West, Sweeting, & Young, 2010).

As transition is a dynamic process, it is vital that transition planning and preparation, along with associated activities, are carried on *across* the educational lifespan (e.g. Akos, 2010; Galton, 2010). This, therefore, implies that preparation should be embedded into everyday life. Organisations and professionals also put on specific activities at the time of a major move, such as starting secondary school. After a review of good transition practice from the UK, Finland, New Zealand, Nigeria, and the US, Jindal-Snape (2010) summarised some examples of good transition practice across the educational stages. These are:

- Induction days lasting at least a few days before and after the move (see entry on *familiarisation*)
- Portfolios from previous school (Peters (2010), see entries on *virtual backpack approach* and *attachment*)
- Opportunities to create friendship networks (see entry on *resilience*)
- Information passed between organisations (especially in the context of nursery, and primary and secondary schools) should focus on educational, social, and emotional aspects
- Opportunities for secure attachment (see entry on *secure attachment*)
- Involving the learner as an active participant (see entry on *agency*)
- Creation of transition teams

- Sharing pedagogy across educational institutions
- Parental participation in the case of children and young people (see entry on *parental participation*)
- Information packs, including photographs and videos of the new environment and people they will interact with in them (see entry on *familiarisation*)
- Practitioners undertaking action research and ongoing evaluation of programme effectiveness
- Interventions involving *emotional intelligence* and *self-esteem*

When the professionals provide these activities, they have sound and well-researched, but not always explicit, theoretical underpinnings. For example, opportunities to create social networks with other children starting the same school or with staff can be linked with resilience theory, as by doing so they can provide opportunities to create strong external protective factors through focus on relationship and networking (see entry on *resilience*). Further, the activities that involve the child as an active participant in transition planning will support the enhancement of internal protective factors, such as child's self-esteem, through increased sense of self-competence and self-worth (Jindal-Snape & Miller, 2008) (see entries on *agency* and *Self-esteem*).

Reflecting on primary–secondary transitions, Galton (2010) summarises transition practice as five bridges of transition, i.e. administrative; social/user friendly; curriculum; teaching and learning; and managing learning. Administrative in this context involves good communication between educational organisations; timely exchange of information about children; reciprocal visits and meetings between teachers and head teachers from primary and secondary school; meetings between primary school teacher and secondary school guidance/support for learning staff and visits by them to the primary school. Social/user friendly practice is one that includes familiarisation with the new environment and people, such as open days and induction events. In terms of curriculum it involves continuity and progression, including starting activity when in primary school and carrying on with it when in secondary school but at a slightly higher level. Teaching and learning on the other hand relates to practice that enhances pedagogical continuity, with teachers using similar approaches and strategies in primary and secondary schools. Managing learning involves preparation for academic life through the development of critical thinking and problem-solving skills. Galton (2010) argues that the idea is to help children develop into 'professional learners'.

These transition practices apply not only to an educational context but also to other transitions such as a major bereavement in the family, preparing for birth, starting a new job, or moving to another country.

Implications for practice

1. It is important that transition planning and preparation takes cognisance of the nature of transition and is not put in place just before and after a major move. Support should be provided to the individual and significant others.
2. Individuals and their families can be involved as active participants in various ways. Their self-esteem, emotional intelligence, agency, and resilience can be enhanced through drama, story-telling, and games-based learning, by providing them with secure exposure to transition-related issues and creating opportunities to tackle them in a safe environment.
3. Some of the creative tools such as story books and board games can also be used by professionals and parents to interact with the young learners, to find out what is worrying them (see entries on **parental participation** and **voice**).
4. Professionals should also be mindful of the families and their own transition needs and put strategies and support systems in place (see entry on **multiple and multi-dimensional transitions theory**).

FURTHER READING

Jindal-Snape, D., & Miller, D. J. (2010). Understanding transitions through self-esteem and resilience. In D. Jindal-Snape (Ed.), *Educational transitions: Moving stories from around the world*. New York & London: Routledge, pp. 11–32.

Kelly, T. B., Tolson, D., Smith, T. D., & McColgan, G. (2010). Using the research process to develop group services for older persons with a hearing disability. In D. M. Steinberg (Ed.), *Orchestrating the power of groups: beginnings, middles, and endings (overture, movements, and finales)*. AASWG Proceedings, Whiting & Birch, pp. 104–117.

transition plans

SEE employment, special educational needs, transition planning and preparation

V

virtual backpack approach

SEE ALSO **attachment, self-esteem**

In a new context, even the most adept and able person can feel a bit de-skilled. Sometimes these messages come from others through the unspoken rules of an organisation or the expectations of others within that organisation. The virtual backpack approach emphasises that the purpose of education is to open the virtual backpack a learner might bring with him or her (Peters, 2010) and avoid de-skilling of a learner. Building on Thomson's (2002) notion of every child carrying a virtual school bag full of knowledge, experiences, and dispositions, and that of Bourdieu (1997) and Brooker (2002) regarding the social and cultural capital every child brings to a school, in the context of early years Peters (2013) emphasised the importance of the significant others valuing the social and cultural capital that a child might bring to the new environment. This applies not only to children and their transitions; it applies to all transitions irrespective of the stage and age. The virtual backpack approach acknowledges the learning journey somebody has been through, and the idea is to build upon what the individual brings with them in terms of skills, abilities, aptitudes, etc.

As opposed to de-skilling of an individual, this asset-based approach would also help with the individual's self-esteem and feelings of attachment with the significant 'artefacts' or 'moments' from the previous context (see entries on *attachment* and *self-esteem*). For example, Peters (2010) describes a child who normally stayed silent in class becoming very animated and interacting with peers when he brought his kindergarten portfolio with him. However, not all professionals have been seen to 'open' these virtual backpacks; even those who do open them might not do so for every child. In a conscious effort to open the virtual backpack of every child and to develop something further, and make professionals aware of it,

Jindal-Snape, Baird and Miller (2011) report on an initiative where a computer game was used for transition purposes, initially with children teaching the teachers how to set up and use consoles. The project that started in primary school was then developed further in secondary school, with the focus of conversation in the class in the first few weeks being on the project and children's achievement, and meetings with guidance staff being organised around the project rather than any issues the child might be facing.

In a university context, in a more concrete way this can be portfolios of work that a learner might bring from the school or further education setting. This can then be built upon during their time in the university, and the learner can take the portfolios with them to an employment context. The virtual pack could also include the life skills that they have acquired such as cooking, budgeting and social skills.

Implications for practice
1. This approach emphasises the importance of valuing and building on the learning from the old context. It reminds us of the importance of first ascertaining what knowledge, skills, and dispositions the newcomer brings with them. It is important therefore to see every learner as an individual rather than making assumptions about their background.
2. As mentioned above, the significant aspects from the previous environment can be used to interact with the learner in the new context as well as providing them with an opportunity to interact with others, e.g. bringing something of significance to them.

FURTHER READING

Peters, S. (2010). Shifting the lens: Re-framing the view of learners and learning during the transition from early childhood education to school in New Zealand. In D. Jindal-Snape (Ed.), *Educational transitions: Moving stories from around the world.* New York: Routledge, pp. 68–84.

Peters, S. (2014). Chasms, bridges and borderlands: A transitions research 'across the border' from early childhood education to school in New Zealand. In B. Perry, S. Dockett, and A. Petriwskyj (Eds.), *Transitions to school - international research, policy and practice.* New York: Springer, pp. 105–116.

voice

SEE ALSO **creative approaches**

Voice is the expression of views and opinions in a way that is meaningful to everyone, with or without using speech. It is seen as a human rights issue, and we have an ethical and moral imperative to listen to the voice of others about matters of significance to them. It is important that as professionals we listen to those who might not always be heard but are the ones most affected, in this context, by transitions. However, as has been seen in the case of transitions of children and young people, especially those who are very young and/or experience additional support needs, their voices are not always heard (Mitchell, 2012). This comes from a lack of consideration of meaningful ways of listening to the voice of individuals for whom traditional ways of expressing their views and opinion might not work (Shucksmith, Spratt, Philip, & McNaughton, 2009).

Some transition researchers and practitioners have argued that for individuals to have positive transition experiences, there should be an increased emphasis on involving those most affected, in planning and preparation for transitions (Galton, 2010; Jindal-Snape, 2012). It is important to gather their perspectives, not only to understand their unique experiences, but also to ensure that they are active participants in determining transition practice and programmes, and feel a sense of control on their transition journey. This is true in the context of transitions practice and research; however, only a few have used alternative ways to engage and listen to voices, for example of the child or young people, in ways that are meaningful to them (e.g. Dockett & Perry, 2011; Jindal-Snape, 2012). Age- and stage-relevant techniques need to be used. Further, voice can be inhibited by the setting or environment, for example by several adults sitting around a large board room table with the young person sitting on their own at one end during post-school transition review meetings (although it is important to be mindful that some young people might prefer this). The adult–child or other power dynamics can have an impact on the ability to express or listen to voice.

In different countries, legislation mandates that young people, for instance, have a voice and say in their transition plans (e.g. The Education (Additional Support for Learning) (Scotland) Act 2004; Individuals with Disabilities Education Act (IDEA), 2004) and that professionals have to make sure that their aspirations, goals, and interests are at the centre. How the young people participate should be dealt with on a case-by-case basis, and appropriate support should be provided to ensure this happens, in consultation with the young people, family members, or their key worker.

Implications for practice

1. The voice of an individual can only be heard effectively in ways meaningful to them. For an example, please refer to entry on **creative approaches.** Please be mindful that this might not be the most effective way of listening to everyone's voice as some can find creative approaches to be a barrier due to stereotypes of aesthetic and finesse attached to them.

FURTHER READING

Jindal-Snape, D. (2012). Portraying children's voices through creative approaches to enhance their transition experience and improve the transition practice, *LEARNing Landscapes*, 6(1), 223–240. Retrieved from www.learninglandscapes.ca/current-issue.

Shucksmith, J., Spratt, J., Philip, K., & McNaughton, R. (2009). *A critical review of the literature on children and young people's views of the factors that influence their mental health*. Edinburgh: NHS Health Scotland.

W

well-being

SEE ALSO **ABCs of acculturation, ecological systems theory, international students' transitions to higher education, migration (international transitions) of children**

A systematic literature review of studies investigating the impact of arts on well-being found that there was no clear definition of well-being and several dimensions were included, such as emotional and psychological well-being, spiritual well-being, physical well-being, and social well-being (Toma, Morris, Kelly, & Jindal-Snape, 2014). It is often used interchangeably with terms such as *happiness, quality of life, flourishing* (Statham & Chase, 2010). It has been measured or reported either in terms of objective measures (e.g. economic indicators) or in terms of subjective well-being (McLellan, Galton, Steward, & Page, 2012). McLellan et al. report that there are four approaches to conceptualising subjective well-being in literature, namely Hedonic Approach (affect and life satisfaction), Eudaimonic Approach (personal growth, development, self-actualisation and motivation), Social Approach (social integration, contribution, coherence and acceptance) and Capability Approach (bodily health, bodily integrity, senses, imagination and thought, emotions, affiliation, control over environment, etc.). Australian Council for Educational Research (ACER) (2010) designed the Social-Emotional Well-being (SEW) Survey, which is a strength-based survey for children and young people in the age range of 3–18 years, that adopts an ecological view (see entry on *ecological systems theory*) of their well-being and assesses seven components; three external components of school life, home life and community life; and four internal components of resilience, positive social skills, positive work management, and engagement skills. Other constructs that have been seen to indicate well-being, or are seen to be *leading* to well-being, include enjoyment, absence of stress or anxiety, self-esteem, self-worth, confidence, empowerment, and voice (Jindal-Snape, Scott, & Davies, 2014).

Therefore, with these loose definitions of well-being it is important to be clear what well-being might mean in different contexts and for the people we are working with. In terms of transitions, depending on the nature and context of transition, emotional and psychological well-being, spiritual well-being, physical well-being, and social well-being, all can be affected. And indeed, across the life course, individuals might experience threat to, or enhancement of, different dimensions of well-being, as well as these dimensions having an impact on each other with the edges blurred (McAdams, Lucas, & Donnellan, 2012). That might be the reason why it is difficult to be specific about well-being and, depending on what is being 'measured' and of course what can actually be 'measured', different disciplines highlight different types of well-being. Dodge, Daly, Huyton, and Sanders (2012) have presented their definition of well-being after reviewing literature and theoretical base. Using the analogy of a seesaw, according to them well-being is the balance point between the resources available to an individual and the challenges faced by them, emphasising that well-being is dynamic, with fluctuations between these challenges and resources, that are psychological, social, and physical. They argue that well-being is not static as, if there are no challenges, it might lead to stagnation again affecting the balance.

McNaught (2011) developed a framework that moves well-being from individual to a more holistic perspective and focuses on individual well-being, family well-being, community well-being, and societal well-being. Well-being is seen as 'dynamically constructed by its actors through an interplay between their circumstances, locality, activities and psychological resources, including interpersonal relations with, for example, families and significant others' (La Placa, McNaught, & Knight, 2013, p. 118).

It is important to see how individuals themselves define well-being or particular domains of well-being. In a study with looked after young people, they were asked to define emotional well-being. They defined *good* emotional well-being according to their feelings (happy, joyful), thoughts (positive thinking), behaviours (smiling, laughing), activities that support well-being (swimming, playing), achievements (praise), relationships (socialising, seeing family, having support), and the importance of safety and stability (feeling safe and secure, comfortable and warm place) (Bazalgette, Rahilly, & Trevelyan, 2015).

As can be seen from the various entries in this book, well-being is at the core of transitions. Researchers have looked at various transitions using the well-being lens. For example, in the context of migration and change of place of residence of people *within* the same country, using a social well-being framework from a life-course perspective, Nowok, van Ham, Findlay, and Gayle (2013) found that move of geographical and social space led to a boost in happiness. This contrasts to mixed outcomes for international migration, although they are similarly dynamic and changeable over time (see entries on ***ABCs of acculturation, international students' transitions to higher education*** and ***migration (international transitions) of children***).

Others have looked at change in well-being over the lifespan, with different trends emerging in the context of ageing due to lack of agreed constructs and differences in samples and methodology (Ulloa, Møller, & Sousa-Poza, 2013). Some studies suggested that subjective well-being is minimum between the mid-30s to early 50s, others suggested that it increases during middle age and peaks around the age of 65, and yet others suggested that it is constant throughout life, with confirmatory and contradictory results from across the world. In the context of educational transitions, West et al. (2010) found that poorer school and peer transitions can have long-term consequences for mental health.

Implications for practice

1. It is important to clearly define what one means by well-being, as it is often used as an all-encompassing term. Well-being is substantially affected by transitions across the life course, as well as well-being having an impact on how different transitions will be experienced. Research suggests that well-being can be enhanced through age- and stage-appropriate interventions, such as creative arts (see entry on ***creative approaches***).

FURTHER READING

Dodge, R., Daly, A. P., Huyton, J., & Sanders, L. D. (2012). The challenge of defining wellbeing. *International Journal of Wellbeing, 2*(3), 222–235.
La Placa, V., McNaught, A., & Knight, A. (2013). Discourse on wellbeing in research and practice. *International Journal of Wellbeing, 3*(1), 116–125.

McNaught, A. (2011). Defining wellbeing. In A. Knight & A. McNaught (Eds.), *Understanding wellbeing: An introduction for students and practitioners of health and social care* (pp. 7–23). Banbury: Lantern Publishing.

Ulloa, B. F. L, Møller, V., Sousa-Poza, A. (2013). How does subjective well-being evolve with age? A literature review. *Population Ageing, 6,* 227–246.

bibliography

Adeyemo, D. A. (2005). The buffering effect of emotional intelligence on the adjustment of secondary school students in transition. *Electronic Journal of Research in Educational Psychology, 3*(2), 79–90.

——— (2007). Moderating influence of emotional intelligence on the link between academic self-efficacy and achievement of university students. *Psychology and Developing Society, 19*(2), 199–213.

———(2010). Educational transition and emotional intelligence. In D. Jindal-Snape (Ed.), *Educational transitions: Moving stories from around the world.* New York: Routledge, pp. 33–47.

Ainsworth, M. D. S (1964). Patterns of attachment behavior shown by the infant in interaction with his mother. *Merrill-Palmer Quarterly of Behavior and Development,* 51–58.

Ainsworth, M. D. S., & Bell, S. M. (1970). Attachment, exploration, and separation: Illustrated by the behavior of one-year-olds in a strange situation. *Child Development, 41,* 49–67.

Ainsworth, M. D. S., Bell, S. M., & Stayton, D. J. (1971). Individual differences in strange-situation behavior of one-year-olds. In H. R. Schaffer (Ed.), *The origins of human social relations.* London and New York: Academic Press, pp. 17–58.

Ainsworth, M. D. S., Blehar, M. C., Waters, E., & Wall, S. (1978). *Patterns of attachment: A psychological study of the strange situation.* Hillsdale, NJ: Erlbaum.

Ainsworth, M. D. S., & Wittig, B. A. (1969). Attachment and exploratory behavior of one-year-olds in a strange situation. In B. M. Foss (Ed.), *Determinants of infant behavior* (Vol. 4, pp. 111–136). London: Methuen.

Akerman, A., & Statham, R. (2011). *Childhood bereavement: A rapid literature review.* London: The Childhood Wellbeing Research Centre.

Akos, P. (2002). Student perceptions of the transition from elementary to middle school. *Professional School Counseling, 5,* 339–345.

———(2004). Advice and student agency in the transition to middle school. *Research in Middle Level Education, 27,* 1–11.

————(2005). The unique nature of middle school counseling. *Professional School Counseling, 9*(2), 95–103.

————(2010). Moving through elementary, middle, and high schools: The primary to secondary shifts in the United States. In D. Jindal-Snape (Ed.), *Educational transitions: Moving stories from around the world*. New York: Routledge, pp. 125–142.

Akos, P., & Galassi, J. (2004). Middle and high school transitions as viewed by students, parents, and teachers. *Professional School Counseling, 7*, 212–221.

Akos, P., & Martin, M. (2003). Transition groups for preparing students for middle school. *The Journal for Specialists in Group Work, 28*(2), 139–154.

Alexander, K. L., & Entwisle, D. R. (1988). Achievement in the first 2 years of school: Patterns and processes. *Monographs of the Society for Research in Child Development, 53*(2), 1–157.

Alexander, R. (Ed). (2010). *Children their world, their education. Final report and recommendations of the Cambridge Primary Review*. New York: Routledge.

Alexson, R. G., & Kemnitz, C. P. (2004). Curriculum articulation and transitioning student success: Where are we going wrong and what lessons have we learned? *Educational Research Quarterly, 28*(2), 19–29.

Anderson, L.W., Jacobs, J., Schramm, S., & Splittgerber, F. (2000). School transitions: Beginning of the end or a new beginning? *International Journal of Educational Research, 33*, 325–339.

Archer, M. S. (2000). *Being human: The problem of agency*. Cambridge: Cambridge University Press.

————(2003). *Structure, agency and the internal conversation*. Cambridge: Cambridge University Press.

————(2007). *Making our way through the world: Human reflexivity and social mobility*. Cambridge: Cambridge University Press.

Association for Children's Palliative Care (ACT). (2007). *The transition care pathway: a framework for the development of integrated multi-agency care pathways for young people with life-threatening and life-limiting conditions*. Bristol: ACT.

Atchley, R. C. (1989). A continuity theory of normal aging. *Gerontologist, 29*(2), 183–190.

Australian Council for Educational Research (ACER). (2010). *Social-Emotional Wellbeing Survey*. ACER: Report for Educational Transformations.

Aziz, A. (2014). *A longitudinal study exploring post-school transitions of young people with learning disabilities perspectives of young people, parents and professionals*. Doctoral thesis, University of Dundee.

Baggs, J. G., Norton, M. H., & Schmitt, C. R. (2004). The dying patient in the ICU: Role of the interdisciplinary team. *Critical Care Clinics, 20*(3), 525–540.

Baker, R. W., McNeil, O. V., & Siryk, B. (1985). Expectation and reality in freshman adjustment to college. *Journal of Counseling Psychology, 32,* 94–103.

Bamber, G., Gittell, J.T., Kochan, A., & von Nordenflycht, A. (2009). *Up in the air: How the airlines can improve performance by engaging their employees.* Ithaca, NY: Cornell University Press.

Bancroft, S., Fawcett, M., & Hay, P. (2008). *Researching children researching the world: 5x5x5=creativity.* Stoke-on-Trent, UK: Trentham.

Bandura, A. (2000). Exercise of human agency through collective efficacy. *Current Directions in Psychological Science, 9,* 75–78.

————(2004). Health Promotion by Social Cognitive Means. *Health Education & Behavior, 31*(2), 143–164.

Bar-On, R. (2006). The Bar-On model of emotional–social intelligence (ESI). *Psychothema, 18,* Supl, 13–25.

Barrett, M. S., & Baker, J. S. (2012). Developing learning identities in and through music: A case study of the outcomes of a music programme in an Australian juvenile detention centre. *International Journal of Music Education, 30*(3), 244–259.

Barron, I. G., & Abdullah, G. (2012). Evaluation of a group-based trauma recovery program in Gaza: Students' subjective experiences. *Journal of Loss and Trauma, 17*(2), 187–199.

————(2015). Intergenerational trauma in the occupied Palestinian territories: Effect on children and promotion of healing. *Journal of Child and Adolescent Trauma, 8*(2), 103–110.

Barron, I. G., Abdallah, G., & Smith, P. (2013). Randomized control trial of a CBT trauma recovery program in Palestinian schools. *Journal of Loss and Trauma, 18*(4), 306–321.

Barron, I.G., Dyregrov, A., Abdallah, G., & Jindal-Snape, D. (2015). Complicated grief in Palestinian children and adolescents. *Journal of Child & Adolescent Behavior, 3*(3), 1–6. doi: 10.4172/2375-4494.1000213.

Barry, M. (2006). *Youth offending in transition: The search for social recognition.* Abingdon: Routledge.

————(2007). Listening and learning: The reciprocal relationship between worker and client. *Probation Journal, 54*(4), 407–422.

————(2009). Promoting desistance amongst young people. In T. Taylor, R. Earle, & R. Hester (Eds.), *Youth justice handbook, theory, policy and practice.* Cullompton: Willan Publishing/The Open University, 158–167.

Baumeister, R. F., Campbell, J. D., Krueger, J. I., & Vohs, K. D. (2005). Does high self-esteem cause better performance, interpersonal success, happiness, or healthier lifestyles? *Psychological Science in the Public Interest, 4,* 1–44.

Baumeister, R. F., & Leary, M. R. (1995). The need to belong: Desire for interpersonal attachments as a fundamental human motivation. *Psychological Bulletin, 117,* 497–529.

Bazalgette, L., Rahilly, T., & Trevelyan, G. (2015). *Achieving emotional wellbeing for looked after children: A whole system approach.* London: NSPCC.

Beech, S. (2016). The multicultural experience? 'Cultural cliques' and the international student community. In D. Jindal-Snape & B. Rienties (Eds.), *Multi-dimensional transitions of international students to higher education.* New York: Routledge, pp. 143–160.

Beresford, B., & Stuttard, L. (2014). Young adults as users of adult healthcare: experiences of young adults with complex or life-limiting conditions. *Clinical Medicine, 14*(4), 404–408.

Bergin, C., & Bergin, D. (2009). Attachment in the Classroom. *Educational Psychology Review, 21,* 141–170.

Berman-Rossi, T., & Kelly, T. B. (2014). Older persons in need of long-term care. In A. Gitterman (Ed.), *Handbook of social work practice with vulnerable and resilient populations.* (3rd edn.). New York: Columbia University Press, pp. 415–440.

Berry, J. W. (1992). Acculturation and adaptation in a new society. *International Migration, 30,* 69–85. doi: 10.1111/j.1468-2435.1992.tb00776.x

———(1997). Immigration, acculturation, and adaptation. *Applied Psychology, 46*(1), 5–34. doi: 10.1111/j.1464-0597.1997.tb01087.x

———(2005). Acculturation: Living successfully in two cultures. *International Journal of Intercultural Relations, 29*(6), 697–712.

———(2006). Acculturative stress. In P. Wong & L. Wong (Eds.), *Handbook of multicultrual perspectives on stress and coping.* New York: Springer, pp. 287–298.

Bethel, A., Szabo, A., & Ward, C. (2016). Parallel lives? Predicting and enhancing connectedness between international and domestic students. In D. Jindal-Snape & B. Rienties, *Multi-dimensional transitions of international students to Higher Education.* New York: Routledge, 21–36.

Beutel, A., & Axinn, W. (2002). Gender, social change, and educational attainment. *Economic Development and Cultural Change, 51,* 109–134.

Beveridge, S. (1999). *Special educational needs in schools* (2nd edn.). New York & London: Routledge.

Beyer, S., Kaehne, A., Grey, J., Sheppard, K., & Meek, A. (2008). *What works? Good practice in transition to employment for young people with learning disabilities.* Cardiff University: Welsh Centre for Learning Disabilities.

Beyer, S., & Robinson, C. (2009). *A review of the research literature on supported employment: A report for the cross-Government learning disability employment strategy team.* London: Department of Health.

Bhugra, D. (2004). Migration and mental health. *Acta Psychiatrica Scandinavica, 109*(4), 243–258.

Biesta, G. J. J., & Tedder, M. (2006). How is agency possible? Towards an ecological understanding of agency-as-achievement. Working paper 5, Exeter: The Learning Lives project.

———(2007). Agency and learning in the lifecourse: Towards an ecological perspective. *Studies in the Education of Adults, 39*, 132–149.

Blackman, N. (2003). *Loss and learning disability.* London: Worth Publishing.

Boal, A. (1995). *The rainbow of desire: The Boal method of theatre and therapy.* London: Routledge.

Bollmer, J., Cronin, R., Brauen, M., Howell, B., Fletcher, P., Gonin, R., & Jenkins, F. (2010). *A study of State's monitoring and improvement practices under the Individuals with Disabilities Education Act.* US Department of Education: National Center for Special Education Research.

Booth, M. Z., & Gerard, J. M. (2014). Adolescents' stage-environment fit in middle and high school: The relationship between students' perceptions of their schools and themselves. *Youth and Society, 46*(6), 735–755.

Bourdieu, P. (1997) The forms of capital. In A. Halsey, H. Lauder, P. Brown, and A. Stuart Wells (Eds.), *Education: Culture, economy and society*, pp. Oxford: Oxford University Press, pp. 42–58.

Bowlby, J. (1988). *A secure base: Parent-child attachment and healthy human development.* London: Routledge.

Brewington, J. O., Nassar-McMillan, S. C., Flowers, C. P., & Furr, S. R. (2004). A preliminary investigation of factors associated with job loss grief. *The Career Development Quarterly, 53*, 78–83.

Britt, C., & Sumsion, J. (2003). Within the borderlands: Beginning early childhood teachers in primary schools. *Contemporary Issues in Early Childhood, 4*(2), 115–136.

Brooker, L. (2002). *Starting school: Young children learning cultures.* Buckingham: Open University Press.

Bronfenbrenner, U. (1979). *The ecology of human development: Experiments by nature and design.* Cambridge, Massachussets: Harvard University Press.

———(1986a). Recent advances in research on the ecology of human development. In R. K. Silbereisen, K. Eyferth, & G. Rudinger (Eds.), *Development as action in context: Problem behavior and normal youth development.* Heidelberg and New York: Springer, pp. 287–309.

———(1986b). Ecology of the family as a context for human development: Research perspectives. *Developmental Psychology, 22*, 723–742.

———(1992). Ecological systems theory. In R. Vasta (Ed.), *Six theories of child development.* London and Philadelphia: Jessica Kingsley Publishers, pp. 187–249.

Bronstein, I., & Montgomery, P. (2011). Psychological distress in refugee children: A systematic review. *Clinical Child and Family Psychology Review, 14*(1), 44–56.

Broström, S. (2000). Transition to school. Paper related to poster symposium on "transition" at EECERA 10th European Conference on Quality in Early Childhood Education, University of London.

Brown, K., & White, K. (2006). *Exploring the evidence base for integrated children's services,* Retrieved December 21 2015, from www.scotland.gov.uk/Publications/Recent.

Bushin, N. (2009). Researching family migration decision-making: A children-in-families approach. *Population Space and Place, 15*(5), 429–443.

Campbell Clark, S. (2000). Work/family border theory: A new theory of work/family balance. *Human Relations, 53*(6), 747–770.

Cebotari, V., & Mazzucato, V. (2016). Educational performance of children of migrant parents in Ghana, Nigeria and Angola. *Journal of Ethnic and Migration Studies, 42*(5), 834–856.

Clark, C. (2007). *Why families matter to literacy: A brief research summary.* London: National Literacy Trust.

Colverd, S., & Hodgkin, B. (2011). *Developing emotional intelligence in the primary school.* New York: Routledge.

Coyner, L., Reynolds, A., & Ou, S. (2003). The effect of early childhood interventions on subsequent special education services: Findings from the Chicago Child–Parent Centers. *Education Evaluation and Policy Analysis, 25*(1), 75–95.

Craft, A., Chappell, K., & Twining, P. (2008). Learners reconceptualising education: widening participation through creative engagement? *Innovations in Education and Teaching International, 45*(3), 235–245.

Creech, A., Hallam, S., Varvarigou, M., McQueen, H., & Gaunt, H. (2013). Active music making: A route to enhanced subjective wellbeing among older people. *Perspectives in Public Health, 133*(1), 36–43.

Cremin, T., Burnard, P., & Craft, A. (2006). Pedagogy and possibility thinking in the early years. *Thinking Skills & Creativity, 1*(2), 108–119.

Crittenden, P. M. (2005). Teoria dell'attaccamento, psicopatologia e psicoterapia: L'approccio dinamico maturativo (The theory of attachment, psychopathology and psychotherapy: The dynamic-maturational approach). *Psicoterapia, 30,* 171–182.

Cruickshank, C.-A., and Barry, M. (2008). *'Nothing has convinced me to stop': Young people's perceptions and experiences of persistent offending,* Glasgow: Who Cares? Scotland.

Cumming, R. (2007). Learning play in the classroom: Encouraging children's intuitive creativity with words through poetry. *Literacy, 41*(2), 93–101.

Dandolo Partners. (2012). *Evaluation of the national partnership on youth attainment and transitions*. A report for the Department of Education. Melbourne: Dandolo Partners.

Daniel, B., & Wassell, S. (2002). *Adolescence: Assessing and promoting resilience in vulnerable children*. London: Jessica Kingsley.

Darling, N. (2007). Ecological systems theory: The person in the center of the circles. *Research in Human Development, 4*, 203–217.

D'Amour, D., Ferrada-Videla, M., San Martin-Rodriguez, L., & Beaulieu, M. D. (2005). The conceptual basis for interprofessional collaboration: Core concepts and theoretical frameworks. *Journal of Interprofessional Care, 19*(1), 116–131.

Davies, D., Jindal-Snape, D., Collier, C., Digby, R., Hay, P., & Howe, A. (2013). Creative learning environments in education—A systematic literature review. *Thinking Skills and Creativity. 8*, 80–91 http://dx.doi.org/10.1016/j.tsc.2012.07.004.

Davies, D., Jindal-Snape, D., Digby, R., Howe, A., Collier, C., & Hay, P. (2014). The roles and development needs of teachers to promote creativity: A systematic review of literature. *Teaching and Teacher Education, 41*, 34–41.

Davydov, V. V., Slobodchikov, V. I., & Tsukerman, G. A. (2003). The elementary school student as an agent of learning activity. *Journal of Russian and East European Psychology, 41*(5), 63–76.

Deci, E. L., Connell, J. P., & Ryan, R. M. (1989). Self-determination in a work organization. *Journal of Applied Psychology, 74*, 580–590.

Deci, E. L., & Ryan, R. M. (2000). The "what" and "why" of goal pursuits: Human needs and the self-determination of behavior. *Psychological Inquiry, 11*, 227–268.

Deckert-Peaceman, H. (2006). *"Big kids go to big school." Changing transitions from early childhood to school. Some methodological considerations towards an international comparison*. AARE Conference 2006, University of South Australia.

Delamont, S. (1991). The hit list and other horror stories. *Sociological Review, 39*(2), 238–259.

Desforges, C., & Abouchaar, A. (2003). *The impact of parental involvement, parental support and family education on pupil achievement and adjustment: A literature review*. Retrieved March 5, 2009, from www.dcsf.gov.uk/research/data/uploadfiles/RR433.pdf.

Dickins, M. (2008). *Listening to young disabled children, Listening as a way of life*. National Children's Bureau. Retrieved November 6, 2015, from www.ncb.org.uk/media/74024/listening_to_young_disabled_children.pdf.

Dockett, S., & Perry, B. (2001). Starting school: Effective transitions. *Early Childhood Research and Practice, 3*(2), Retrieved November 1, 2008 from http://ecrp.uiuc.edu/v3n2/dockett.html.

————(2003). Children's views and children's voices in starting school. *Australian Journal of Early Childhood, 28*(1), 12–17.

————(2005). 'You need to know how to play safe': children's experiences of starting school. *Contemporary Issues in Early Childhood, 6*(1) 4–18.

Dockett, S., Perry, B., & Howard, P. (2000). *Guidelines for transition to school.* Paper presented at the Australian Research in Early Childhood Education Annual Conference, Canberra, Australia.

Dodge, R., Daly, A. P., Huyton, J., & Sanders, L. D. (2012). The challenge of defining wellbeing. *International Journal of Wellbeing, 2*(3), 222–235.

Doel, M., & Kelly, T. B. (2014). *A-Z of groups and groupwork* (Professional keywords). Basingstoke: Palgrave Macmillan.

Doka, K. (Ed.). (2002). *Disenfranchised grief: New directions, challenges, and strategies for practice.* Champaign, IL: Research Press.

Doug, M., Adi, Y., Williams, J., Paul, M., Kelly, D., Petchey, R., & Carter, Y. H. (2011). Transition to adult services for children and young people with palliative care needs: A systematic review. *BMJ Supportive & Palliative Care, 1*(2), 167–173.

Dowdney, L. (2011). Children bereaved by parent or sibling death. In D. Skuse, H. Bruce, L. Dowdney and D. Mrazek (Eds.), *Child psychology and psychiatry: Frameworks for practice* (2nd edn.). Chichester, UK: John Wiley & Sons Ltd, 92–98.

Drugli, M. B., & Undheim, A. M. (2012). Partnership between parents and caregivers of young children in full-time daycare. *Child Care in Practice, 18*(1), 51–65.

Dunlop, A.-W. (2002). Perspectives on children as learners in the transition to school. In H. Fabian & A.-W. Dunlop (Eds.), *Transitions in the early years.* London: Routledge Falmer, pp. 98–110.

Dunlop, A.-W., Lee, P., Fee, J., Hughes, A., Grieve, A., & Marwick, H. (2008). Positive behavior in the early years: Perceptions of staff, service providers and parents in managing and promoting positive behavior in early years and early primary settings. Retrieved October 11, 2014, from www.scotland.gov.uk/Publications/2008/09/12112952/0.

Eccles, J. S., Adler, T. F., Futterman, R., Goff, S. B., Kaczala, C. M., Meece, J., & Midgley, C. (1983). Expectancies, values and academic behaviors. In J. T. Spence (Ed.), *Achievement and achievement motives.* San Francisco: W.H. Freeman, pp. 75–146.

Eccles, J. S., & Midgley, C. (1990). Changes in academic motivation and self-perception during early adolescence. In R. Montemayor, G. R. Adams, & T. P. Gullotta (Eds.), *From childhood to adolescence: A transitional period?* London: SAGE, pp. 134–155.

Eccles, J. S., Lord, S., & Midgley, C. (1991). What are we doing to early adolescents? The impact of educational contexts on early adolescents. *American Journal of Education*, 99(4), 521–542.

Eccles, J. S., Midgley, C. Wigfield, A. Buchanan, C. M., Reuman, D., Flanagan, C., & MacIver, D. (1993). Development during adolescence: The impact of stage-environment fit in young adolescents' experiences in schools and families. *American Psychologist*, 48, 90–101.

Eccles J. S., & Wigfield, A. (1995). In the mind of the actor: The structure of adolescents' achievement task values and expectancy-related beliefs. *Personality and Social Psychology Bulletin*, 21, 215–225.

————(2002). Motivational beliefs, values, and goals. *Annual Review of Psychology*, 53, 109–132.

Eccles, J. S., Wigfield, A., Harold, R. D., & Blumenfeld, P. C. (1993). Age and gender differences in children's self- and task perceptions during elementary school. *Child Development*, 64, 830–847.

Eccles, J. S., Wigfield, A., & Schiefele, U. (1998). Motivation to succeed. In W. Damon (Series Ed.) & N. Eisenberg (Vol. Ed.), *Handbook of child psychology*, Vol. 3: Social, emotional, and personality development (5th edn.). New York: Wiley, pp. 1017–1095.

Ecclestone, K. (2007). Lost and found in transition: The implications of 'identity', 'agency' and 'structure' for educational goals and practices. Keynote presentation to *Researching Transitions In Lifelong Learning Conference*, University Of Stirling, Scotland, 22–24 June 2007.

Ecclestone, K., Biesta, G. J. J., & Hughes, M. (2010). Transitions in the lifecourse: The role of identity, agency and structure. In K. Ecclestone, G. J. J. Biesta, & M. Hughes (Eds.), *Transitions and learning through the lifecourse*. London: Routledge, pp. 1–15.

Edwards, G. (2010). Mixed-Method Approaches to Social Network Analysis. ESRC National Centre for Research Methods Review paper. Retrieved January 2, 2016, from www.ncrm.co.uk: ESRC NCRM. eScholarID:78728

Ebberwein, C. A., Krieshok, T. S., Ulven, J. C., & Prosser, E. C. (2004). Voices in transition: Lessons on career adaptability. *The Career Development Quarterly*, 52, 292–308.

Elder, Jr., G. H. (1998). The life course as developmental theory. *Child Development*, 69(1), 1–12.

Emond, R. (2014). Longing to belong: Children in residential care and their experiences of peer relationships at school and in the children's home. *Child and Family Social Work*, 19, 194–202.

Engeström, Y. (2006). Development, movement and agency: Breaking away into mycorrhizae activities. In K. Yamazumi (Ed.), *Building activity theory in practice: Toward the next generation*. Osaka: Center for Human Activity Theory, Kansai University. Technical Reports No. 1.

Epstein, J. (2001). *School, family, and community partnerships: Preparing educators, and improving schools.* Boulder, CO: Westview Press.

Erikson, E. (1950). *Childhood and society.* New York: Norton.

——(1968). *Identity: Youth and crisis.* New York: Norton.

Evangelou, M., Taggart, B., Sylva, K., Melhuish, E., Sammons, P., & Siraj-Blatchford, I. (2008). *Effective Pre-school, Primary and Secondary Education 3-14 Project (EPPSE 3-14). What makes a successful transition from primary to secondary school?* Nottingham: DCSF Publications.

Fabian, H. (2000). Small steps to starting school. *International Journal of Early Years Education, 8*(2), 141–153.

Fabian, H., & Dunlop, A.-W. (Eds.) (2002). *Transitions in the early years. Debating continuity and progression for children in early education.* London: Routledge Falmer.

——(2006). Outcomes of good practice in transition processes for children entering primary school. Paper commissioned for the EFA Global Monitoring Report 2007, Strong foundations: early childhood care and education. Retrieved October 9, 2015, from http://unesdoc.unesco.org/images/0014/001474/147463e.pdf.

——(2007). *Outcomes of good practice in transition processes for children entering primary school.* Working Paper 42. Bernard van Leer Foundation: The Hague, The Netherlands.

Fan, X. T., & Chen, M. (2001). Parental involvement and students' academic achievement: A meta-analysis. *Educational Psychology Review, 13,* 1–22.

Fauth, B., Thomson, M., & Penny, A. (2009). *Associations between childhood bereavement and children's background experiences and outcomes: Secondary analysis of the mental health of children and young people in Great Britain, 2004 data.* London: NCB.

Ferber, A., Onyeije, C. I., Zelop, C. M., Oōreilly-Green, C., & Divon, M. Y. (2002). Maternal pain and anxiety in genetic amniocentesis: Expectation versus reality. *Ultrasound Obstet Gynecol, 19,* 13–17.

Finn, J., & Kohler, P. (2010). Transition outcomes project: Perceptions of school personnel explored through a multiple case study. *Journal of Ethnographic and Qualitative Research, 4,* 95–107.

Fitzpatrick, K. M., & Yoels, K. M. (1992). Policy, school structure, and sociodemographic effects on statewide high school dropout rates. *Sociology of Education, 65,* 76–93.

Ford, J., & Gledhill, T. (2002). Does season of birth matter? The relationship between age within the school year (season of birth) and educational difficulties among a representative general population of children and adolescents (aged 5–15) in Great Britain. *Research in Education, 68,* 41–47.

Forrest, W., & Hay, C. (2011). Life-course transitions, self-control and desistance from crime. *Criminology & Criminal Justice, 11*(5), 487–513.

Fortune-Wood, J. (2002). Transitions without school. In H. Fabian & A. -W. Dunlop (Eds.), *Transitions in the early years. Debating continuity and progression for children in early education.* London: Routledge Falmer, pp. 135–145.

Fredrickson, B. L. (2004). The broaden-and-build theory of positive emotions. *The Royal Society, 359*, 1367–1377. http://dx.doi.org/10.1098/rstb.2004.1512.

Galton, M. (2010). Going with the flow or back to normal? The impact of creative practitioners in schools and classrooms. *Research Papers in Education, 25*(4), 355–375.

———(2010). Moving to secondary school: What do pupils in England say about the experience? In D. Jindal-Snape (Ed.), *Educational transitions: Moving stories from around the world.* New York: Routledge, pp. 107–124.

Galton, M., & Morrison, I. (2000). Concluding comments. Transfer and transition: The next steps. *International Journal of Educational Research, 33*(4), 443–449.

Galton, M., & Willcocks, J. (Eds.). (1983). *Moving from the primary school.* London: Routledge and Kegan Paul.

Galton, M., Gray, J., & Ruddock, J. (1999). *The impact of school transitions and transfers on pupil progress and attainment.* DfEE Research Report No. 131. Norwich: HMSO.

———(2003). *Transfer and transition in the middle years of schooling (7–14): Continuities and discontinuities in learning.* Department for Education and Skills, Research Report RR443. Nottingham: DfES Publications.

Galton, M., Morrison, I., & Pell, T. (2000). Transfer and transition in English schools: Reviewing the evidence. *International Journal of Educational Research, 33*, 340–363.

Gerrard, B., Young, H., & Lambe, L. (2014). *Bereavement and loss: Supporting bereaved parents and carers who have cared for someone with profound and multiple learning disabilities.* Dundee: PAMIS.

Gilligan, R. (2000). Adversity, resilience and young people: The protective value of positive school and spare time experiences. *Children and Society, 14*, 37–47.

Giordano, P.C., Cernkovich, S.A., & Rudolph, J.L. (2002). Gender, Crime, and Desistance: Toward a Theory of Cognitive Transformation. *American Journal of Sociology, 107*(4), 990–1064.

Goleman, D. (1995). *Emotional intelligence.* London: Bloomsbury.

Görgens-Ekermans, G., Delport, M., & Du Preez, R. (2015). Developing Emotional Intelligence as a key psychological resource reservoir for sustained student success. *SA Journal of Industrial Psychology/SA Tydskrif vir Bedryfsielkunde, 41*(1), Art. #1251, 13 pages. Retrieved December 10, 2015, from http://dx.doi.org/10.4102/sajip.v41i1.1251.

Gorton, H. (2012). *"Are they ready? Will they cope?" An exploration of the journey from pre-school to school for children with additional support needs who had their school entry delayed.* Dundee: Doctoral thesis. Retrieved April 4, 2015, from http://discovery.dundee.ac.uk/portal/files/2112743/Gorton_dedpsych_2012.pdf.

Government of India. (2006). *Status of education and vocational training in India*, NSS 61st Round (July 2004–June 2005). New Delhi: National Sample Survey Organisation.

Graham, C., & Hill, M. (2003). Negotiating the transition to secondary school. SCRE, Spotlight 89. Retrieved March 2, 2006, from www.scre.ac.uk/spotlight/spotlight89.html.

Greco, V., Sloper, P., Webb, R., & Beecham, J. (2005). *An exploration of different models of multi-agency partnerships in key worker services for disabled children: Effectiveness and costs.* Report for Department of Education and Skills, Research Report RR656.

Griebel, W., & Niesel, R. (2000). The children's voice in the complex transition into kindergarten and school. Paper presented at 10th European Conference on Quality in Early Childhood Education, London, United Kingdom.

Gulliford, M., Naithani, S., & Morgan, M. (2006). What is 'continuity of care'? *Journal of Health Services Research & Policy, 11*(4), 248–250.

Gunnar, M., Kryzer, E., Phillips, D., & van Ryzin, M. (2010). The rise in cortisol in family day care: Associations with aspects of care quality, child behavior and child sex. *Child Development, 81*, 851–869.

Gutman, L. M., & Eccles, J.S. (2007). Stage–environment fit during adolescence: Trajectories of family relations and adolescent outcomes. *Developmental Psychology, 43*(2), 522–537.

Hackman, J. R. (2002). *Leading teams: Setting the stage for great performance.* USA: Harvard Business School Press.

Hanna, B. (2014). The organisational context of professional and inter-professional ethics. In D. Jindal-Snape and E. F. S. Hannah (Eds.), *Exploring the dynamics of personal, professional and interprofessional ethics, pp..* Bristol: Policy Press, 35–51.

Hannah, E. F. S., Gorton, H., & Jindal-Snape, D. (2010). Small steps: Perspectives on understanding and supporting children starting school in Scotland. In D. Jindal-Snape (Ed.), *Educational transitions: Moving stories from around the world.* New York: Routledge, pp. 51–67.

Hannah, E. F. S., & Topping, K. J. (2012). Anxiety levels in students with Autism Spectrum Disorder making the transition from primary to secondary school, *Education and training in autism and developmental disabilities, 47*(2), 198–209.

Hannah, E. F., & Topping, K. (2013). The transition from primary to secondary school: perspectives of students with autism spectrum disorder and their parents. *International Journal of Special Education*, 28(1), 145–160.

Hasson, F., Spence, A., Waldron, M., Kernohan, G., McLaughlin, D., Watson, B., & Cochrane, B. (2009). Experiences and needs of bereaved carers during palliative and end-of-life care for people with chronic obstructive pulmonary disease. *Journal of Palliative Care*, 25(3), 157–163.

Healy, D. (2014). Becoming a desister: Exploring the role of agency, coping and imagination in the construction of a new self. *British Journal of Criminology*, 54(5), 873–891.

Heath, S., Fuller, A., & Johnston, B. (2009). Chasing shadows: defining network boundaries in qualitative social network analysis. *Qualitative Research*, 9(5), 645–661.

Hemelt, S. W., & Marcotte, D. (2013). High school exit exams and dropout in an era of increased accountability. *Journal of Policy Analysis and Management*, 32(2), 323–349.

Herrera, M., Sani, F., & Bowe, M. (2010). Perceived continuity and group identification: Implications for social well-being. *Revista de Psicologia Social*, 25(2), 203–214.

Hernandez Nanclares, N., Rienties, B., & Van den Bossche, P. (2012). Longitudinal analysis of knowledge spillovers in the classroom. In P. Van den Bossche, W. H. Gijselaers, and Richard G. Milter (Eds.), *Learning at the crossroads of theory and practice*. Dordrecht: Springer, pp. 157–175.

HM Government. (2011). *Supported employment and job coaching: Best practice guidelines*. London: Department of Health.

Hobbs, C., Todd, L., & Taylor, J. (2000). Consulting with children and young people: Enabling educational psychologists to work collaboratively. *Educational and Child Psychology*, 17(4) 107–115.

Holcomb, T. F. (2010). Transitioning into retirement as a stressful life event. In T. W. Miller (Ed.), *Handbook of stressful transitions across the lifespan*. New York: Springer, pp. 133–146.

Holland, J., & Edwards, R. (Eds.) (2014). *Understanding families over time*. Basingstoke: Palgrave Macmillan.

Horn, E. A. D., Crews, J. A., & Harrawood, L. K. (2013). Grief and loss education: Recommendations for curricular inclusion. *Counselor Education and Supervision*, 52(1), 70–80.

Hudson, B., Hardy, B., Menwood, M., & Wistow, G. (1999). In pursuit of interagency collaboration in the public sector: What is the contribution of theory and research? *Public Management*, 1, 235–260.

Iyer, J., Jetten, J., Tsivrikos, D., Postmes, T., & Haslam, S. A. (2009). The more (and the more compatible) the merrier: Multiple group memberships and identity compatibility as predictors of adjustment after transitions. *British Journal of Social Psychology, 48,* 707–733.

Jackson, C. (2003). Transitions into higher education: Gendered implications for academic self-concept. *Oxford Review of Education, 29*(3), 331–346. 10.1080/03054980307448.

Jacobs, J. E., Lanza, S., Osgood, D. W., Eccles, J. S., & Wigfield, A. (2002). Changes in children's self-competence and values: Gender and domain differences across grade one through twelve. *Child Development, 73,* 509–527.

Jadue-Roa, D. S., & Whitebread, D. (2011). Young children's experiences through transition between Kindergarten and First Grade in Chile and its relation with their Developing Learning Agency. *Educational and Child Psychology, 29*(1), 32–46.

Jain, L. (2008). *Dropout of girl-child in schools.* New Delhi: Northern Book Centre.

James, R. (2002). Students' changing expectations of higher education and the consequences of mismatches with the reality. In P. Coaldrake & L. Stedman (Eds.), *Responding to student expectation.* Paris: OECD, pp. 71–83. www1.oecd.org/publications/e-book/8902041E.PDF.

Jee, S. H., & Cabana, M. D. (2006). Indices for continuity of care: A systematic review of the literature. *Medical Care Research and Review, 63*(2), 158–188.

Jeynes, W. H. (2007). The relationship between parental involvement and urban secondary school student academic achievement: A meta-analysis. *Urban Education, 42*(1), 82 - 110.

Jindal-Snape, D. (2005). Self-evaluation and recruitment of feedback for enhanced social interaction by a student with visual impairment. *Journal of Visual Impairment and Blindness, 99*(8), 486–498.

———(Ed.) (2010a). *Educational transitions: Moving stories from around the world.* New York & London: Routledge.

———(2010b). Setting the scene: Educational transitions and moving stories. In D. Jindal-Snape (Ed.), *Educational transitions: Moving stories from around the world.* New York: Routledge, pp. 1–8.

———(2010c). Moving on: Integrating the lessons learnt and the way ahead. In D. Jindal-Snape (Ed.), *Educational transitions: Moving stories from around the world.* New York & London: Routledge, pp. 223–244.

———(2012). Portraying children's voices through creative approaches to enhance their transition experience and improve the transition practice, *LEARNing Landscapes, 6*(1), 223–240. Retrieved June 16, 2013, from www.learninglandscapes.ca/current-issue.

———(2013). Primary-secondary transition. In S. Capel, M. Leask, & T. Turner, *Learning to teach in the secondary school: A companion to school experience* (6th edn.). New York: Routledge, pp. 186–198.

Jindal-Snape, D., Baird, L., & Miller, K. (2011). *A longitudinal study to investigate the effectiveness of the Guitar Hero project in supporting transition from P7-S1*. Dundee: Report for Learning and Teaching Scotland.

Jindal-Snape, D., & Booth, H. (2010). International doctoral students' experience of transitions: Examples of video case studies to facilitate transitions. Proceedings of S-ICT Conference, Student mobility and ICT: World in transition, 1st–2nd November 2010, The Hague, Netherlands.

Jindal-Snape, D., Davies, D., Collier, C., Howe, A., Digby, R., & Hay, P. (2013). The impact of creative learning environments on learners: A systematic literature review. *Improving Schools, 16*(1), 21–31.

Jindal-Snape, D., Douglas, W., Topping, K. J., Kerr, C., & Smith, E. F. (2006). Autistic spectrum disorders and primary-secondary transition. *International Journal of Special Education, 21*(2), 18–31. Retrieved March 21, 2007, from www.internationalsped.com/documents/03Jindalsnape.doc.

Jindal-Snape, D., & Fernandes, F. L. (2013). *Wave of friendship: Olympics legacy*. Dundee: University of Dundee.

Jindal-Snape, D., & Foggie, J. (2008). A holistic approach to primary-secondary transitions. *Improving Schools, 11*, 5–18.

Jindal-Snape, D., & Hannah, E. F. S. (2013). Reconceptualising the inter-relationship between social policy and practice: Scottish parents' perspectives. In A. Kienig and K. Margetts (Eds.), *International perspectives on transitions to school: Reconceptualising beliefs, policy and practice*. Abingdon: Routledge, pp. 122–132.

———(Eds.) (2014a). *Exploring the dynamics of personal, professional and interprofessional ethics*. Bristol: Policy Press.

———(2014b). Understanding the dynamics of personal, professional and interprofessional ethics: A possible way forward. In D. Jindal-Snape and E. F. S. Hannah (Eds.), *Exploring the dynamics of personal, professional and interprofessional ethics (pp)*. Bristol: Policy Press, pp. 315–333.

———(2014c). Promoting resilience for primary-secondary transitions: supporting children, parents and professionals. In A. B. Liegmann, I. Mammes, & K. Racherbäumer (Eds.), *Facetten von übergängen im bildungssystem: nationale und internationale ergebnisse empirischer forschung*. Munster: Waxmann, pp. 265–277.

Jindal-Snape, D., & Ingram, R. (2013). Understanding and supporting triple transitions of international doctoral students: ELT and SuReCom Models. *Journal of Perspectives in Applied Academic Practice, 1*(1), 17–24.

Jindal-Snape, D., Johnston, B., Pringle, J., Gold, L., Grant. J., Scott, R., Carragher, P., & Dempsey, R. (2015). *Multiple and multi-dimensional transitions: Understanding the life transitions of young adults cared for by CHAS and the impact on their parents, siblings and professionals*. Dundee: Final Report for Children's Hospice Association Scotland.

Jindal-Snape, D., & Miller, D. J. (2008). A challenge of living? Understanding the psycho-social processes of the child during primary-secondary transition through resilience and self-esteem theories. *Educational Psychology Review, 20*, 217–236.

———(2010). Understanding transitions through self-esteem and resilience. In D. Jindal-Snape (Ed.), *Educational transitions: Moving stories from around the world*. New York & London: Routledge, pp. 11–32.

Jindal-Snape, D., & Mitchell, D. (2015). Supporting transition from primary to secondary school: Perspectives of pupils, parents and teachers. *Teacher Education Policy in Europe Conference*. Teacher Education Policy in Europe (TEPE) Conference, Dundee, United Kingdom, 14–16 May 2015.

Jindal-Snape, D., & Rienties, B. (Eds.) (2016). *Multi-dimensional transitions of international students to Higher Education*. New York: Routledge.

Jindal-Snape, D., Roberts, G., & Venditozzi, D. (2012). Parental involvement, participation and home-school partnership: Using the Scottish lens to explore parental participation in the context of transitions. In M. Soininen & T. Merisuo-Storm (Eds.), *Home-school partnership in a multicultural society*. Publications of Turku University Faculty of Education B80, pp. 73–101.

Jindal-Snape, D., Scott, R., & Davies, D. (2014). *'Arts and smarts': Assessing the impact of arts participation on academic performance during school years. Systematic literature review.* Glasgow: Glasgow Centre for Population Health.

Jindal-Snape, D., Snape, N., & Snape, A. (2011a). *Shall we play?* Pre-school to primary school transition story book. Retrieved October 5, 2015, from www.dundee.ac.uk/media/dundeewebsite/eswce/documents/research/transitions/play.pdf.

Jindal-Snape, D., Snape, A., & Snape, N. (2011b). *Neena's school uniform*. Pre-school to primary school transition story book. Retrieved October 5, 2015, from www.dundee.ac.uk/media/dundeewebsite/eswce/documents/research/transitions/school-uniform.pdf.

Jindal-Snape, D., & Sweeney, S. (2011). *Professionals' beliefs and training needs*. Dundee: Report for STAGES (Support: Trauma And Grief-Enabling Schools) pilot project monitoring group.

Jindal-Snape, D., & Topping, K. J. (2010). Observational analysis within case study designs. In S. Rodrigues (Ed.), *Using analytical frameworks for classroom research*. New York: Routledge, pp. 19–37.

Jindal-Snape, D., Vettraino, E., Lowson, A., & McDuff, W. (2011). Using creative drama to facilitate primary–secondary transition, *Education 3-13, 4*, 383–394. Retrieved October 5, 2015, from http://dx.doi.org/10.1080/03004271003727531.

Jovanovic, J. (2011). Saying goodbye: An investigation into parent–infant separation behaviours on arrival in childcare. *Child Care in Practice, 17*(3), 247–269, doi: 10.1080/13575279.2011.571237.

Kaehne, A. (2010). Multiagency protocols in Intellectual Disabilities Transition Partnerships: A survey of Local Authorities in Wales. *Journal of Policy and Practice in Intellectual Disabilities, 7*(3), 182–188.

Kaehne, A., & Beyer, S. (2009). Transition partnerships: the views of education professionals and staff in support services for young people with learning difficulties. *British Journal of Special Education, 36*(2), 112–119.

———(2008). Carer perspectives on the transition of young people with learning disabilities to employment. *Journal on Developmental Disabilities, 14,* 91–100.

Kapp, K. M. (2012). *The gamification of learning and instruction: Game-based methods and strategies for training and education.* San Francisco, CA: Pfeiffer, John Wiley & Sons.

Kashima, E. S., & Sadewo, G. R. P. (2016). Need for cognitive closure and acculturation of international students: Recent findings and implications. In D. Jindal-Snape and B. Rienties, *Multi-dimensional transitions of international students to higher education.* London: Routledge, pp. 37–52.

Keep, E. (2012). *Youth transitions, the labour market and entry into employment: Some reflections and questions.* UK: SKOPE Research Paper No. 108.

Kelly, T. B., Tolson, D., Smith, T. D., & McColgan, G. (2010). Using the research process to develop group services for older persons with a hearing disability. In D. M. Steinberg (Ed.), *Orchestrating the power of groups: beginnings, middles, and endings (overture, movements, and finales).* AASWG Proceedings, Whiting & Birch, pp. 104–117.

Keup, J. R. (2007). Great expectations and the ultimate reality check: Voices of students during the transition from high school to college. *NASPA Journal, 44*(1), 3–31.

Kimmel, K., & Volet, S. (2012). University students' perceptions of and attitudes towards culturally diverse group work: Does context matter? *Journal of Studies in International Education, 16*(2), 157–181. doi: 10.1177/1028315310373833.

King, S. (2013). Early desistance narratives: A qualitative analysis of probationers' transitions towards desistance. *Punishment & Society, 15*(2), 147–165.

Kirby, E., Broom, A., & Good, P. (2014). The role and significance of nurses in managing transitions to palliative care: A qualitative study. *BMJ Open,* 4:e006026 doi: 10.1136/bmjopen-2014-006026.

Kirk. S., & Fraser, C. (2014). Hospice support and the transition to adult services and adulthood for young people with life–limiting conditions and their families: A qualitative study. *Palliative Medicine, 28*(4), 342–352.

Klein, P., Kraft, R., & Shoet, C. (2010). Behaviour patterns in daily mother-child separations: Possible opportunities for stress reduction. *Early Child Development and Care, 180,* 387–396.

Kosovich, J. J., Hulleman, C. S., Barron, K. E., & Getty, S. (2015). A practical measure of student motivation: Establishing validity evidence for the expectancy-value-cost scale in middle school. *Journal of Early Adolescence, 35*(5–6), 790–816.

Krackhardt, D., & Stern, R. N. (1988). Informal networks and organizational crises: An experimental simulation. *Social Psychology Quarterly, 51*(2), 123–140.

Krause, K., Hartley, R., James, R., & McInnis, G. (2005). The first year experience in Australian universities: Findings from a decade of national studies. Centre for Study of Higher Education, University of Melbourne. Retrieved December 10, 2015, from www.cshe.unimelb. edu.au/researchproj.html.

Lam, M., & Pollard, A. (2006). A conceptual framework for understanding children as agents in the transition from home to kindergarten. *Early Years, 26*(1), 123–141.

La Placa, V., McNaught, A., & Knight, A. (2013). Discourse on wellbeing in research and practice. *International Journal of Wellbeing, 3*(1), 116–125.

Laub, J. H., & Sampson, R. J. (2003). *Shared beginnings, divergent lives: Delinquents boys to age 70.* Cambridge, MA: Harvard University Press.

Ledger, E., Smith, A. B., & Rich, P. (2000). Friendship over the transition from early childhood centre to school. *International Journal of Early Years Education, 8*(1), 57–69.

Levine, S. (2006). Getting in, dropping out, and staying on: Determinants of girls' school attendance in the Kathmandu Valley of Nepal. *Anthropology and Education Quarterly, 37*, 21–41.

Liabo, K., Newman, T., Stephens, J., & Lowe, K. (2001). *A review of key worker systems for disabled children and the development of information guides for parents, children and professionals.* Wales: Office of R&D for Health and Social Care, Cardiff.

Liddle, J. L., Parkinson, L., & Sibbritt, D. W. (2012). Painting pictures and playing musical instruments: Change in participation and relationship to health in older women. *Australasian Journal on Ageing, 31*(4), 218–221.

Lindebaum, D., & Cartwright, C. (2011). Leadership effectiveness: the costs and benefits of being emotionally intelligent. *Leadership & Organization Development Journal, 32*(3), 281–290.

Lloyd, C., & Serin, R. (2012). Agency and outcome expectancies for crime desistance: Measuring offenders' personal beliefs about change. *Psychology, Crime and Law, 18*, 543–565.

Lucey, H., & Reay, R. (2000). Identities in transition: Anxiety and excitement in the move to secondary school. *Oxford Review of Education, 26*, 191–205.

Luthar, S. S. (2006). Resilience in development: A synthesis of research across five decades. In D. Cicchetti & D. J. Cohen (Eds.), *Developmental psychopathology: Risk, disorder, and adaptation*. New York: Wiley, pp. 739–795.

Lynch, J., & Smith, G. D. (2005). A life course approach to chronic disease epidemiology. *Annual Review of Public Health, 26*, 1–35.

MacEachern, A. D., Miles, E., & Jindal-Snape, D. (2014). Personal, professional and interprofessional ethics in policing in a child protection context. In D. Jindal-Snape & E. F. S. Hannah (Eds.), *Exploring the dynamics of personal, professional and interprofessional ethics*. Bristol: Policy Press, pp. 183–197.

Main, M., & Solomon, J. (1990). Procedures for identifying infants as disorganized/disoriented during the Ainsworth strange situation. In M. T. Greenberg, D. Cichetti, & E. M. Cummings (Eds.), *Attachment in the preschool years: Theory, research and intervention*. Chicago: University of Chicago Press, pp. 121–160.

Margetts, K. (2002). Transition to school - complexity and diversity. *European Early Childhood Education Research Journal, 10*(2), 103–114.

———(2006). *Teachers should explain what they mean: What new children need to know about starting school*. Paper presented at the EECERA 16th Annual conference, Reykjavik, Iceland, 2006.

———(2007). Understanding and supporting children: Shaping transition practices. In A.-W. Dunlop & H. Fabian (Eds.), *Informing transitions in the early years: Research, policy and practice*. Maidenhead: Open University Press, pp. 107–119.

Marsh, H. W., Trautwein, U., Lüdtke, O., Baumert, J., & Köller, O. (2007). The big-fish-little-pond effect: Persistent negative effects of selective high schools on self-concept after graduation. *American Educational Research Journal, 44*(3), 631–669.

Marsh, K. (2012). 'The beat will make you be courage': The role of a secondary school music program in supporting young refugees and newly arrived immigrants in Australia. *Research Studies in Music Education, 34*(2), 93–111. doi: 10.1177/1321103x12466138.

Marso, R. N., & Pige, F. L. (1991). *Factors associated with longitudinal changes in teachers' attitude toward teaching during training and the first year of teaching*. Paper presented at the annual meeting of the Association of Teacher Educators, 16–20 February 1991.

Maruna, S. (2001). *Making good: How ex-convicts reform and rebuild their lives*. Washington, DC: American Psychological Association Books.

Maruna, S., Immarigeon, R., & LeBel, T. P. (2004). Ex-offender reintegration: Theory and practice. In S. Maruna & R. Immarigeon (Eds.), *After crime and punishment: Pathways to offender reintegration*. Cullompton: Willan, pp 65–87.

Masten, A. S. (1994). Resilience in individual development: Successful adaptation despite risk and adversity. In M. C. Wang & E. W. Gordon (Eds.), *Educational resilience in inner-city America: Challenges and prospects*. Hillsdale, NJ: Erlbaum, pp. 3–25.

Matthews, L. (2007). Can the process of transition for incoming secondary pupils be supported through a creative art project? *International Journal of Art & Design Education, 26*(3), 336–344.

Maume, M. O., Ousey, G. C., & Beaver, K. (2005). Cutting the grass: A reexamination of the link between marital attachment, delinquent peers, and desistance from marijuana use. *Journal of Quantitative Criminology, 21,* 27–53.

Mayer, K., Amendum, S., & Vernon-Feagans, L. (2010). The transition to formal schooling and children's early literacy development in the context of the USA. In D. Jindal-Snape (Ed.), *Educational transitions: Moving stories from around the world.* New York: Routledge, pp. 85–103.

Mayer, J. D., DiPaulo, M., & Salovey, P. (1990). Perceiving affective content in ambiguous visual stimuli: A component of emotional intelligence. *Journal of Personality Assessment, 54,* 772–781.

Mayer, J. D., Salovey, P., & Caruso, D. R. (2002a). *Mayer–Salovey–Caruso Emotional Intelligence Test (MSCEIT) item booklet.* Toronto, Ontario, Canada: MHS Publishers.

———(2002b). *Mayer–Salovey–Caruso Emotional Intelligence Test (MSCEIT) user's manual.* Toronto, Ontario, Canada: MHS Publishers.

McAdams, K. K., Lucas, R. E., & Donnellan, M. B. (2012). The role of domain satisfaction in explaining the paradoxical association between life satisfaction and age. *Social Indicators Research,* 295–303.

McKenzie, D., & Rapoport, H. (2011). Can migration reduce educational attainment? Evidence from Mexico. *Journal of Population Economics, 24*(4), 1331–1358. doi: 10.1007/s00148-010-0316-x.

McLellan, R., Galton, M., Steward, S., & Page, C. (2012). *The impact of creative initiatives on wellbeing: A literature review.* Newcastle upon Tyne, UK: Creativity, Culture and Education.

McNaught, A. (2011). Defining wellbeing. In A. Knight, & A. McNaught (Eds.), *Understanding wellbeing: An introduction for students and practitioners of health and social care.* Banbury: Lantern Publishing, pp. 7–23.

Miller, D. J., & Daniel, B. (2007). Competent to cope, worthy of happiness? How the duality of self-esteem can inform a resilience-based classroom environment. *School Psychology International*, 28(5), 605–622.

Miller, D. J, Hudson, A., Shimi, J., & Robertson, D. (2012). Signature pedagogy in early years education: A role for COTS game-based learning. *Computers in the Schools*, 29(1–2), 227–247.

Miller, D. J., & Robertson, D. P. (2010). Using a games console in the primary classroom: Effects of 'Brain Training' programme on computation and self-esteem. *British Journal of Educational Technology*, 41(2), 242–255.

Miller, D. J., & Robertson, D. P. (2011). Educational benefits of using game consoles in a primary classroom: A randomised controlled trial. *British Journal of Educational Technology*, 42(5), 850–864.

Miller, K., Wakefield, J. R. H., & Sani, F. (2015). Identification with social groups is associated with mental health in adolescents: Evidence from a Scottish community sample. *Psychiatry Research*, 228(3), 340–346.

Miller, T. W. (Ed.) (2010). *Handbook of stressful transitions across the lifespan.* New York: Springer.

Mitchell, F. (2012). Self-directed support and disabled young people in transition. *Journal of Integrated Care*, 20(1), 51–61.

Mittelmeier, J., & Kennedy, J. J. (2016). Adapting Together: Chinese Student Experience and Acceptance at an American University. In D. Jindal-Snape & B. Rienties, *Multi-dimensional transitions of international students to higher education.* London: Routledge, pp. 161–180.

Mittler, P. (2007). Education – The missing link at transition. *Tizard Learning Disability Review*, 12(2), 14–21.

Mruk, C. (1999). *Self-esteem: Research, theory and practice.* London: Free Association Books.

Murphy, S. A., Chung, I.-J., & Johnson, L. C. (2002). Patterns of mental distress following the violent death of a child and predictors of change over time. *Research in Nursing & Health*, 25, 425–437.

Murphy, S. A., Johnson, C., Cain, K. C., Gupta, A. D., Dimond, M., Lohan, J., et al. (1998). Broad-spectrum group treatment for parents bereaved by the violent deaths of their 12- to 28- year-old children: A randomized controlled trial. *Death Studies*, 22, 209–235.

Murphy, S. A., Johnson, L. C., Wu, L., Fan, J. J., & Lohan, J. (2003). Bereaved parents outcomes 4 to 60 months after their children's deaths by accident, suicide, or homicide: A comparative study demonstrating differences. *Death Studies*, 27(1), 39–61.

Muszynski, J., & Jindal-Snape, D. (2015). *Investigation into the holistic transition experience and support needs of first year undergraduates.* Poster session presented at 2nd International Conference on Enhancement and Innovation in Higher Education, Glasgow, United Kingdom.

Neal, J. W., & Neal, Z. P. (2013). Nested or networked? Future directions for ecological systems theory. *Social Development, 22*, 722–737.

Nelson, K. J., Kift, S. M., & Clarke, J. A. (2008). Expectations and realities for first year students at an Australian university, 11th Pacific Rim First Year in Higher Education Conference 2008, 30 June–2 July 2008, Hobart.

Newman, T., & Blackburn, S. (2002). *Transitions in the lives of children and young people: Resilience factors*. Edinburgh: Scottish Executive Education Department.

Ng, J. Y. Y., Ntoumanis, N., Thøgersen-Ntoumani, C., Deci, E. L., Ryan, R. M., Duda, J. L., & Williams, G. C. (2012). Self-determination theory applied to health contexts: A meta-analysis. *Perspectives on Psychological Science, 7*(4), 325–340.

Nicholson, N. (1987). The transition cycle: A conceptual framework for the analysis of change and human resources management. *Research in Personnel and Human Resources Management, 5*, 167–222.

Niesel, R., & Griebel, W. (2001). Transition to schoolchild: What children tell about school and what they teach us. Paper presented at 11th European Conference on Quality in Early Childhood Education, Alkmaar, Netherlands.

Nowok, B., van Ham, M., Findlay, A. M., & Gayle, V. (2013). Does migration make you happy? A longitudinal study of internal migration and subjective well-being. *Environment and Planning, 45*(4), 986–1002.

O'Brien, J. (2004). If Person-centred planning did not exist, valuing people would require its invention. *Journal of Applied Research in Intellectual Disabilities, 17*, 11–15.

OECD. (2015). *OECD employment outlook 2015*. Paris: OECD Publishing.

Office of the Surgeon General (US). (2001). *Youth violence: A report of the surgeon general*. Rockville (MD): Center for Mental Health Services (US).

Ouyang, Z., Sang, J., Li, P., & Peng, J. (2015). Organizational justice and job insecurity as mediators of the effect of emotional intelligence on job satisfaction: A study from China. *Personality and Individual Differences, 76*, 147–152.

Oxenbridge, S., & Evesson, J. (2012). *Young people entering work: A review of the research*. Research Paper for ACAS, Ref: 18/12. ISBN 978-1-908370-29-7.

Parker, J. D. A., Hogan, M. J., Eastabrook, J. M., Oke, A., & Wood, L. M. (2006). Emotional intelligence and student retention: Predicting the successful transition from high school to university. *Personality and Individual Differences, 41*, 1329–1336.

Parkes, C. M. (1971). Psycho-social transitions: A field of study. *Social Science & Medicine, 5*(2), 101–115.

Peters, S. (2010). Shifting the lens: Re-framing the view of learners and learning during the transition from early childhood education to school in New Zealand. In D. Jindal-Snape (Ed.), *Educational transitions: Moving stories from around the world*. New York: Routledge, pp. 68–84.

———(2010). *Literature review: Transition from early childhood education to school*. New Zealand: Ministry of Education.

———(2014). Chasms, bridges and borderlands: A transitions research 'across the border' from early childhood education to school in New Zealand. In B. Perry, S. Dockett & A. Petriwskyj (Eds.), *Transitions to school: International research, policy and practice*. New York: Springer, pp. 105–116.

Phillip, M., Lambe, L., & Hogg, J. (2005). *The well-being workshop, recognising the emotional and mental wellbeing of people with profound and multiple learning disabilities: A training resource for family carers and support staff*. London: Foundation for People with Learning Disabilities.

Pietarinen, J., Pyhältö, K., & Soini, T. (2010). A horizontal approach to school transitions: A lesson learned from Finnish 15-year-olds. *Cambridge Journal of Education, 40*(3), 229–245.

Pietarinen, J., Soini, T., & Pyhältö, K. (2010). Learning and well-being in transitions – how to promote pupils' active learning agency? In D. Jindal-Snape (Ed.), *Educational transitions: Moving stories from around the world*. New York: Routledge, pp. 143–158.

Pilnick, A., Clegg, J., Murphy, E., and Almack, K., (2010). Questioning the answer: Questioning style, choice and self determination in interactions with young people with intellectual disabilities. *Sociology of Health and Illness, 32*(3), 415–436.

Qualter, P., Whiteleya, H. E., Hutchinson, J. M., & Pope, D. J. (2007). Supporting the development of emotional intelligence competencies to ease the transition from primary to high school. *Educational Psychology in Practice: Theory, research and practice in educational psychology, 23*(1), 79–95.

Ramey, S. L., & Ramey, C. T. (1999). *Going to school*. New York: Goddard Press.

Rasheed, S. A. (2006). Person-centered planning: Practices, promises and provisos. *The Journal for Vocational Special Needs Education, 28*(3), 47–59.

Raymond, E., & Grenier, A. (2015). Social participation at the intersection of old age and lifelong disability: Illustrations from a photo-novel project. *Journal of Aging Studies, 35*, 190–200.

Reedy, C. K., & McGrath, W. H. (2010). Can you hear me now? Staff-parent communication in child care centers. *Early Child Development and Care, 180*, 347–357.

Reyes, O., Gillock, K. L., Kobus, K., & Sanchez, B. (2000). A longitudinal examination of the transition into senior high school for adolescents from urban, low-income status, and predominantly minority backgrounds. *American Journal of Community Psychology, 28*(4), 519–544.

Ribbens McCarthy, J., & Jessop, J. (2005). *The impact of bereavement and loss on young people*. York: Joseph Rowntree Foundation.

Rice, F., Frederickson, N., Shelton, K., McManus, C., Riglin, L., & Ng-Knight, T. (N.D.). The School Transition and Adjustment Research Study (STARS). Retrieved November 11, 2015, from www.ucl.ac.uk/stars.

Richardson, M. J., & Tate, S. (2013). Improving the transition to university: Introducing student voices into the formal induction process for new geography undergraduates. *Journal of Geography in Higher Education, 37*(4), 611–618.

Richardson, T. D. (2015). *Collaborative practice during the school to postschool transition in Scotland: The perspectives of professionals, young people and their families*. Doctoral thesis. Dundee: University of Dundee.

Riddell, S., Edward, S., Weedon, E., & Ahlgren, L. (2010). *Disability, skills and employment: A review of recent statistics and literature on policy and initiatives*. Research Report 59. Manchester: Equality and Human Rights Commission.

Rienties, B., Alcott, P., & Jindal-Snape, D. (2014). To let students self-select or not: That is the question for teachers of culturally diverse groups. *Journal of Studies in International Education, 18*(1), 64–83.

Rienties, B., Heliot, Y., & Jindal-Snape, D. (2013). Understanding social learning relations of international students in a large classroom using social network analysis. *Higher Education, 66*(4), 489–504. doi: 10.1007/s10734-013-9617-9.

Rienties, B., Hernandez Nanclares, N., Jindal-Snape, D., & Alcott, P. (2013). The role of cultural background and team divisions in developing social learning relations in the classroom. *Journal of Studies in International Education, 17*(4), 322–353. doi: 10.1177/1028315312463826.

Rienties, B., & Jindal-Snape, D. (2016). A social network perspective on ABC of international and host-national students. In D. Jindal-Snape & B. Rienties, *Multi-dimensional transitions of international students to higher education*. London: Routledge, pp. 53–70.

Rienties, B., Johan, N., & Jindal-Snape, D. (2014). A dynamic analysis of social capital-building of international and UK students. *British Journal of Sociology of Education*. doi: 10.1080/01425692.2014.886941.

————(2015). Bridge building potential in cross-cultural learning: A mixed method study. *Asia Pacific Education Review, 16*(1), 37–48.

Rienties, B., Beausaert, S., Grohnert, T., Niemantsverdriet, S., & Kommers, P. (2012). Understanding academic performance of international students: The role of ethnicity, academic and social integration. *Higher Education, 63*(6), 685–700. doi: 10.1007/s10734-011-9468-1.

Rienties, B., & Nolan, E.-M. (2014). Understanding friendship and learning networks of international and host students using longitudinal Social Network Analysis. *International Journal of Intercultural Relations, 41*, 165–180. doi: 10.1016/j.ijintrel.2013.12.003.

Rienties, B., & Tempelaar, D. T. (2013). The role of cultural dimensions of international and Dutch students on academic and social integration and academic performance in the Netherlands. *International Journal of Intercultural Relations, 37*(2), 188–201. doi: 10.1016/j.ijintrel.2012.11.004.

Robertson, J., Emerson, E., Hatton, C., Elliot, J., McIntosh, B., Swift, P., & Joyce, T. (2005). *The impact of person centred planning.* Institute for Health Research, Lancaster University.

Robins, R. W., Hendin, H. M., & Trzesniewski, K. H. (2001). Measuring global self-esteem: Construct validation of a single item measure and the Rosenberg Self-Esteem scale. *Personality and Social Psychology Bulletin, 27,* 151–161.

Robinson, V., Timperley, H., & Bullard, T. (2000). *Strengthening education in Mangere and Otara evaluation: Second evaluation report.* Auckland: The University of Auckland.

Roccas, S., & Brewer, M. B. (2002) Social identity complexity. *Personality and Social Psychology Review, 6*(2), 88–106.

Roeser, R. W. (2005). Stage-environment fit theory. In C. B. Fisher & R. M. Lerner (Eds.), *Encyclopedia of applied developmental science.* Thousand Oaks, CA: Sage, pp. 1055–1059.

Rosenberg, M. (1989). *Society and the adolescent self-image, Revised edition.* Princeton, NJ: Princeton University Press.

Rosenberg, M. (1986). Self-concept from middle childhood through adolescence. In J. Suls & A.G. Geenwald (Eds.), *Psychological perspectives on the self,* Vol. 3, pp. 107–136. Hillsdale, NJ: Lawrence Erlbaum Associates.

Ross, C. E., & Broh, B. A. (2000). The roles of self-esteem and the sense of personal control in the academic achievement process. *Sociology of Education, 73,* 270–284.

Rothchild, J. (2005). Processes of gendering and the institutionalization of gender in the family and school: A case study From Nepal. In M. T. Segal and V. P. Demos (Eds.), *Advances in Gender Research.* Bingley: Emerald Group Publishing Limited, pp. 265–296.

Rubery, J., Grimshaw, D., & Marchington, M. (2010). Blurring boundaries and disordered hierarchies: Challenges for employment and skills in networked organisations. UKCES Praxis Paper No. 6. Wath-upon-Dearne: UK Commission for Employment and Skills.

Rudisill, J. R., Edwards, J. M., Hershberger, P. J., Jadwin, J. E., & McKee, J. M. (2010). Coping with job transitions over the work life. In T. W. Miller (Ed.), *Handbook of stressful transitions across the lifespan.* New York: Springer, pp. 111–131.

Rudolph, K. D., Lambert, S. F., Clark, A. G., & Kurlakowsky, K. D. (2001). Negotiating the transition to middle school: The role of self-regulatory processes. *Child Development, 72,* 929–946.

Rutter, M. (1979). Protective factors in children's responses to stress and disadvantage. In M. W. Kent & J. E. Rolf (Eds.), *Primary prevention of psychopathology. Social competence in children* (Vol. 3, pp. 49–74). Hanover, NH: University Press of New England.

———(1985). Resilience in the face of adversity. Protective factors and resistance to psychiatric disorder. *The British Journal of Psychiatry*, 147(6), 598–611.

———(1987). Parental mental disorder as a psychiatric risk factor. In R. Hales & A. Frances (Eds). *American Psychiatric Association Annual Review* (Vol. 6). Washington, DC: American Psychiatric Press, Inc., pp. 647–663.

———(1987). Psychosocial resilience and protective mechanisms. *American Journal of Orthopsychiatry*, 57, 316–331.

Ryan, R. M., & Deci, E. L. (2000). Self-determination theory and the facilitation of intrinsic motivation, social development, and well-being. *American Psychologist*, 55, 68–78.

Ryan, R. M., Patrick, H., Deci, E. L, & Williams, G. C. (2008). Facilitating health behavior change and its maintenance: Interventions based on self-determination theory. *The European Health Psychologist*, 10(1), 2–5.

Salas, E., Rosen, M. A., Burke, C. S., & Goodwin, G. F. (2009). The wisdom of collectives in organizations: an update of competencies. In E. Salas, G. F. Goodwin and C. S. Burke, *Team effectiveness in complex organizations: Cross-disciplinary perspectives and approaches.* London: Routledge, pp. 39–79.

Salovey, P., & Mayer, D. (1990). Emotional intelligence. *Imagination, Cognition and Personality*, 9, 185–211.

Sanderson, H., Thompson, J., & Kilbane, J. (2006). The emergence of person centred planning as evidence based practice. *Journal of Integrated Care*, 14(2), 18–25.

Sani, F., Bowe, M., Herrera, M., Manna, C., Cossa, T., Miao, X., & Zhou, Y. (2007). Perceived collective continuity: seeing groups as entities that move through time. *European Journal of Social Psychology*, 37(6), 1118–1134.

Sani, F., Herrera, M., Wakefield, J. R. H., Boroch, O., & Gulyas, C. (2012). Comparing social contact and group identification as predictors of mental health. *British Journal of Social Psychology*, 51(4), 781–790.

Sani, F., Madhok, V. B., Norbury, M., Dugard, P., & Wakefield, J. R. H. (2015a). Greater number of group identifications is associated with lower odds of being depressed: Evidence from a Scottish community sample. *Social Psychiatry and Psychiatric Epidemiology*, 50(9), 1389–1397.

Sani, F., Madhok, V. B, Norbury, M., Dugard, P., & Wakefield, J. R. H. (2015b). Greater number of group identifications is associated with healthier behaviour: Evidence from a Scottish community sample. *British Journal of Health Psychology*, 20(3), 466–481.

Santariano, W. A. (2006). *Epidemiology of aging: An ecological approach.* Burlington, MA: Jones & Bartlett Learning.

Schacter, J., Thum, Y., & Zifkin, D. (2006). How much does creative teaching enhance elementary school students' achievement? *Journal of Creative Behavior*, 40(1), 47–72.

Schoon, I. (2006). *Risk and resilience: Adaptations in changing times.* Cambridge: Cambridge University Press.

Shucksmith, J., Spratt, J., Philip, K., & McNaughton, R. (2009). *A critical review of the literature on children and young people's views of the factors that influence their mental health.* Edinburgh: NHS Health Scotland.

Schutte, N. S., Marlouff, J. M., Hall, L. E., Haggerty, D. D., Cooper, J. T., Golden, C. J., et al. (1998). Development and validation of measure of emotional intelligence. *Personality and Individual Differences*, 25, 167–177.

Schwartz, S. J., Unger, J. B., Zamboanga, B. L., & Szapocznik, J. (2010). Rethinking the concept of acculturation: Implications for theory and research. *American Psychologist*, 65, 237–251.

Seaton, M., Marsh, H. W., & Craven, R. G. (2009). Earning its place as a pan-human theory: Universality of the big-fish-little-pond effect across 41 culturally and economically diverse countries. *Journal of Educational Psychology*, 101(2), 403–419.

Simpkins, S. D., Fredricks, J. A., & Eccles, J. S. (2012). Charting the Eccles' expectancy-value model from mothers' beliefs in childhood to youths' activities in adolescence. *Developmental Psychology*, 48, 1019–1032.

Sitzmann, T. (2011). A meta-analytic examination of the instructional effectiveness of computer-based simulation games. *Personnel Psychology*, 64, 489–528.

Skardhamar, T., Monsbakken, C. W., & Lyngstad, T. H. (2014). Crime and the transition to marriage: The role of the spouse's criminal involvement. *British Journal of Criminology*, 54, 411–427.

Skyrme, G. (2016). 'It's about your journey, it's not about uni': Chinese international students learning outside the university. In D. Jindal-Snape & B. Rienties, *Multi-dimensional transitions of international students to higher education.* London: Routledge, pp. 91–105.

Smith, K., Lavoei-Tremblay, M., Richer, M. C., & Lanctot, S. (2010). Exploring nurses' perceptions of organizational factors of collaborative relationships. *The Health Care Manager*, 29(3), 271–278.

Smith, R. A., & Khawaja, N. G. (2011). A review of the acculturation experiences of international students. *International Journal of Intercultural Relations*, 35(6), 699-713. doi: 10.1016/j.ijintrel.2011.08.004.

Snape, J. B., & Jindal-Snape, D. (2009). *Managing motivation and job satisfaction of scientists: Impact of organisational change and transitions at a research institute.* Saarbrucken, Germany: VDM Verlag.

So, T. (2010). *What empirically tested research underpins career transition interventions?* Report for Meyler Campbell. Cambridge: Meyler Campbell.

Sole, C., Mercadal-Brotons, M., Gallego, S., & Riera, M. (2010). Contributions of music to aging adults' quality of life. *Journal of Music Therapy*, 47(3), 264–281.

Stash, S., & Hannum, E. (2001). Who goes to school? Educational stratification by gender, caste and ethnicity in Nepal. *Comparative Education Review*, 45, 354–378.

Stipek, D. (2002). At what age should children enter kindergarten? A question for policy makers and parents [Electronic Version]. *Society for Research in Child Development Social Policy Report*, 16, 1–20.

Statham, J., & Chase, E. (2010). *Childhood wellbeing: a brief overview*. London: Childhood Wellbeing Research Centre, Briefing Paper 1.

Swanborn, P. G. (2010). *Case study research: What, why and how*. London: SAGE.

Sweeney, S., & Boge, P. (2014). Personal, professional and interprofessional ethical issues in the context of supporting children affected by bereavement. In D. Jindal-Snape and E. F. S. Hannah (Eds.), *Exploring the dynamics of personal, professional and interprofessional ethics*. Bristol: Policy Press, pp. 199–213.

Suh, S., & Suh, J. (2006). Educational engagement and degree attainment among high school dropouts. *Educational Research Quarterly*, 29, 11–20.

Tafarodi, R. W., & Milne, A. B. (2002). Decomposing global self-esteem. *Journal of Personality*, 70, 443–483.

Tafarodi, R. W., & Vu, C. (1997). Two-dimensional self-esteem and reactions to success and failure. *Personality and Social Psychology Bulletin*, 23, 626–635.

Tajfel, H., & Turner, J. C. (1986). The social identity theory of inter-group behaviour. In S. Worchel, & L. W. Austin (Eds.), *Psychology of intergroup relations*. Chicago: Nelson-Hall, pp. 7–24.

Teixeira, P., Carraca, E., Markland, D., Silva, M., & Ryan, R. M (2012). Exercise, physical activity, and self-determination theory: A systematic review. *International Journal of Behavioral Nutrition and Physical Activity*, 9, 78. doi: 10.1186/1479-5868-9-78.

Tempelaar, D. T., & Verhoeven, P. S. (2016). Adaptive and maladaptive emotions, behaviours, and cognitions in the transition to university: The experience of international full degree students. In D. Jindal-Snape & B. Rienties, *Multi-dimensional transitions of international students to higher education*. London: Routledge, pp. 200–217.

The Scottish Government. (2009). Education (Additional Support for Learning) Act (Amendment). Edinburgh: The Scottish Government.

Thomson, P. (2002). *Schooling the rustbelt kids: Making the difference in changing times*. Sydney: Allen & Unwin.

Tizard, B., & Hughes, M. (2002). *Young children learning* (2nd edn.). Oxford: Blackwell.

Toma, M., Morris, J., Kelly, C., & Jindal-Snape, D. (2014). *The impact of art attendance and participation on health and wellbeing: Systematic literature review.* Glasgow: Glasgow Centre for Population Health.

Tonner, S., & Jindal-Snape, D. (2015). *Familiarisation with the new environment, staff and friendship formation: Using QR whodunnit mystery activity for students transitioning into HE.* Paper presented at 2nd International Conference on Enhancement and Innovation in Higher Education, Glasgow, United Kingdom.

Topping, K. J., & Foggie, J. (2010). Interactive behaviors for building independence in exceptional youth. In D. Jindal-Snape (Ed.), *Educational transitions: Moving stories from around the world.* New York: Routledge, pp. 107–124.

Tsujita, Y. (2009). *Deprivation of education: A study of slum children in Delhi, India,* Background paper prepared for the Education for All Global Monitoring Report 2010, UNESCO.

Turner, J. C., Hogg, M. A., Oakes, P., Reicher, S., & Wetherell, M. S. (1987). *Rediscovering the social group: A self-categorization theory.* Oxford: Basil Blackwell.

Ulloa, B. F. L, Møller, V., & Sousa-Poza, A. (2013). How does subjective wellbeing evolve with age? A literature review. *Population Ageing, 6,* 227–246.

US Department of Education. (2004). Individuals with Disabilities Education Act (IDEA), Retrieved December 10, 2015, from, http://idea.ed.gov.

Van Gennep, A. (1960). *The rites of passage.* Chicago: University of Chicago Press.

Vathi, Z., & Duci, V. (2015). Making other dreams: The impact of migration on the psychosocial wellbeing of Albanian-origin children and young people upon their families' return to Albania. *Childhood,* 1–16. doi: 10.1177/0907568214566078.

Vernon-Feagans, L., Odom, E., Panscofar, N., & Kainz, K. (2008). Comments on Farkas and Hibel: A transactional/ecological model of readiness and inequality. In A. Booth & A. C. Crouter (Eds.), *Disparities in school readiness.* New York: Lawrence Erlbaum Associates, pp. 61–78.

Vignoles, V. L., Schwartz, S. J., & Luyckx, K. (2011). Introduction: Toward an integrative view of identity. In S. J. Schwartz, K. Luyckx, & V. L. Vignoles (Eds.), *Handbook of identity theory and research.* New York: Springer, pp. 1–27.

Visher, C. A., & Travis, J. (2003). Transitions from prison to community: Understanding individual pathways. *Annual Review of Sociology, 29,* 89–113.

Vogel, J. F., Vogel, D. S., Cannon-Bowers, J., Bowers, C. A., Muse, K., & Wright, M. (2006). Computer gaming and interactive simulations for learning: A meta-analysis. *Journal of Educational Computing Research, 34*(3), 229–243.

Vogler, P., Crivello, G., & Woodhead, M. (2008). *Early childhood transitions research: A review of concepts, theory, and practice.* Working Paper No. 48. The Hague, The Netherlands: Bernard van Leer Foundation.

Wang, C., & Burris, M. A. (1997). Photovoice: Concept, methodology, and use for participatory needs assessment. *Health Education and Behavior, 24*(3), 369–387.

Wang, C. C., Yi, W. K., Tao, Z. W., & Carovano, K. (1998). Photovoice as a participatory health promotion strategy. *Health Promotion International, 13*(1), 75–86.

Wang, J. (2009). A study of resiliency characteristics in the adjustment of international graduate students at American universities. *Journal of Studies in International Education, 13*(1), 22–45. doi: 10.1177/1028315307308139.

Ward, C., Bochner, S., & Furnham, A. (2001). *The psychology of culture shock* (2nd edn.). New York: Routledge.

Ward, C. (2001). The A, B, Cs of acculturation. In D. Matsumoto (Ed.), *The handbook of culture and psychology* (pp. 411–446). New York: Oxford University Press.

Warmington, P., Daniels, H., Edwards, A., Brown, S., Leadbetter, J., Martin, M., & Middleton, D. (2004). *Interagency collaboration: A review of the literature,* Bath: Learning in and for Interagency Working Project.

Waters, E. (1978). The reliability and stability of individual differences in infant-mother attachment. *Child Development, 49,* 483–494.

Waters, E., Merrick, S., Treboux, D., Crowell, J., & Albersheim, L. (2000). Attachment security in infancy and early adulthood: A twenty-year longitudinal study. *Child Development, 71*(3), 684–689.

Wehmeyer, M. L. (2005). Self-determination and individuals with severe disabilities: Re-examining meanings and misinterpretations. *Research and Practice in Severe Disabilities, 30,* 113–120.

Wehmeyer, M. L., Abery, B., Mithaug, D. E., & Stancliffe, R. (2003). *Theory in self-determination: Foundations for educational practice.* Springfield, IL: Charles C. Thomas Publishing Company.

Wertheimer, A. (2007). *Person Centred Transition Reviews – A national programme for developing person centred approaches to transition planning for young people with special educational needs.* London: Valuing people support team.

Wesley, P. (2001). *Smooth moves to kindergarten.* Chapel Hall: Chapel Hill Training Outreach Project Incorporated.

West, P., Sweeting, H., & Young, R. (2010). Transition matters: Pupils' experiences of the primary–secondary school transition in the West of Scotland and consequences for well-being and attainment. *Research Papers in Education, 25*(1), 21–50.

Whitebread, D., Coltman, P., Jameson, H., & Lander, R. (2009). Play, cognition and self-regulation: What exactly are children learning when they learn through play? *Educational & Child Psychology, 26*(2), 40–52.

Wigfield, A. (1994). Expectancy-value theory of achievement motivation: A developmental perspective. *Educational Psychology Review, 6*, 49–78.

Wigfield, A., & Eccles, J. S. (1992). The development of achievement task values: A theoretical analysis. *Developmental Review, 12*, 265–310.

———(2000). Expectancy–value theory of achievement motivation. *Contemporary educational psychology, 25*(1), 68–81. doi: 10.1006/ceps.1999.1015.

Wigfield, A., Eccles, J. S., MacIver, D., Reuman, D. A., & Midgley, C. (1991). Transitions during early adolescence: Changes in children's domain-specific self-perceptions and general self-esteem across the transition to junior high school. *Developmental Psychology, 27*, 552–565.

Wigfield, A., & Tonks, S. (2002). Adolescents' expectancies for success and achievement task values during middle and high school years. In F. Pajares & T. Urdan (Eds.), *Academic motivation of adolescents*. Greenwich, CT: Information Age, pp. 53–82.

Williams-Diehm, K., Wehmeyer, M. L., Palmer, S. B.,Soukup, J. H., & Garner, N. W. (2008). Self-determination and student involvement in transition planning: A multivariate analysis. *Journal on Developmental Disabilities, 14*(1), 27–39.

Wise, P. H. (2003). Framework as metaphor: The promise and peril of MCH life-course perspective. *Maternal Child Health Journal, 7*, 151–156.

Wolfe, J. (1997). The effectiveness of business games in strategic management course *Work. Simulation & Gaming, 28*(4), 360–376.

Wood, L., Ivery, P., Donovan, R., & Lambin, E. (2013). 'To the beat of a different drum': Improving the social and mental wellbeing of at-risk young people through drumming. *Journal of Public Mental Health, 12*(2), 70–79.

Xenikou, A., & Furnham, A. (2012). *Group dynamics and organizational culture: Effective work groups and organizations*. Basingstoke: Palgrave Macmillan.

Yaeda, J. (2010). Transition from secondary school to employment in Japan for students with disabilities. In D. Jindal-Snape (Ed.), *Educational transitions: Moving stories from around the world*. New York: Routledge, pp. 205–220.

Yaeda, J., & Jindal-Snape, D. (2011). Post-school transitions of students with disabilities: The Japanese experience. *International Journal of Humanities and Social Science, 1*(17), 112–117.

Yin, R. K. (2009). *Case study research: Design and methods* (5th edn.). California: SAGE.

Young, H., Gerrard, B., & Lambe, L. (2014). *Bereavement and loss: Supporting bereaved people with profound and multiple learning disabilities.* Dundee: PAMIS.

Zaidi, A. (2014). *Life cycle transitions and vulnerabilities in old age: A review.* Occasional Paper, UNDP Human Development Report Office, Retrieved December 14, 2015, from http://hdr.undp.org/en/content/life-cycle-transitions-and-vulnerabilities-old-age-review.

Zeedyk, M. S., Gallagher, J., Henderson, M., Hope, G., Husband, B., & Lindsay, K. (2003). Negotiating the transition from primary to secondary school: Perceptions of pupils, parents and teachers. *School Psychology International, 24,* 67–79.

Zeidner, M., & Schleyer, E. J. (1999). The big-fish-little-pond effect for academic self-concept, test anxiety, and school grades in gifted children. *Contemporary Educational Psychology, 24*(4), 305–329.

Zell, E., & Alicke, M. D. (2011). Age and the better-than-average effect. *Journal of Applied Social Psychology, 41,* 1175–1188.

Zhou, Y., Jindal-Snape, D., Topping, K., & Todman, J. (2008). Theoretical models of culture shock and adaptation in international students in higher education. *Studies in Higher Education, 33*(1), 63–75. doi: 10.1080/03075070701794833.

Zhou, Y., Todman, J., Topping, K., & Jindal-Snape, D. (2010). Cultural and pedagogical adaptation during transition from Chinese to UK Universities. In D. Jindal-Snape (Ed.), *Educational transitions: Moving stories from around the world.* London: Routledge, pp. 186–204.

Zhou, Y., Topping, K., & Jindal-Snape, D. (2009). *Cultural and educational adaptation of Chinese students in the UK.* Saarbrucken, Germany: VDM Verlag.

Zhou, Y., Topping, K. J., & Jindal-Snape, D. (2011). Intercultural adaptation of Chinese postgraduate students and their UK tutors. In L. Jin & M. Cortazz, *Researching Chinese Learners - skills, perceptions & intercultural adaptations.* London: Palgrave Macmillan, pp. 233–249.

Zimmer-Gembeck, M. J., Chipuer, H. M., Hanisch, M., Creed, P. A., & McGregor, L. (2006). Relationships at school and stage-environment fit as resources for adolescent engagement and achievement. *Journal of Adolescence, 29*(6), 911–933.

Zwarenstein, M., Goldman, J., & Reeves, S. (2009). *Interprofessional collaboration: Effects of practice-based interventions on professional practice and healthcare outcomes (Review),* Retrieved November 16, 2012, from www.thecochranelibrary.com/view/0/index.html.

index